TEACHING COMMUNICATION AND MEDIA STUDIES

Designed for communication/media educators and graduate students, *Teaching Communication and Media Studies* is a practical and conceptual guide to teaching university courses in communication and media studies. Relying on her extensive experience instructing graduate students on the ins and outs of teaching, Jan Fernback discusses theoretical and applied topics central to contemporary mediated communication instruction, offering instructors at all levels strategies they can use to create a successful classroom experience.

Fernback also considers the logic, design, and delivery of courses in communication and media studies, while encouraging readers to reflect on their own strategic pedagogical decisions. Supplemented with interviews of successful communication instructors and sample exercises, this book is a must-have resource for all those teaching communication and media studies courses, regardless of level of experience.

Jan Fernback is Associate Professor of Media Studies at Temple University, where she created a communication pedagogy curriculum for PhD students. Her current work examines issues of privacy and surveillance online and in mobile technologies, the impact of information/communication technologies on urban revitalization efforts, institutional uses of ICTs, and the meaning of virtual community in contemporary culture.

TEACHING COMMUNICATION AND MEDIA STUDIES

Pedagogy and Practice

Jan Fernback

NEW YORK AND LONDON

First published 2015
by Routledge
711 Third Avenue, New York, NY 10017

and by Routledge
2 Park Square, Milton Park, Abingdon, Oxon OX14 4RN

Routledge is an imprint of the Taylor & Francis Group, an informa business

Library of Congress Cataloging in Publication Data
Fernback, Jan, 1964-
Teaching communication and media studies : pedgagogy and practice / Jan Fernback.
pages cm
Includes bibliographical references and index.
1. Mass media—Study and teaching (Graduate) I. Title.
P91.3.F375 2015
302.2071'1—dc23 2014027603

ISBN: 978-0-415-88663-5 (hbk)
ISBN: 978-0-415-88664-2 (pbk)
ISBN: 978-0-203-69448-0 (ebk)

Typeset in 10/12 Bembo
by codeMantra

Printed and bound in the United States of America by Publishers Graphics, LLC on sustainably sourced paper.

CONTENTS

LIST OF FIGURES AND TABLES

ACKNOWLEDGMENTS

Many thanks to my students who continually inspire and amaze me. I owe a great debt to colleagues who agreed to be interviewed or otherwise shared their wisdom. They are Kim Bissell, Bonnie Brennan, John Campbell, Terry Harpold, Jarice Hanson, Tom Johnson, Jack Klotz Jr., Matthew Lombard, Brian McFadden, Andrew Mendelson, Dustin Morrow, Adrienne Shaw, Maria Simone, William Walter, and Kristine Weatherston. I am particularly grateful to Nancy Morris whose invaluable feedback helped shape this book and my teaching. The many conversations we've had and work we've done together are woven throughout this book. Generous thanks to Erica Wetter at Routledge for her continued support. Lastly, my family and friends have encouraged and sustained me, particularly my husband, David Hollar. Thank you all.

1

TEACHING COMMUNICATION AND MEDIA STUDIES: INTRODUCTION

Media and communication educators, like the students they teach, understand the extent to which contemporary experience is mediated. The everyday environment is awash in mobile computers, smartphones, mp3 players, HD radio and television, online social networking, text messaging, microblogging, sundry digital applications, and myriad forms of print and video content. Since mediated communication envelops us, educators must engage with mediated communication in order to be relevant to and attentive to modern realities. As divisions between producers and audiences disintegrate, effective communication becomes increasingly crucial to contemporary living and working. Media and communication educators recognize that teaching about media, about communication, is a sometimes frustrating exercise in metacommunication. How does communication challenge yet create social tensions such as racism, homophobia, sexism, or ageism? How are media integrated into our psychological, sociocultural, political, economic, technological, and historical lives? These questions are addressed by media studies and communication studies as each field considers the communicative process, message content, symbolic meaning, and impact of message reception. Media and communication related fields in the academy are more relevant now than ever as university educators struggle with pedagogical issues of the day—critical thinking, facility with technology, relativistic epistemology—that are typically addressed in communication and related disciplines. The ubiquity of communication and media-related issues in our world illustrates the primacy of communication/media studies in any university student's education.

Communication and media studies address structure, intent, content, and interpretation of all types of messages. All human action is grounded in communication. This is why it is essential to grasp the basics of all forms of communication. Communication is culture; it is part of a system of cultural practices that create, maintain, and transmute society. As James Carey (1989) and others have claimed, "our minds and lives are shaped by our total experience" (p. 33) or by symbols of experience; those symbols are communication. Our cultural realities are communicated through various means, including the media. We use stories of our culture to be entertained, to learn, to understand values, to grasp how society works. Ideally, audiences have a responsibility to question the storytellers and to reflect on the meanings of messages and what they say about culture. This book is about tying together the need to understand the ways and means of communication/media studies with pedagogies that strategically address media and communication topics. For reasons to be explained later in this introduction, the book uses the terms "mediated communication" and "communication/media studies" interchangeably. The term "communication" refers generally to "mediated communication" and not to rhetorical studies.

This book is written for a broad range of instructors in the academy: graduate students and faculty who teach media studies, communication, RTF (radio, television, film), journalism, American studies, anthropology, sociology, cultural studies, English, or other disciplines that engage with media as a content area. Thus, this book seeks to position the educator within the academy but outside rigid disciplinary boundaries. Graduate student teaching assistants as well as newer faculty and those who wish to revitalize their teaching or keep up with changing technological and social realities will find this book useful as they engage in the teaching of media-related content. The book accounts for broad approaches to media as means of communication between senders and receivers; as industries or organizations; as agents of social change and globalization; as agents of social stability and powerful sources of social meaning; as devices of surveillance; as commodities produced by media sub-industries; as cultural products with social, economic, historical, political, and technological significance.

Ideas about media are central to any pedagogical practice. Media-saturated environments make media studies a necessity, and communication education "is an essential component of every student's plan of study," according to Dickson (2000, p. 188). Morreale and Pearson (2008) find that education in communication is essential for both professional and personal success. Their analysis shows that knowledge of communication is crucial for holistic personal development, responsible involvement in activities of the citizenry, and addressing concerns of contemporary life. Kincheloe (2004) claims a vision of pedagogy that is grounded in social justice and includes a reconceptualization of education as it relates to community, marginalized groups, and the nature of knowledge (p. 6). To that list, I add "how we live in the world" as an essential educational axiom that acknowledges our media-inundated existence. As educators, we must formulate ideas about enacting our educational values into our pedagogical approaches. John Dewey said, "[Education] has to do with the perpetuation of positive values of inherited culture by embodying them in the dispositions of individuals who are to transmit culture into the future" (Brown, 1970, p. 53). Thus, faculty develop identities as both educators and as scholars. These identities sometimes fail to intersect as cleanly as we may like, for institutional realities sometimes dictate that one cannot always teach one's research. This book provides an opportunity for graduate student educators and faculty to contemplate our academic identities as it explores both the practical modalities of teaching and the philosophical presumptions about how/what/why we teach.

Media studies and communication faculty prepare students to consume media critically *and* to become professional communicators. Communication majors' central focus is learning how to make and interpret media, but most undergraduate students will (and *should*, according to Morreale and Pearson, 2008) take at least one communication-related course. This reality poses a particular set of challenges to the educator that this book seeks to address. *First*, the number of media courses in the academy, across disciplines, is growing while the object of study is continually changing. As mediated content changes form based on interactivity, delivery systems change based on technological advancement and political will, and content producers change based on decentralization and user sophistication (and the viral nature of user-produced content and other things), the ways in which faculty engage with these changes must be grounded in some universal principles of effective education. Like faculty in technologically driven fields and other professional fields, media and communication educators must keep pace with rapid changes while preparing students to work in evolving arenas.

Second, media and communication studies are interdisciplinary to the extent that it can be difficult to create academic boundedness. Drawing from too many disciplines to list, faculty must teach an amazing breadth without sacrificing depth. This quality lends the field a theoretical richness but a potentially schizophrenic identity. Scholarship in media studies and communication is widely varied, and providing an overview of the field to beginning students can be daunting to the most experienced faculty. How is expertise judged? What methods of inquiry are most appropriate? How do faculty and students create professional and scholarly identities around an area of the academy that seems like it encompasses nearly everything? How is the field defined? These questions lead to the *third* point—that many people within the academy do not understand the field and what our faculty and students do. Communication in general is sometimes regarded only in terms of performativity (usually public speaking), whereas media studies are often trivialized as either theoretically bereft or akin to trade school. These misunderstandings speak to the likelihood that general pedagogy texts will not address the field's specific character and needs. Communication and media studies have successfully articulated cross-disciplinary conversations about theory, research, and teaching in our own journals. The field's success in these endeavors must be translated for others inside and outside the academy in order to demonstrate the value in learning about our subject material.

Fourth, communication and media studies are relatively new in the academy in comparison with many of the established fields and disciplines from which media studies/communication have emerged. This creates issues of academic legitimacy in the minds of many schools, particularly those traditional liberal arts colleges and universities without communication or media studies programs. For the purposes of pedagogy at both the graduate and undergraduate levels, this means faculty must instill in students an academic identity that values the unique contributions of communication to the world of scholarship, to the professional workplace, and to the culture as a whole.

Perhaps because of the questions surrounding the legitimacy of the field and due to the sheer omnipresence of the media, the *fifth* challenge deals with the persistent assumption among many outside of communication and media studies that the media are easily understood. Our own students often demonstrate these attitudes early in their educational careers. Everyone consumes media, but not all attempts to theorize issues of media and communication are equally valid. To reach beyond platitudes about the entertainment purposes of media or the audience pulse-taking purposes of ratings systems, faculty in the field must communicate to students and others in the academy the importance of media as an object of study.

Sixth, many academic disciplines suffer from what might be termed the scholarly/professional faculty split, and this gulf particularly impacts pedagogy in communication and media studies. Partly owing to the field's interdisciplinary theoretical richness, some communication/media studies faculty focus on scholarship without having the experience of working in the media industries. Simultaneously, some professional communication/media studies faculty focus on those practices without full grounding in theories that probe the psychological-sociocultural importance of communication. That split often emphasizes a gulf in understanding both the symbolic and material aspects of, for example, communication technologies. Faculty examine the meanings users ascribe to technologies such as smartphones or social media, but faculty also probe the material realities of how and why those technologies are used by consumers. Thus, while our field unites theory and practice across the curriculum to our students' advantage, that scholarly/professional faculty split may present undergraduates with a variety of perspectives and contexts whose relationships may not be elucidated to them. Some students endure theoretically driven coursework to get their hands on production equipment or on portfolio projects. Some students stumble through production-oriented coursework in order to engage with topics that interrogate their own assumptions about the place of communication industries in the culture. This could impede students from integrating their studies in ways that enhance the development of their professional identities. Moreover, the breadth of approaches to teaching media studies and communication may create confusion among students who may not recognize connections among disparate viewpoints among individual faculty that implicitly underlie our teaching. The sophisticated student may grasp differences between an institutional perspective on media studies and a psychological approach to communication, or a critical theoretical orientation and a symbolic interactionist perspective, but many students miss the nuanced contradictions and correspondences between approaches that characterize the scope of the field. How do communication and media studies faculty create context-specific pedagogies that build upon general instructional theories and methods?

Healey (2000) suggests an investment in both high-quality, discipline-specific teaching and in the scholarship of teaching. These are means to contribute to the progression of a discipline. Approaching teaching in the same rigorous and contextual form as research is approached will yield enhanced student learning. The interplay between discipline-based research and student learning, according to Healey, is key to developing context-specific pedagogies that "attract and stimulate students to study the subject; transmit the values and traditions of the discipline; develop and promote good discipline-based pedagogic practice; encourage reflection on teaching styles and strategies; and enhance the reputation of the discipline" (p. 173). Healey's points are general, and they do not account for the need for faculty to cultivate an academic identity that incorporates both research and teaching. Nonetheless, Healey provides a valuable point of departure for linking discipline, teaching, scholarship, and identity. Healey and Jenkins (2003) offer several reasons for discipline-based pedagogy. Among these: faculty identity centers primarily around their subject; certain disciplines use specific types of teaching, such as lab work or internships, which require distinct pedagogical skills; disciplinary epistemology is transmitted through the curriculum; and disciplinary content must be contextualized and translated into "real world" pedagogies for students.

Young (2010), however, finds that few teaching and learning issues are discipline-specific. Young argues that universally suitable ideas about teaching may be contextualized into various disciplines, but most teaching issues transcend the disciplines. Although certain pedagogical issues may be intensified by the character of a particular discipline, Young advocates the use of discipline-specific research to "provide understanding of the particular significance of more generic issues and the ways in which these are played out for students and lecturers in a particular subject" (p. 122). Young's arguments are intriguing, but they are ultimately based on an instrumental assumption about teaching. Faculty engage in the practice of knowledge production so that students can learn, but a more holistic approach to pedagogy regards the development of an academic identity as vital for all scholars to craft over the course of a career. Students benefit from the development of faculty identities that include both research and teaching.

In an attempt to forge scholarship with pedagogical practice, Sprague (1993) offers suggestions for a context-specific pedagogy for communication. Her suggestions emerge from a recognition that knowledge is produced in the process of teaching, and that process is inseparable from prior content knowledge. Our evolving understandings of discipline-specific content are based in research we conduct in our field. Thus, theory is never separate from practice; theory is our everyday lived experience. A context-specific pedagogy, for example, recognizes theories of institutional power dynamics in the teaching of media law classes. Among Sprague's (1993) guidelines, a discipline-specific pedagogy recognizes that communication is a complex process; that competency with all types of communication arises from a learned understanding of communicative patterns. That understanding is achieved only through immersion within communicative environments and practice with communicative skills. Our pedagogy must recognize the process or the form, in addition to the content.

Another of Sprague's guidelines recognizes the performativity of communication. Although she articulates this guideline in interpersonal and oral terms, it can be expanded to encompass mediated communication. She urges scholars to consider oral discourse as a valuable epistemology, and those same aspects of performativity are evident in much of contemporary mediated discourse. It has a recognizable form in which meaning resides. For example, scholars may analyze the aspects of performance on social networking sites such as Facebook in terms of how they communicate identity; or scholars may investigate the cultural meaning of how various prototypical roles are performed on reality programs. A communication-specific pedagogy may value the conscious interrogation of *how* communicative subjects perform. Another discipline-specific pedagogical guideline acknowledges that much communicative behavior is automatic and unconscious, and thus, our pedagogy must explore the interaction between conscious and unconscious learning. This tenet applies to mediated communication in that naturalized, unquestioned, or habituated behaviors appear in the form of templates that overlay much mediated communication. For example, news values dictate the form of reportage; the profit motive narrows the variety and quality of mediated messages; and accepted institutional, technological, and policy constraints result in oligopolistic patterns of delivery of major media. This communicative shorthand, evident in human and mediated communication, has implications for learning that build upon what we already know about cognitive apprehension of knowledge.

Next, Sprague (1993) asserts that communication is linked to cultural identity. Language both creates and reflects culture, and "language performed through speech is a powerful social marker as well as one of the primary expressions of self" (p. 117). Mediated communication serves these same functions as, for example, news media codes communicate trust and authority while advertising creates brand identity. For both human and mediated communication, culture-specific codes are established to display communicative competence. Defining those codes is a powerful function that shapes identity. Discourses that neglect to observe codes of cultural competence are marginalized. A discipline-specific pedagogy would illuminate the clash between personal identity and discursive competence in some contexts, whether, for example, individual code-switching or rebranding a web site. The creation of identities is a powerful communicative act that must be embraced in our pedagogies. Lastly, a discipline-specific pedagogy recognizes the connection between communication and power, according to Sprague. Human and mediated discourses serve or resist extant power arrangements, and these processes must be examined from critical and ethical perspectives. Moreover, Sprague suggests, the metacommunicative nature of teaching communication requires that our pedagogies be dissected for both those metamessages and for how they model social arrangements. Subjecting ourselves to such examination is a difficult but necessary by-product of teaching communication and media studies.

Sprague's (1993) valuable insights provide a foundation for the approach to this book. Because the process of teaching is linked to the content areas we teach, pedagogical techniques alone do not lend themselves to a one-size-fits-all ethos. Teaching is a skill but equally important is the substance of our courses. Our activities as faculty best serve ourselves and our students when they are integrated. Research informs teaching (and vice versa) not just in terms of content but also in terms of perspective. One who researches psychological processes involved in message reception cannot reasonably or ethically ignore those research findings in the quotidian realities of the classroom. How differently might a symbolic interactionist, a critical theorist, and a former general manager of a television station approach course content or pedagogical philosophy? Among other pedagogical concerns, classroom dynamics, grading, and teaching styles have all been influenced by research in communication and media studies from audience reception theories to theories of communicative action to theories of institutional power structures. Teaching and scholarship converge to shape our identities within the academy.

For communication and media studies faculty and graduate students, identity issues are close to the surface. Some within the field dispute turf claims or argue over disciplinary heritage. Because faculty enter the field from multiple disciplines, those diverse influences impact our perceptions on the nature of communication and media studies in the academy. While this fact could be seen as an argument against a discipline-specific pedagogy as a means to identity formation within the academy, other discipline-specific aspects of academic life influence faculty identities such as departmental structures, object of study, non-academic experiences, and scholarship. Thus, a clarification of terminology is necessary here. I have been using the terms communication/media studies to characterize the investigation of actions designed to convey meaning and attain understanding. I view mediated and interpersonal communication, along with Lievrouw (2009), as commingled areas of study. We develop identities as scholars, researchers, and teachers based upon our assumptions about our own objects of study. This book approaches pedagogy in communication/media studies as a converged field. Lievrouw (2009) claims that divisions between interpersonal and mediated communication "obscure the shifting, contingent nature of communication in everyday experience, social formations, and culture" (p. 303). Using Gumpert and Cathcart's (1986) term "mediation" to bridge the divide, Lievrouw argues that the process, form, and content of communication intersect in mutually implicated communicative customs, technologies, and social structures. When we conceive of communication as action within networked systems and relations, we recognize that so-called boundaries between interpersonal and media communication become obfuscatory. Lievrouw essentializes this nexus, claiming that "any satisfactory theory of communication today must account for its dual social and technical nature, and for the experience of communication as a seamless and continually negotiated web of meaning, practices, tools, resources, and relations" (p. 317). Lievrouw's stance emphasizes the theoretical; however, this stance can be more broadly applied: pedagogy in the field is served by identification of this nexus between interpersonal and mediated communication. If, for example, the two-step flow (Katz & Lazarsfeld, 1955) provided a model for individual interpretation of mediated content as well as a model for the transmission of institutional content through social arrangements and relationships, our teaching must acknowledge that sociocultural and relational contexts shape negotiated understanding of content. In other words, an individual's understanding of a particular scene in a film results not just from individual perspectives but from that person's place in and relationship to a host of social institutions. Pedagogical communication about communication cannot separate interpersonal from mediated actions. Our identities as educators are therefore inseparable from our identities as scholars. Each classroom is a microcosm of our research and theory, of our actions and experiences.

Faculty form academic identities in micro and macro ways—through departmental and collegial associations, through institutional structures and culture, and through the norms and standards of the profession. To the extent that academic identity is informed by disciplinary norms, structures, and culture, educators can accept or dismiss disciplinary ways of being in the academy. Disciplinary commonalities and differences of method, language, epistemology, history, and theoretical orientation define our academic identities. Part of the purpose of this book is to help faculty to cultivate academic identities that incorporate the crux of what we do—knowledge production, acquisition, contestation, and dissemination—in ways that include pedagogical philosophy and practice. Many academics first become interested in the academy through teaching in the exposure to talented faculty who serve as role models in the realm of ideas. Teaching is a means to continue learning about captivating subjects. Moreover, faculty in higher education are fostered from graduate programs that are discipline or field specific rather than from graduate education programs. Constructing an argument that pedagogy, as an essential part of faculty identity, is not separate from other disciplinary actions, Malcolm and Zukas (2000) speculate about a world in which research is isolated in such a way.

> [U]niversities might have generalist, non-academic 'research developers' who would educate academics in research methodology, methods of analysis, research ethics, writing and so on. ... They would not necessarily

> be researchers themselves, but could offer part-time courses assessed by themselves, which would certify academics as qualified research practitioners. This imagined reality seems ludicrous to us, of course, because we understand research as an aspect of specialist knowledge production, not as a set of generalist techniques.
>
> (p. 54)

Malcolm and Zukas (2000) lament that conversation about teaching in higher education is "characterized by 'quick-fix' empiricism and technicist discourse" (p. 54). The aim of this book is to aid in the consideration of pedagogy as an integral element of disciplinary culture as students/faculty of media studies and communication develop and reassess their academic identities. This book regards teaching as a focus of academic work, not a by-product of it.

Elsewhere, Malcolm and Zukas (2007) claim that "Teachers' pedagogic identities involve the negotiation of meaning, with learners, as members of a disciplinary community of pedagogic practices, just as research identities involve the negotiation of meaning with other disciplinary actors" (p. 17). For them, pedagogy is "a collective engagement with learners in knowledge production" (p. 18) rather than the mere transmission of knowledge. Extending this notion, the practice of explaining what one knows to various constituencies—students, the media, peers, members of the public—is a connection with public life beyond the academy. It is a part of keeping students and these other constituencies interested in lifelong learning. For communication faculty, it's about making sure all groups understand the importance of examining, evaluating, and analyzing the role of media and communication in everyday life. And in this respect, this book focuses on pedagogical strategies that are both unique to communication/media studies and broad enough to encompass all aspects of university teaching with a view toward helping faculty to construct or renegotiate their academic identities. For some broader perspectives on faculty identity within the academy, this book features brief interviews of successful communication instructors corresponding to the book's chapters.[1]

Note

1 All interview data stem from personal communication with the author. Interviewees graciously provided permission for their words to be used throughout this book.

References

Brown, L. M. (Ed.). (1970). *Aims of education*. New York, NY: Teacher's College Press.

Carey, J. (1989). *Communication as culture: Essays on media and society*. Boston, MA: Unwin Hyman.

Dickson, T. (2000). *Mass media education in transition*. Hillsdale, NJ: Lawrence Erlbaum.

Gumpert, G., & Cathcart, R. (1986). *Inter/Media: Interpersonal communication in a media world* (3rd ed.). Oxford, UK, and New York, NY: Oxford University Press.

Healey, M. (2000). Developing the scholarship of teaching in higher education: A discipline-based approach. *Higher Education Research & Development, 19*(2), 169–189.

Healey, M., & Jenkins, A. (2003). Discipline-based educational development. In H. Eggins & R. Macdonald (Eds.), *The scholarship of academic development* (pp. 47–57). Buckingham, UK: Open University Press.

Katz, E., & Lazarsfeld, P. (1955). *Personal influence: The part played by people in the flow of mass communications*. Glencoe, IL: Free Press.

Kincheloe, J. L. (2004). *Critical pedagogy: Primer*. New York, NY: Peter Lang.

Lievrouw, L. A. (2009). New media, mediation, and communication study. *Information, Communication & Society, 12*(3), 303–325.

Malcolm, J., & Zukas, M. (2000). Becoming an educator: Communities of practice in higher education. In I. McNay (Ed.), *Higher education and its communities* (pp. 51–64). Buckingham, UK: Open University Press.

Malcolm, J., & Zukas, M. (2007). Poor relations: Exploring discipline, research and pedagogy in academic identity. In M. Osborne, M. Houston, & N. Toman (Eds.), *The pedagogy of lifelong learning: Understanding effective teaching and learning in diverse contexts* (pp. 15–25). London, UK: Routledge.

Morreale, S. P., & Pearson, J. C. (2008). Why communication education is important: The centrality of the discipline in the 21st century. *Communication Education, 57*(2), 224–240. DOI: 10.1080/03634520701861713

Sprague, J. (1993). Retrieving the research agenda for communication education: Asking the pedagogical questions that are "embarrassments to theory." *Communication Education, 42*(2), 106–122.

Young, P. (2010). Generic or discipline-specific? An exploration of the significance of discipline-specific issues in researching and developing teaching and learning in higher education. *Innovations in Education and Teaching International, 47*(1), 115–124.

2

THE "WHY" BEFORE THE "HOW": TEACHING PHILOSOPHY

John Dewey was among the first American scholars to recognize that problems of communication are inextricably linked to problems of community and democracy, that the felt nature of daily life is evident in communicative activities and how those activities manifest themselves in communities. In *Democracy and Education*, Dewey (1916) notes that "Society not only continues to exist by transmission, by communication, but it may fairly be said to exist in transmission, in communication. There is more than a verbal tie between the words common, community, and communication. Men live in a community in virtue of the things which they have in common; and communication is the way in which they come to possess things in common" (p. 4). Dewey's work is integral to the study of social life as a form of communication—a view that supports much of the North American academy's contemporary focus on *active learning*. This pedagogical initiative envisions learning as a communal activity beyond the transmission of information, beyond the "stand and deliver" method of teaching. Active learning holds that students learn better when participating in learning activities rather than simply receiving information. Meyers and Jones (1993) identify these activities as talking and listening, reading, writing, and reflecting. For the communication classroom, this means involving students in media creation and analysis to understand their roles as both media creators/practitioners and media consumers. It encourages the development of higher-order thinking skills through student practice. Active learning is about more than student engagement; it is about using that engagement to create actual experiences and to build understanding. Examples of active learning activities in a communication classroom might be participating in the development of a class wiki on ethical journalism practices, collaborating on the editing of a class-created documentary film, or participating in an online game where students debate legal issues in media. Because media are cultural artifacts, active learning encourages students to be deliberators of culture as opposed to mere cultural users.

Dewey's progressive view of communication as the foundation that undergirds true community and a democratic way of life symbolizes his educational philosophy. In *The Public and Its Problems*, Dewey (1927) claims that a crisis of community life exists which arises from a public failure to recognize that a democratic social order, based on communicative activity, is the primary locus of associative life in the Western world. Communication is, for Dewey, the embodied practice of participating in the collective experience of public life; that embodiment can take the form of scientific inquiry, artistic creation, and physical agency within the local community. Throughout *The Public and Its Problems* Dewey asserts that this practice results in what he refers to as a collective "intelligence" or "common sense" that expresses the deeper meaning of the seemingly quotidian experience of public life. Dewey proclaims that we must look to scientists and artists (as expert communicators) to reveal these deeper meanings to us. His educational philosophy was thus one of learning how to live in the world and of social consciousness and reconstruction.

Through his works on education and democracy, Dewey illustrates the need for a pedagogy that is grounded in one's personal philosophy. What is the role of education in society? What is the role of the educator? What is the role of the student? How and why should certain material be taught? How is education juxtaposed against and integrated with other social institutions? How do disciplinary characteristics insist upon a specific set of pedagogical approaches? Dewey and other educational philosophers recognized the necessity for a guiding principle from which specific techniques and practices can arise. Attention to the 'why' of teaching clarifies the 'how' and eases the creation of teaching practices. The 'why' is commonly articulated through the development of a teaching philosophy; this chapter is devoted to exploring some ideas that may inspire a teaching philosophy for communication and media studies faculty.

A teaching philosophy is a set of organizing, essential tenets that orient the instructor's educational activities. In suggesting some educational philosophies for communication faculty, Briggs and Pinola (1985) argue that a pedagogical philosophy should be used as a reference point for consistency and to guide the newer instructor. A philosophy, they claim, represents a commitment to one's principles and does not serve as a justification after the fact for failure or success in the classroom.

A pedagogical philosophy that can be connected to one's research or creative endeavors within the academy contributes to a coherent, robust identity as an educator. Establishing a grounded, pedagogical philosophy provides a consistency of approach that may help stabilize professional identity in the face of certain challenges. Those challenges could include institutional constraints, ideological conditions, criticism from internal or external constituencies, or disciplinary struggles.

Background for a Pedagogical Philosophy

The term *philosophy* is used here to refer loosely to a set of guiding principles that shape an educator's approach to teaching and to education in general. A philosophy is an important first step in articulating a vision for what can be accomplished in the classroom and in the curriculum. It allows us to connect our various roles within the academy and encourages self reflexivity about those roles. Because, as James Carey (1989) notes, *communication is culture,* a variety of philosophies are applicable to the scope of media studies education. Any philosophy of communication is linked to the cultural *zeitgeist* as media produce and reproduce a culture. Simultaneously, communication faculty are responsible for engaging students to reflect on the implications for both consuming and producing media. This role may lead to what Denski (1991, 1994) refers to as "schizophrenia," in that a scholarly critique of media as hegemonic cultural systems may be difficult to reconcile for those also teaching production courses in which students learn to reproduce (and celebrate) those systems of social control. For faculty seeking to provide students with social capital—with a recognition of power imbalances—and to help students develop professionally, the schizophrenia may be alleviated by enacting a philosophy melding theory and practice in a media-centric communication landscape. Sholle and Denski (1994) suggest a "reflexive" approach to the academy in which faculty consider themselves as educators and citizens. The dichotomies they see characterizing media and communication education such as teaching/research, production/research, "real world"/"ivory tower," theory/practice, and scholar/practitioner may be dislocated with a reflexive consideration of how our roles as educators and citizens can be complementary. The ability to recognize those traditional divisions as byproducts of an uninformed perspective on the role of communication and media in cultural production is the beginning of a holistic philosophy that considers theory and practice, teaching and research, professional identity and citizenship (Sholle & Denski, 1994). For communication faculty in particular, a pedagogical philosophy that acknowledges the role of the contemporary university in the professional development of students while emphasizing deep and critical examination of communication in culture may best contribute to a democratic, comprehensive education.

To ensure that our pedagogical philosophies are relevant as well as robust, communication faculty must recognize that the media and communicative practices themselves inspire our approach to education. For example, how do students' (as producers as well as consumers) relationships with media impact our classroom practices? So much of students' daily activities are centered around communication—texting, posting to Facebook or YouTube, blogging, and interacting with the world at large through social media—that our approaches to pedagogy cannot ignore their profound immersion in media environments. What cognitive, affective, or behavioral consequences of this immersion might be considered in our pedagogical philosophies? How does that immersion change student expectations for active learning models? What cultural politics are at play that may shape our educational approaches? As educators and students spend more time with communication and information technologies, teaching practices expand. Teaching philosophies may expand as well.

Some Philosophies for Communication/Media Pedagogy

Briggs and Pinola (1985) suggest five traditional educational philosophies for communication educators: idealism, which emphasizes the student's ideal behaviors as a responsibility to the whole society; realism, which centers on empirical observation of concrete reality; existentialism, which seeks to develop the student's individual essence; neo-thomism, which is a search for eternal truth to create internal discipline; and experimentalism, which values subjective experience in developing students' motivations toward positive social change. Briggs and Pinola provide a self-assessment inventory to help educators ascertain their philosophical preferences. Elements of these philosophies underlie other frameworks, including some that are oriented toward active learning. Overall, they can be seen as a useful starting point from which to consider other orienting positions. Whether aligned with philosophies of social change, of ideal existence, of absolute moral authority, of empirical epistemology, or of individual uniqueness, the media studies instructor can connect communicative thought and behavior through these principles to actual practices in the classroom. Some examples follow in conjunction with an examination of several philosophies that inform contemporary communication education. These philosophies are possible grounding foundations that will likely be combined by an educator working through her/his own philosophy. An instructor's philosophy may ultimately be a syncretism that unifies various elements of a few philosophies in concert with one's academic identity.

Critical Pedagogy

Critical pedagogy stresses social critique as a means to social justice. It assumes that inquiry is not value-free or acontextual; it engages with the links between knowledge and power. Critical pedagogy seeks to expose and confront dominant ideologies of oppression rather than reproduce them. Paulo Freire's ideas have inspired critical pedagogies through critiques of social institutions and through a commitment to social transformation based on the liberation of marginalized populations. In his classic work, *Pedagogy of the Oppressed*, Freire (1970) argues that educational institutions are sites of political struggle in that they often replicate the existing social order and train students to accept dominant ideologies uncritically. In his "banking model" (p. 58), students are empty containers waiting to receive deposits of knowledge from educators. His notion of critical pedagogy, however, regards students as co-creators of knowledge in a form of "liberating" education. In *The Politics of Education*, Freire (1985) articulates in more detail the means of the liberation enterprise. He notes that various political, economic, and social disadvantages contribute to the illiteracy of oppressed people. Because illiteracy is a political problem, it must be remedied through critical reasoning, curiosity, and activism that can lead to human emancipation and ultimate social change. For Freire, the teacher's role is to assist students in framing community issues in larger sociocultural and political contexts as a first attempt to confront these issues. The educator understands how students construct meaning; these meanings are communally interpreted and the educator helps students create strategies for empowerment.

In Fassett and Warren's (2007) elucidation of critical communication pedagogy, the classroom can be a site of social influence; students can shape one another and their actions can have consequences. Since communication as a field typically engages with issues of diversity, identity, culture, power, and socioeconomic status, it can provide a basis from which to enact transformative agendas (Fassett & Warren, 2007). Such agendas often relate to identities of difference according to Brooks and Ward (2007):

> Critical pedagogy combines the realm of media practice with a theoretically informed critical analysis of media institutions, practices, and texts. At its core is a curriculum that, among other strategies and goals, synthesizes theory and practice. Therefore, pedagogy goes beyond teaching philosophy and technique to embrace all activities that determine what constitutes knowledge—what is important to know, how it is known, and how this construction and production of knowledge formulates social identities. In a critical pedagogy, a primary goal is to give students an active and critical voice.
>
> (p. 246)

For Sholle and Denski (1994), critical pedagogies are vital means by which to invalidate what they see as media education's "acritical and celebratory indoctrination into the mechanisms and techniques" of social control (p. 8). Thus, media studies must interrogate the connections between communication curricula and media institutions. The means of enacting that interrogation includes, according to Sholle and Denski, engaging with media as popular texts—as sites of conflict over meaning in everyday life between dominant and subaltern groups. As indicated by Sprague (1990) critical pedagogy is embodied in the communication curriculum through

> identification of sexism in language, the exposure of ideological assumptions in media, and the empowering of individuals to resist subtle intimidation in interpersonal encounters. Students learn to look beyond what is said. They ask also "What is *not* said? Why? Who profits from keeping communication the way it is now? How could changing communication patterns change social reality?" [emphasis in original].
>
> (p. 25)

A media/communication focused critical pedagogy also might ask: In what ways can mediated communication function to control and reproduce accepted knowledge? How do media normalize and subjectify the populace? How do media industries influence the structure of curricula and pedagogical practices? In light of these questions, Bragg (2007) posits that students acquire not just cultural meaning but also cultural capital from a concentrated critique of the media that truly values student interpretations and their lived experiences. Moreover, she advocates a critical learning based on social relationships forged in the classroom: "media teaching would do better to acknowledge that learning and change always require others" (p. 68), whether the others are experienced as tools for thinking, as affirmations of what we already know, or as unintended pathways toward new understandings. Bragg entreats educators to regard the media as resources for sense-making and cultural capital rather than as sources of ideological dominion. An example of a Freirean approach to a critical communication pedagogy designed to increase cultural capital is Solorzano's (1989) study of "Chicano gang films" and media stereotyping. Using Freire's method of reciprocal dialogue between students and teacher, the group collaborates to identify, analyze, and rectify a social problem. Solorzano's students identified negative ethnic stereotypes and organized boycotts and picketing of the films. Solorzano reports success in that students were empowered as a group and attained critical curiosity and problem-solving abilities, and that Hollywood had curtailed the release of additional Chicano gang films.

A colleague at Temple University, John Campbell (July, 2011), articulates a philosophy consonant with some of the tenets of critical pedagogy. He states:

> To motivate students to really want to learn, we have to first change how they view knowledge. In essence, we as educators must alter their value system. This is especially true if we want our students to become critical thinkers; individuals who will question existing power relations and social hierarchies. In my introductory courses, I provide students with a different conceptualization of knowledge on the first day of class by associating knowledge and understanding with something they already value: economic capital. Our capitalistic society has been good indeed at teaching undergraduate students the value of economic capital. Educators can use this existing value system as a starting point for helping students to reconsider the importance they place on knowledge.
>
> I encourage students to think of knowledge—all forms of knowledge—as a resource much like economic capital. However, unlike material resources, this particular resource is never exhausted, cannot be lost in a recession, and can be readily shared without any reduction in its worth. Having framed the forthcoming discussion in these terms, I introduce them to a simplified version of Pierre Bourdieu's (1984) concept of cultural capital. I explain how Bourdieu found a strong correlation between cultural capital and economic

> capital. Those who had greater levels of cultural capital tended to have greater levels of economic capital. Although Bourdieu never suggested that knowledge could be directly transformed into material wealth, his work does indicate a relationship between the amount of knowledge an individual possesses and that individual's potential for economic success. As many undergraduates have trouble relating to abstractions, I use multiple examples from my life and the lives of friends, acquaintances, and associates who have employed cultural capital to enhance their economic, social, and political status and to enrich their lives. I also explain to my students during the first class that as with economic capital, not all forms of cultural capital are of equal worth. I suggest that the most valuable form of cultural capital they can obtain in college is critical thinking skills. Given that critical thinking skills can be employed in every aspect of their lives, I present this form of cultural capital as a vital resource in achieving a truly successful life (and I'm careful to point out that "success" is not measured merely by how much money one makes). I believe that as students develop their critical thinking, they will take greater responsibility for their own education and greater initiative in expanding their knowledge base.

Critical pedagogy differs from deontological approaches to education in that it seeks the maximization of social justice as a collective good. For the communication curriculum, a critical perspective questions institutional realities, provides students with tools to challenge their own assumptions in addition to the normative assumptions of the wider culture, and considers human emancipation to be an ultimate goal of education. The critical perspective recognizes value in the student's voice beyond the traditionally accepted discourses of media production. Instead, the critical perspective finds value in helping students to express, in literate ways, their own experiences so that they may reposition themselves as contributors to the larger community and to culture.

Constructivist Pedagogy

Constructivist pedagogical perspectives are built around the notion that knowledge is socially constructed. People use culture to create knowledge that is historically and contextually bound and built on prior knowledge. Constructivist pedagogy is consequently concerned with the *process* of the validation and legitimization of knowledge as well as the devaluation or delegitimization of other types of knowledge. For Lattuca (2006), "constructivist pedagogy therefore emphasizes the active learner—who discusses, questions, debates, hypothesizes, investigates, and argues in order to understand new information" (p. 355). The instructor helps students to discover meaning. Constructivism connects to Dewey's notions about learning as a process of communal and contextual sense-making. Kincheloe (2005) merges constructivist pedagogy with critical pedagogy in order to challenge the politics of knowledge through critical inquiry. In this regard, constructivist pedagogy views teaching and research to be inextricably connected; both enterprises focus on empowering people from a position of partnership rather than superiority or dominion. And both enterprises focus on a contextual understanding of "how things came to be" (Kincheloe, 2005). In general, constructivist pedagogical perspectives eschew the expository methods of transmitting so-called universal truths in the classroom in favor of constructing knowledge through experience.

A media/communication focused constructivist pedagogy might ask: In what ways do media shape our constructions of reality? How have developments in communication technology and surrounding institutions influenced our awareness of the world? In what ways does language—whether visual, nonverbal, written, symbolic, or aural—direct our apprehension of knowledge? How can field experiences with media be integrated into the curriculum? Are the meanings we construct and refine from communicative activities utterly subjective? What role do communication-institutional conditions play in our knowledge construction? These questions can form the foundation for a style that, as Lattuca (2006) reminds us, "is not about *delivering content*. It is the act of designing experiences that encourage and enable learning" (p. 356). Lattuca's examples include the development of a framework for analysis of ethical situations in journalism in which the instructor poses questions that serve as tools for students to create strategic processes for analyzing case studies. Students can work together in class to critique these processes, modifying their frameworks as they collaborate. Eventually students are able to build critical and collaborative skills while learning to consider alternative ethical solutions and to refine their own ethical convictions. Because the constructivist approach holds that the material world and the self are formed through an iterative, communicative process, students can reform their understanding of various concepts as contexts change.

For communication faculty, constructivist pedagogy provides a natural symbiosis with the notion of participatory culture. As students develop proficiencies with the cultural products of communication such as remixes, blogs, video game modding, fan fiction, machinima, podcasting, and so on, they actively construct their own meanings, identities, and knowledge. Jenkins, Purushotma, Weigel, Clinton, and Robison (2009) note that participatory culture encourages an environment of collaboration, creativity, and civic connection among people who build and publish media. Students relate to media as raw materials for reimagining and reconstructing rather than solely as a final authority. Jenkins et al. (2009) also report the benefits of such participatory culture as "opportunities for peer-to-peer learning, a changed attitude toward intellectual property, the diversification of cultural expression, the development of skills valued in the modern workplace, and a more empowered conception of citizenship" (p. xii). These benefits reflect, in part, a constructivist orientation toward learning. The goal of a constructivist approach to media studies is for students to create meaning and knowledge about communication through the process of experimenting with ideas, working through problems collaboratively, questioning self-perceptions, reevaluating prior knowledge, and constructing new information.

Dustin Morrow (July, 2011), professor in the Department of Theater and Film at Portland State University, exemplifies this approach to his teaching. He explains the "why" before the "how" when discussing his academic identity:

> When I'm writing as an academic, I'm processing previously written texts on a subject, as well as related works—reorganizing, reinventing, and adding to them. But I am also thinking about the classroom—what I have learned from students and their responses to the materials I have presented, and what I have gained from the act of teaching itself. In my creative activities, I am primarily producing works in response to what I experience in the world around me, of which such a large part is my life as an educator. I am a teacher and a media producer—these two identities frame how I process the world around me and how I use/re-work/re-create any knowledge and experience I have gained.

Professor Morrow values that iterative process of knowledge creation in all aspects of his academic life. He also displays constructivist tactics in his ideas about classroom learning:

> The best teachers are good listeners. ... Students must be empowered to experiment, to take creative risks—once they have mastered the skills they need to create, and the protocols used in the professional market they'll enter upon graduation, they must be encouraged to do something new, to take chances in the pursuit of intellectual and creative growth. ... Even in media production classes, I'm strongly in favor of writing exercises like creative journals and reasoned, analytical responses to texts and work. In the act of committing ideas to paper, even in something as short as an informal one-page essay, students are required to develop and organize their thoughts, which necessitates a significant level of wrestling with the material. But whether it is through writing or classroom discussion, students should always be responding to everything that is happening in a course—my comments, the comments and work of their classmates, the technologies, the written and audiovisual texts, and the processes of creating, presenting and discussing work. It is in this act of response that they become critical thinkers. As important as realizing an accomplished production is, the value of the producer is limited if he/she can't competently evaluate and discuss the work.

This collaborative, active approach is useful in preparing students to contribute to participatory culture. Students can engage with multiple instruments in media environments in order to invent, remix, and enjoy knowledge production as opposed to observing those environments from an outsider position. Similarly, Andrew Mendelson (August, 2011), a journalism professor at Temple University, has created an approach to teaching and research that centers on visual literacy. He uses tenets of visual literacy as guiding principles in his courses; these principles are tools he uses to both construct pedagogical strategies and to discern patterns in mediated images and texts. Mendelson's philosophy forms the foundation of an iterative process of continual modification in both his teaching and his research as he incorporates successful strategies and jettisons unsuccessful ones. His "end game" is to "remember that it's always about the 'why.'" Both of these philosophies indicate the formation of academic identities that flow consistently between teaching activities and research/creative pursuits.

Multicultural Pedagogy

Another philosophy that resonates with the field of media studies is multicultural pedagogy. This perspective emphasizes diverse perspectives, negotiated meanings, and citizenship. Concerned with awareness of various cultures and cultural differences, multicultural pedagogy has moved, in recent years, beyond tolerance and cultural sensitivity to seek cultural equality, encouragement of cultural difference rather than "color-blindness," and meaningful socioeconomic change for groups historically subjected to discrimination. It is about a mutual respect and esteem for distinct cultures based on the notion of equal value (Rothenberg, 2007; May & Sleeter, 2010). Multicultural pedagogy contests any type of marginalization whether resulting from arrangements of race, sexuality, class, ability, gender, age, or religion. McLaren (1999) advocates a critical dimension to multicultural pedagogy that "challenges educators to develop a concept of unity and difference that reconfigures the meaning of difference as political mobilization rather than cultural authenticity" (p. 29). For the communication classroom, multicultural pedagogy considers how media institutions and students' communicative patterns may promote tenets of equality and democracy. This includes issues of free expression in a contemporary media environment. Sharma (2010) explores the use of popular media as a site for students to become active in the critical examination of their own knowledge and histories in order to examine everyday differences. Low (2011) talks about using hip-hop and spoken word culture as a pedagogical strategy designed to probe the cultural roots of and responses to racism in North America. The goal of this strategy is to create knowledge of and respect of social difference and cultural identity in ways that speak to students through popular media. Students engage with hip-hop texts in critical ways to examine the politics of identity and representation. Citing an unpublished 2009 dissertation by Eloise Tan, Low lays out a typology of hip-hop pedagogies mandating that they are:

1. Rooted in hip-hop culture while recognizing that its histories and ideologies are socially produced and at times must be challenged and reworked.
2. Socially conscious of how hegemony operates within society, while paying particular attention to how hegemony and power operate within hip-hop culture to marginalize populations it seeks to liberate.

3. Responsive to marginalization whether it be through structures of gender, class, race, religion, sexuality, or ability.
4. Culturally productive by encouraging learners to be producers of their own hip-hop culture.
5. Inclusive of multiliteracies across forms of media, technology, and culture. (p. 22)

A media/communication focused multicultural pedagogy might ask: How can media be created in ways that value cultural difference? How do differing communication practices contribute to cultural unity and cultural division? In what ways does individual identity arise from communication? What meanings about social differences can we take away from popular culture? How does language of difference or of tolerance or of "color blindness" work to propel or encumber social equality?

Additional Pedagogical Philosophies and Communication

Because communication studies/media studies are founded on interdisciplinary inquiry, some of the philosophies mentioned by Briggs and Pinola (1985) are interlaced in the pedagogical practices of communication faculty. Idealist notions of education, based on Platonic ideals, advocate a holistic approach in the development of a well-balanced individual who can serve society. Because idealist pedagogy requires the instructor to model responsibility to society at large, a communication faculty member may stress the development of an ethical sensibility regarding communicative actions. Notions of social responsibility in the media have arisen from idealist philosophical perspectives. Alternatively, realist educational philosophy, based on an Aristotelian value of reason, stresses pedagogical responses to concrete realities of the material world. The realist instructor focuses on empirically verifiable constructs in an attempt to articulate basic laws of the world. Realism in communication pedagogy might emphasize a problem-solving approach to communication issues from a core curriculum of tested knowledge. This may include, for example, the teaching of skills demanded by employers in current media marketplaces.

Existentialist pedagogy emphasizes individual truth and conceives of the instructor's role as a facilitator to student development. The instructor is a resource for students on individual pathways of discovery; there are no learning outcomes to define the parameters of a class. For the communication educator, existentialist approaches may include individualized field studies in which students enact communication behaviors, skills, attitudes, or ideas that they believe contribute to their development. Almost any media/communication subject might be examined this way, as the instructor provides individualized critique and challenges to ideas.

Lastly, some communication educators embrace a type of postmodern approach to pedagogy in which the underlying assumptions governing the philosophical aspects of the educational enterprise are questioned. Universities are constituted by culture and they serve culture, and are therefore terrain for critique according to the postmodern approach. Aronowitz and Giroux (1991) describe a pedagogical philosophy that questions modernist educational ideals accentuating social responsibility, citizenship, progress, and human development. They argue that the culture of education privileges white, male, upper- and middle-class perspectives, and that a radical critique is the means by which those dominant perspectives can be politicized and demystified. For them,

> Postmodern criticism … offers the promise of deterritorializing modernism and redrawing its political, social and cultural boundaries, while simultaneously affirming a politics of racial, gender, and ethnic difference. … In effect, postmodern criticism calls attention to the shifting boundaries related to the increasing influence of the electronic mass media and information technology, the changing nature of class and social formations in postindustrialized capitalist societies, and the growing transgression of boundaries life and art, high and popular culture, and image and reality.
>
> (pp. 58–59)

Their idea of shifting boundaries is a challenge to pedagogy to reformulate traditional conceptualizations of truth so that multiple perspectives, unhinged from prevailing hierarchies, are represented and valued. For media and communication educators, a postmodern philosophy confronts the discourses of cultural representations. Who is represented and who is excluded? How are they represented? In what ways do these representations signal dominant ideas or challenge them? Who creates these representations? What interests are promoted through them? Students are encouraged to place themselves within their own histories and narratives in order to construct a larger critique of knowledge that is historically and socially conscious. Educators thus reposition and validate alternative social narratives and voices by exploring them in the classroom. Aronowitz and Giroux (1991) stress an educational agenda that serves democracy and justice by privileging cultural pluralism and multiple student voices.

William Walter (June, 2011), a writing instructor at the University of Florida, talks about helping students to "find their voice" through an online class game in which students practice argumentation and persuasion through role playing. The game crafts a model whereby students must accept a non-traditional, postmodern approach to assignments and grading:

> I'm about them finding their voice but also familiarizing themselves with the professional writing context, which is why I devised this dual model that I call parallax pedagogy. You approach the same target but from two different orientations, which creates a bit of dissonance. The online game was designed to help students find their voice through their desires in these various position papers. But for students who weren't comfortable with that, they could take a creative writing approach through the role playing and character development. … I have a certain belief that the indoctrination

> of certain pedagogical models from elementary school on to high school really does kill students' belief in their own writing; it kills their confidence. They start to look at writing as an anxious experience as opposed to one that is communicative and involving. ... That's my motivation to do these courses—I'm almost desperate to unlock a little creativity and get them to stop thinking like that, at least in the humanities.

Professor Walter's techniques reveal his conviction that the traditional educational agenda might be better served by an approach that values students' authentic viewpoints and "desires." He adds:

> The humanities are oriented in personal gain—figuring out how to approach life from a position that is not locked down. When students are just getting into college, that's the malleable point. Beyond that, students have locked down their agendas about what they should want and what they should be. They have shut down to the openness, to the questioning. They're missing the glory of college. We aren't trying to program them! ... The detachment is the primary idea of my teaching philosophy. Re-instilling a sense of desire in students is *very* important to me. The institutionalization has restricted to a great degree the ability to do that in the classroom because even if you do these various assignments that are more experimental—the "Victor Vitanza" approach—it's still within the physical classroom, and you can never breach the institutional demands while you're in the physical classroom. I'm very interested in whether it is possible to destabilize an institutional space.

For Professor Walter, this destabilization is endemic to the notion that prevailing hierarchies of knowledge can indeed be challenged and potentially reconstituted.

Philosophy and Goals

Whatever "why" guides one's teaching philosophy, it connects to the overall goals an instructor wants to achieve with students. Sprague (1990) identifies four common goals for communication education that are born of philosophies often applied to communication. First, transmitting cultural knowledge is a goal that aims to enculturate students in the liberal educational tradition. For communication, this goal emphasizes a knowledge of great works of communication and media (speeches, films, and other important cultural products). Second, developing students' intellectual skills is a means of strengthening the learning process such that students become analytical, critical thinkers. For communication, this goal centers on a broad knowledge of communicative practices, processes, and critiques. Third, providing students with career skills is a goal often cited by parents and students as a rationale for a college education. For communication, this perspective responds to industry needs but is sometimes disparaged as anti-intellectual or too focused on the vocational. Last, reshaping the values of society is a goal that resonates with several philosophies examined in this chapter. It promotes the notion that students can be agents of social transformation and human emancipation. For communication, this goal is reflected in the study of ideology in rhetoric and in media. Together with general philosophies for communication/media studies, these goals can lend shape to both the actual practices and professional identities of communication instructors.

Briggs and Pinola (1985) remind us that "an educational philosophy helps educators in communication become true professionals through a commitment to principles, consistency, and responsibility" (p. 314). Thus, a teaching philosophy is a systematic, thoughtful representation of one's academic identity. It clarifies our own goals and values. It helps us to make decisions about teaching practices. It helps us locate ourselves within (or without) disciplinary and institutional cultures. A solid philosophy is dynamic, and it accounts for questions about communication in culture such as, what is the purpose of teaching media/communication studies? How might students grasp the central role of media as cultural storytellers? How do media colonize our public spaces? What is the connection between communication and identity? In what ways does communication both contribute to and challenge social change or social stability?

A solid philosophy also addresses questions of pedagogy such as, how do educators provide vocational skills in communication without sacrificing ethical critique of communicative practices? How is the curriculum representative of the best interests of multiple constituencies? How might students be taught to create media in responsible ways? These are questions of perennial importance that may be revisited as we continue to shape and reshape our own teaching philosophies. Instructors may be most comfortable borrowing from the underlying motivations of discrete philosophies and melding them into one reflective of their individual identity. Albert Einstein is credited with reworking a Chinese proverb into the question, "What does a fish know about the water in which he swims all his life?" In our media-soaked society, media and communication constitute that water. Students must learn to recognize the water and to make the imperceptible perceptible. An understanding of the why before the how for each communication educator will establish our ability to approach the task of aiding students in grasping the water.

References

Aronowitz, S., & Giroux, H. (1991). *Postmodern education: Politics, culture and social criticism.* Minneapolis, MN: University of Minnesota.

Bourdieu, P. (1984). *Distinction: A social critique of the judgment of taste.* Cambridge, MA: Harvard University Press.

Bragg, S. (2007). What Kevin knows: Students' challenges to critical pedagogical thinking. In A. Nowak, S. Abel, & K. Ross (Eds.), *Rethinking media education: Critical pedagogy and identity politics* (pp. 57–73). Cresskill, NJ: Hampton.

Briggs, N., & Pinola, M. (1985). A consideration of five traditional educational philosophies for speech communication. *Central States Speech Journal, 36*, 305–314.

Brooks, D. E., & Ward, C. J. (2007). Assessing students' engagement with pedagogies of diversity. *Journalism & Mass Communication Educator, 62*(3), 244–262.

Carey, J. (1989). *Communication as culture: Essays on media and society*. Boston, MA: Unwin Hyman.

Denski, S. (1991). Critical pedagogy and media production: The theory and practice of the video documentary. *Journal of Film and Video, 43*(3), 3–17.

Denski, S. (1994). Building bridges: Critical pedagogy and media studies. *Journal of Communication Inquiry, 18*(2), 65–76.

Dewey, J. (1916). *Democracy and education: An introduction to the philosophy of education*. New York, NY: Macmillan.

Dewey, J. (1927). *The public and its problems*. New York, NY: Henry Holt.

Fassett, D. L., & Warren, J. T. (2007). *Critical communication pedagogy*. Thousand Oaks, CA: Sage.

Freire, P. (1970). *Pedagogy of the oppressed* (M. G. Ramos, Trans.). New York, NY: Seabury.

Freire, P. (1985). *The politics of education: Culture, power, and liberation* (D. Macedo, Trans.). South Hadley, MA: Bergin & Garvey.

Jenkins, H., Purushotma, R., Weigel, M., Clinton, K., & Robison, A. J. (2009). *Confronting the challenges of participatory culture: Media education for the 21st century*. Cambridge, MA: MIT Press.

Kincheloe, J. L. (2005). *Critical constructivism primer*. New York, NY: Peter Lang.

Lattuca, L. R. (2006). The constructivist pedagogy we're looking for. *Journalism & Mass Communication Educator, 60*(4), 354–358.

Low, B. E. (2011). *Slam school: Learning through conflict in the hip-hop and spoken word classroom*. Stanford, CA: Stanford University Press.

May, S., & Sleeter, C. E. (2010). *Critical multiculturalism: Theory and praxis*. New York, NY: Routledge.

McLaren, P. (1999). Introduction: Traumatizing capital: Oppositional pedagogies in the age of consent. In M. Castells, R. Flecha, P. Freire, H. A. Giroux, D. Macedo, & P. Willis (Eds.), *Critical education in the new information age* (pp. 1–36). Lanham, MD: Rowman & Littlefield.

Meyers, C., & Jones, T. B. (1993). *Promoting active learning: Strategies for the college classroom*. San Francisco, CA: Jossey-Bass.

Rothenberg, P. (2007). Half-empty or half-full? "Diversity" in higher education today. *Liberal Education, 93*(1), 44–49.

Sharma, S. (2010). Critical multiculturalism and cultural and media studies. In S. May & C. E. Sleeter (Eds.), *Critical multiculturalism: Theory and praxis* (pp. 113–123). New York, NY: Routledge.

Sholle, D., & Denski, S. (1994). *Media education and the (re)production of culture*. Westport, CT: Bergin & Garvey.

Solorzano, D. G. (1989). Teaching and social change: Reflections on a Freirean approach in a college classroom. *Teaching Sociology, 17*, 218–225.

Sprague, J. (1990). The goals of communication education. In J. A. Daly, G. W. Friedrich, & A. L. Vangelisti (Eds.), *Teaching communication: Theory, research and methods* (pp. 19–38). Hillsdale, NJ: LEA.

3
TECHNOLOGY AND MEDIA/ COMMUNICATION PEDAGOGY

In the communication and media studies curriculum, technology is often the object of study. Beyond the economic, political, cultural, or historical ramifications of technological development in media and communication, our curricula consider specific technologies of design and delivery as social phenomena, as tools in the creative process, and as the environments in which our students live. Communication students are often adept at shooting and editing their own video, experimenting with audio technologies, microblogging, and constructing their digital selves through social media. They have learned to create and share knowledge collaboratively, technologically. Because technological considerations are now an essential thread running through all areas of communication pedagogy, this chapter references current and emerging technologies used in the classroom. This chapter is about conceptualizing the use of technology in teaching about communication rather than the use of specific technologies. This chapter also questions some of the institutional and cultural imperatives to embrace technology uncritically. All instructors have proclivities with specific pedagogical techniques and methods—and that includes specific technologies as well. In other words, consider what works for you and is consistent with your teaching philosophy, teaching goals, and academic identity. With Bates and Poole (2003), this chapter uses a definition of *technology* that encompasses non-direct means of interacting with students. Technology can therefore be used to supplement face-to-face courses or to structure online or hybrid courses. Whatever type of course, this chapter focuses on constructing sound pedagogical practices involving technology.

In some respects, using technology is a highly effective means for presenting information and for creating collaborative learning environments for media and communication students. Many of our students seek professional careers in

communication, and many of our faculty have professional experienc
industries. Within the academy, communication faculty use technology
istrative work and in research endeavors. Since these activities inform our
the incorporation of technology into our pedagogical strategy complem
academic identities. Our faculty are researchers in media labs, scholars examining social uses/misuses of technology, and practitioners with media contacts and jobs. Moreover, many academic practices are deeply interwoven with technology, creating a culture influenced by standardization, individualization, globalization, and capitalization. Hence, we don't hesitate to consider our own immersion in technological environments. It rings true to unify our teaching with our everyday environments.

New communication technologies abound in higher education classrooms, and faculty and students have abundant opportunities to engage them in the educational enterprise. With the rise in institutional investments in technological infrastructure, university faculty are expected to integrate technology into their teaching. Not only are private, online universities proliferating, but all of higher education has witnessed the impact of presentation software, course management software, and other information and communication technologies (ICTs). The ideology of the information society prizes novelty and innovation in the form of information capital. Thus, faculty may be subject to institutional mandates to show proficiency with ICTs in order to demonstrate to various constituencies basic competence in the information environment. The use of sophisticated courseware for managing individual classes is one manifestation of these ICT imperatives. Moreover, some educational literature (Turney, Robinson, Lee, & Soutar, 2009; Mayer, 2001) argues that effective pedagogy includes the use of multimedia in the active learning process. Beyond institutional considerations, individual faculty may want to reflect on the degree to which technology enhances the communication classroom and supports learning activities. Our students learn to create communication and media, and they learn to critique communication and media. Faculty have an obligation to consider technologies of media and communication in the classroom.

Some scholars (Quinlan, 2011; Richardson, 2006) argue that blogs and similar technologies are constructivist pedagogical tools because they create knowledge in collaborative ways that reach beyond a particular course. But because technology is integrated into students' lives, it is a vital part of their learning. Thus, instructors embracing nearly any pedagogical philosophy can find technology to be an essential part of their teaching portfolio. Technology inside the classroom can be used to enhance debates and exchanges of viewpoints. It can be used to provoke thought and as a means to see things anew. It can be deconstructed as an object of study and as a content delivery system. It can be used to question social inequalities. It can be used in communication/media classrooms as a tool for enhancing students' social capital since they are positioned to understand and use technology as well as to critique it. How might one use technology to complement a postmodern philosophy, or a constructivist philosophy, or a critical pedagogy? These philosophical perspectives differ with regard to their technological epistemologies in addition to their pedagogical assumptions. So, instructors can ask: Why does our political culture emphasize hyper-individualism and libertarianism at the expense of the community while our educational culture stresses collaborative thought and cooperative work efforts? What are the benefits of the investment in technology when students using laptops in the classroom are attentive to social media rather than class activities? What critiques surround the cultural narrative of progress that subsumes technological development? As technologies develop and become commonplace, learners' relationships with those technologies adjust, and they experience education differently as the culture at large contends with these shifts.

Such shifts are addressed by Boyer (2011), who contends that the conveniences of ICTs have "transformed the communicational and social relations of university life" (p. 183) in ways that sometimes obscure the focus on the university community of knowledge exchange in favor of commercial interests. Boyer argues that "digital ICTs destabilize the local communitarianism of traditional campus life through their accelerated temporality of productivity, through the individualizing property of their interfaces, and through their immense capacity to translocalize real-time academic communication" (p. 182). Thus, while we gain the ability to work rapidly and globally on our scholarship and teaching, that rapidity is stressed over quality, and, for Boyer, "[f]or all of the emancipatory moments and empowering aspects we associate with digital communication and information, it remains true that it catalyzes alienation just as commonly" (p. 183). It may be that our students are so distracted by their personal use of technologies like social media that they cannot conceive of how those communal technologies of entertainment may have educational utility.

Traxler (2012), in discussing the increasing use of social media within the classroom, notes that they are

> creating more and more places and modes that people can inhabit, where communities can form, where ideas, identities, images and information can be produced, stored, shared, transmitted and consumed and thus these technologies, each in their different ways, transform rather than merely reproduce the nature of learning. Each of these technologies may also have its own rules, for example concerning privacy, expressed in the appropriate terms and conditions to which users sign up. These may be at odds with their indigenous communities' custom and practice and with educators' own expectations.
>
> (p. 199)

Here, Traxler raises questions about the ethics of using technologies from outside the classroom in which students are so heavily socially and emotionally invested. But he also illuminates the possibilities for expanded modes of learning that are not only transformative, but culturally bound. The use of *au courant* social media in this way is particularly pertinent for media/communication students who are discovering that communication is culture.

Why Use Technology?

The communication/media studies classroom has transcended debates about technological affordances within higher education. Communication faculty recognize, with Jenkins, Purushotma, Weigel, Clinton, and Robison (2006), that faculty and student relationships with technology are implicated in the classroom. We must consider the interplay among communication technologies, the cultures surrounding various technologies, the political, economic, and legal imperatives that accompany them, and how they fit not only into media systems but also into our classrooms and into our students' lives. If we accept an epistemology of active learning and of engaging with questions of culture in communication, we accept the notion that our curricula have space for creating culture through technology—what Jenkins (2002) terms "participatory culture." He argues that "Participatory culture is emerging as the culture absorbs and responds to the explosion of new media technologies that make it possible for average consumers to archive, annotate, appropriate, and recirculate media content in powerful new ways. A focus on expanding access to new technologies carries us only so far if we do not also foster the skills and cultural knowledge necessary to deploy those tools toward our own ends" (2009, p. 8). Thus, students can be encouraged to participate in culture through an educational process that embraces technology. Whether in class or on their own, communication students often participate in cultural creation through remixing, fan fiction, machinima, podcasting, open source, or blogging. Types of knowledge that can be denoted in digital form and instantly shared are often privileged in both academic and popular circles. Communication and media faculty and students are at the forefront of critical examination of this epistemology.

According to Jenkins et al. (2006), participatory culture epitomizes optimal informal learning spaces. These so-called "affinity spaces"[1] that emerge as students create informal knowledge cultures speak to students on deep levels in which they are actively engaged. Such spaces might include wikis, fan fiction sites, or YouTube. Affinity spaces augment learning "because they are sustained by common endeavors that bridge differences—age, class, race, gender, and educational level—and because people can participate in various ways according to their skills and interests, because they depend on peer-to-peer teaching with each participant constantly motivated to acquire new knowledge or refine their existing skills, and because they allow each participant to feel like an expert while tapping the expertise of others" (2009, p. 10). This wisdom need not be interpreted in celebratory terms. A critical engagement with media, both in its creation and in its consumption, enhances the value of participatory culture for learning—in particular, peer learning. As Jenkins (2002) argues, participatory culture is characterized by:

1. Technologies empowering consumers with the ability to appropriate and reconfigure mediated content.
2. Subcultures forming around do-it-yourself media creation and the discourses arising from the D-I-Y ethos.

3. Global economic tendencies toward more democratized media companies that encourage audience interactivity and endorse the flow of images, narratives, and ideas over many media channels. (see p. 157)

These characteristics help evince an epistemological rationale for engaging with technology in the media studies/communication learning environment.

If we accept that technology is itself a process and not merely an artifact, as suggested by Amiel and Reeves (2008), we can embrace the nature of participatory culture as it speaks to learning. Technology continually develops and changes through the interplay of social, political, and human agents in addition to technical advances. Student-created culture will only increase as part of this evolutionary process. Media conglomerates will respond to new audience capabilities and technological realities by continuing to participate in the flow of images and narratives, and the learning environment will continue to integrate these notions into a full examination of communication and media as object of inquiry, and as tool (or a set of practices), and as process. The principles that guide the deployment of technology include a commitment to its ubiquity in contemporary higher education. For media and communication educators, this commitment is assumed, and participatory culture is increasingly the norm as students create and distribute their own narratives using social media technology that's inexpensive and easy to acquire. As technologies continue to evolve, the nature and products of participatory culture evolve and vice versa. Technologies themselves are by-products of a sociopolitical system that values technological progress. Participatory culture responds to these sociopolitical realities through its own narratives about progress that emerge from the ethos of DIY subcultures. That system views technological progress as a natural and vital outgrowth of the passage of time.

The full integration of technology into the learning experience represents a hybrid space of knowledge creation that breaches the walls of the classroom in expansive ways. Students are encouraged to share with one another and with the instructor and to invite the "outside" world in through the use of laptops or tablet devices with web access. They can instantly access external knowledge that pertains to what's being discussed or created in the classroom. They may even be encouraged to share the ideas of the classroom outside by microblogging during class or by creating a game that has use beyond the confines of the course. The group can work to construct knowledge together. The instructor is part of the group. The consequence of these actualities for the learning environment is that public culture is enhanced when students learn to become discriminating judges of information sources and when they transfer their skills at navigating various media from informal settings (gaming, blogging) to academic settings. For example, instructors can direct students in the use of social bookmarking sites for reviewing and evaluating literature on a communication phenomenon, and through the process of collaborative knowledge building, students generate materials for class discussion and evaluation. This allows students to foster skills of inquiry while simultaneously reflecting on their own learning process.

Oblinger and Oblinger (2005) find that college students immersed in technological environments develop "hypertext minds" (p. 2.4) comfortable with non-linear modes of thinking and assembling chunks of information from myriad sources. Traits that characterize these students include an intuitive ability to communicate visually; an aptitude for integrating hybridized physical and virtual environments; a capacity for learning through discovery; dispersed attention; and facility with rapid response (see p. 2.5). These traits suggest shallow, imprecise thinking that is dependent on collective effort. They also suggest the potential for originality and resourcefulness. A plan for integrating various technologies into any course might account for these characteristics but should principally be cognizant of their epistemological implications. Oblinger and Oblinger (2005) argue that students expect technology to be integrated into their courses—particularly for convenience and customization—but they also desire the social interaction of the face-to-face classroom in the learning process. They are comfortable with multiple modalities in the classroom. Beetham and Oliver (2010) see an evolution in epistemological worthiness in higher education to include networked knowledge, multimedia literacy, collaborative learning, and critical awareness. They suggest ways for educators to respond to this evolution, by rethinking some conventional academic routines of knowledge production and by encouraging students to respect some academic traditions. Strategies they advocate include the development of:

- Authentic contexts for practice, including digitally mediated contexts;
- Individual support for development, recognising [sic] learners' different prior experiences and practices;
- Making explicit academic practices and expectations of meaning-making;
- Anticipating and helping learners manage conflict between different practices and contexts. (p. 165)

For media and communication students, applications of these strategies might include allowing them to dictate the extent to which they prefer to use social media in learning contexts while highlighting the possibilities for formal and informal learning in these spaces. Or, students might write about their experiences as authors of their own intellectual property and as users of others'.

Communication and media faculty must consider the purpose of education when making judgments about the use of technology in our courses. What values are we promoting? How do we reconcile the interdisciplinary nature of communication as a field? Are technologies used in learning to encourage critique or subversion or liberation or connection or career training? Technologies themselves do not possess inherent characteristics that make them useful. The use of specific technologies may derive from social practices or they may be designed as a result of socioeconomic-political pressures. Human agency may drive technological practices in unintended ways. Technological tools may redirect systems of social activity as deployed in specific institutional contexts. The adoption of branded courseware may, for example, enhance students' educational experience by consolidating learning activities and materials into one unit, but the social good is not part of the consideration of the adoption of course management products. Instead, the institutional imperative to embrace technology in an economically prudent way most likely guides the adoption of a particular brand of courseware and its attendant add-on features. Similarly, university administrations must appear, to various constituencies (parents, students, legislators), to endorse the values of interactivity and technological progress. Corporations producing these technologies are responding to the perceived needs of universities and their constituencies by satisfying the demand for the new and the progressive technologies.

Our ways of knowing are not detached from the practices surrounding technology, so perhaps our understanding of and interaction with technology is shaped by the cultural practices surrounding the development and employment of technological artifacts in educational settings. Might the use of tablet devices in the classroom both create and respond to a particular epistemology about the interactive nature of tablet technology? Because technology is an object of study in media and communication, we are obligated to grasp the value-laden nature of technology, both as process and product. We are obligated to assume a critical stance toward the role of technological practices in the educational enterprise. Accordingly, educational principles and goals should guide the use of technology. Amiel and Reeves (2008) reinforce this critical stance, arguing, "Gone unquestioned, the values promoted by the technological process are clear. Technology mediated by powerful interest groups is based on and promotes efficiency, speed, control, and reliability—values that primarily emphasize economic utility" (p. 33). Education should be about human agency, discovery, empowerment, fulfillment, and potential rather than economic efficiency.

In response, the edupunk ethos, founded by Jim Groom (Young, 2008), eschews the use of corporate educational technologies such as Blackboard. Edupunk promotes an ethic of DIY defiance against corporatized higher education and in favor of original, independent approaches to thinking and learning (Young, 2008). The idea is that corporatized courseware and its predetermined menus cuts off the possibilities of the web and creates isolated spaces that remove paths toward exploration outside the courseware. Edupunk reminds educators that, while Blackboard may be useful, it is not the panacea that some university administrators might believe it is. Groom (Young, 2008) prefers that students question the assumptions underlying the conventions of packaged courseware. For media and communication students, this ethos seems like a matter of course. Our students are skilled at selecting and manipulating raw materials online to reappropriate for use in sampling, remixing, or mashups. Using these selection, repurposing, and sharing skills in academic ways is a valuable learning activity. Some institutions are recognizing this value through the expansion of the boundaries of learning—establishing learning communities and global partnerships, widening access to libraries, and course content sharing—to develop models of an "edgeless university" (Bradwell, 2009).

Educators must work to design a strategy for the use of technology that takes into consideration their teaching philosophies and course goals. Educators must similarly reflect on that strategy in order to keep it fresh and mindful of those goals. This symbiotic process is advocated by Amiel and Reeves (2008), who claim that, "integrating technologies into the classroom leads to substantial changes in social organization, student-teacher relationships, and a myriad of other factors ..." (p. 35). When students are educated about the design and implementation of educational technologies, a participatory culture of deliberation, collaboration, and inquiry develops. This outlook on technology privileges the value of education as a social good in a democratic society.

Technology in a Media-saturated Environment

Students in communication/media and in related disciplines learn with technology and through technology as they are awash in the ubiquity of media. These students are quite aware that they "live within social media," as mine often declare. They tend to grasp the nature of technologies as communicative devices and as objects of study and critique. They are savvy about popular discourses about media culture such as those regarding citizen journalism or digital surveillance. Thus, students expect to encounter technology in media/communication curricula, and they expect to use it in deep ways that challenge their preconceptions and current skill levels. They often expect to be entertained and engaged by technology. They are multitaskers, and at least one of those multiple tasks involves some type of technology. They are members of multiple personal and organizational networks. They are part of a culture of technology; technology is part of their identity. Sherry Turkle (2011) argues that digital technologies have become the "architect of our intimacies," beginning in adolescence. For our students, their immersion in social media spaces in which they are "always on" means that their conception of self has become more collaborative because "we are together even when we are alone" (p. 169). They must undergo identity management from an early age and in multiple mediated and non-mediated milieus. Simultaneously, our students have been influenced by institutional imperatives that revere technology. Universities seduce applicants with technological marvels, and once enrolled, students understand that technological literacy is mandated. This amalgamation of expectations, characteristics, and imperatives creates opportunities for educators to embrace technology in the classroom in innovative ways.

To illustrate, Dustin Morrow (July, 2011), who teaches media production, describes his approach to using technology to teach technology:

> Part of teaching media production is teaching technology, which doesn't have to be as dry and challenging as it seems. There are few things more frustrating than listening to an instructor drone on, "This button does

> this and this button does that." I learn new software and new equipment extremely quickly because I find that understanding technology is largely intuitive—when I'm learning a new program, I try to imagine why the author of the software laid it out as he/she did, and similarly, when I'm learning a new piece of equipment I wonder why the engineer constructed it in a particular way. These are questions I bring up when teaching technology, and I have found that it always helps students learn more quickly.

Professor Morrow demonstrates a discovery-based, collaborative approach to the use of technology in the classroom that accounts for our students' involvement with technology and with participatory culture. This mode of teaching speaks to the DIY subcultures that characterize participatory culture. Students connect with the instructor, with one another, and with outside sources to learn. To students who are "always on" and whose identities are in many ways intertwined with digital technologies, a critical mastery of techniques for learning technological skills seems indispensable.

Some scholars (notably Boon & Sinclair, 2009) question the efficacy of social media spaces such as Facebook for educational purposes. They find that the variability of identities in these spaces leads to issues of trust and veracity, ultimately leading to conflict and detachment for some students. They implicate the architecture of sites like Facebook for this phenomenon, claiming that they are "designed for and prefer the novel, popular, and phatic over the meaningful, factual, and content-driven, [such that] academics might find themselves faced with questionable levels of engagement and difficulty in achieving meaningful, deep learning for their students" (p. 108). Such a critique is constructive, for it cautions instructors that social media spaces may have limitations as educational spaces. Nevertheless, it is incumbent upon educators to exploit the possibilities of participatory culture to engage students meaningfully with the technological society.

Using wikis routinely in his writing classes, Terry Harpold (June, 2011 & May, 2014), an English professor at the University of Florida, describes ways that he builds on the ethos of participatory culture to create valuable learning experiences for his students:

> I'm less interested in building online tools for propping up a course—blogs, listservs and the like—than in resituating the course more fully within a digital context, where the discussion continues to operate, to generate new meanings, after the event of the class meeting. The wiki offers the possibility of elaborating on, redirecting classroom exchanges, taking them into new lines of thought that didn't emerge in the class. I encourage students to be open to, and to recognize in my mode of teaching, the force of what the French call *l'esprit d'escalier*—"staircase wit": the clever argument or rejoinder that occurs to you only after the party is over, as you descend the staircase—or in this case, after you leave the classroom. One of the ways we foster this is to assign on a rotating basis a couple of students to take notes

> directly in the wiki during class. I'll go back to these notes afterwards, and edit and expand on them, and after that other students will also edit and expand on the notes. Over time, this accretes into a brambly but surprisingly productive collection of the lecture notes, a richer, more expansive and more dynamic document than any one student could produce, or that I could give the students if I just gave them a copy of (ugh!) PowerPoint lecture slides.
>
> They need to grow accustomed to writing in a more freeform, branching, and *entangled* mode than they are generally accustomed to. "Everything is deeply intertwingled," as Ted Nelson has said: in the wiki environment, writing is locally lucid and well-defined, but globally-linked and errant. I encourage them to link to other students' writing, to revise and elaborate that writing, and to learn to read not only the current version of any page in the wiki, but also the audit trail of prior edits, so as to see how the current page emerged—which ideas were introduced, discarded, and modified along the way. Above all, I want them to see their writing in this environment as something that is dynamic and mutable. The outcome of this effort is much more complex than a blog, which is really a form of journal writing—something they already know about and can master pretty easily. The wiki challenges them to consider writing and reading as dynamic, unfinished processes.

Harpold's use of wikis reveals a means by which instructors can create course content that is greater than the sum of its parts through participatory culture. Knowledge is created, reworked, added to, and re-created again. That knowledge is generated by instructors, students, supplemental online materials, and invited experts. Richardson (2006) identifies this process, echoing Harpold, in terms of the social construction of knowledge, arguing that "information created and published in this way takes on a new social context that requires us to change the way we think about what we ask our students to produce, not as something to be "finished" but as something to be added to and refined by those outside the classroom who may interact with it" (p. 129). This collective practice of knowledge construction is not just a benefit of social learning but a personal benefit as well as students gain new strategies for understanding and interpretation.

Because the media environments in which we live are technologically enabled, instructors wishing to be technologically innovative in their teaching understand that student writing may encompass more than written text. According to Richardson (2006), the products of student writing could include multiple genres—video, audio, HTML, digital photography—that create expansive textual meaning. The Internet was designed as a system of connected networks, horizontally integrated and collaborative. As part of our mediated environment, social media, wikis, virtual worlds, blogs, and microblogs use the wisdom of the Internet's design to model cooperative educational spaces. Course texts are supplemented or even crafted by the learning process when instructors use these tools. The system of knowledge construction is a leaky one, and knowledge flows readily in multiple directions, not just from instructor to student. Our students are awash in information, and communication/media studies educators understand that students can easily accumulate more information. What students need help with is managing that information in ways that enable them to learn, critique, create, and reflect. Moreover, classroom engagement with social media and other digital tools permits faculty to highlight the ways in which those tools might be manipulating student perceptions, interactions, lifestyles, and values, in addition to the social contexts of their lives.

Using Technology in the Active-learning Classroom

The active-learning classroom experience focuses on learning as a public endeavor. The focus is on how students learn. Active learning does not eschew lecture as a mode of content delivery; rather, it seeks communal engagement with content in ways as diverse as talking, writing, or reflecting. Students are actively engaged rather than passively receptive. They are provided occasions to absorb, incorporate, employ, and reflect upon course materials. Active learning techniques allow for the development of "affinity spaces" (Gee, 2004)—those informal cultures of public knowledge produced when students experiment and engage collectively with materials outside the domain of course content in accordance with their own reservoirs of expertise. Students captivated in these ways cultivate a personal stake in the generation of knowledge. In the media/communication curriculum, opportunities abound for the use of technology in creating active learning environments. Social media, wikis, podcasts, or class blogs are evident here, but open source content (Slideshare, for example), online gaming, or video/audio simulations can be innovative means for maximizing technological resources. Students might collaborate on developing film or video content ratings standards, experimenting with communication ethics scenarios, constructing visual projects involving new spatial realities, or programming a local video news operation. Such activities produce experiences that, in Dewey's (1916) conception, foster community and enhance learning. The emphasis is on constructing knowledge collectively and not just consuming it individually.

Because educators are most likely resistant to technologically deterministic approaches to the integration of technology into the communication classroom, active learning places the student at the center of the learning enterprise. Technology serves the learner. This is where the creativity of the communication/media instructor is paramount. Constructing an immersive course game, for example, puts the student at the crux of learning activity. Students who create media and who analyze it as part of their studies understand that interacting with media technologies in active ways is an inherent part of the learning process. They use skills of reading and writing, coupled with technology, to interrogate the technologies themselves as sociotechnical systems. They not only create meaning, but they contest meaning within digital forms of expression and representation. Contending with technologies that they use in production helps students not only to learn in flexible ways that engage multiple senses (see Mayer, 2001) but to engage with the object of their studies in meaningful, personal ways.

One way to accomplish this is for faculty to use simple technologies in teaching how to create mediated communicative messages. For example, some universities have created special YouTube channels for the sharing of student content—a useful interface for collaboration and for the promotion of a deeper understanding of material. Instructors can use Skype in the classroom to instigate dialogues between outside experts and students. Or, an instructor might create a video or audio file on some foundational subject so that students might experiment on their own in order to master the content while working collaboratively in a classroom setting. Jack Klotz (June, 2012), who teaches audio production at Temple University, has used this technique so his students might practice course material individually or within small groups. He uses a field recorder to record himself reciting the directions for the basic operation of that same field recorder while in front of the class. He uploads the recording to Blackboard for continued student reference. The environment allows for a customizable and flexible means for Professor Klotz to deliver the material while the possibilities for student interaction with that material expand. They may construct mental techniques for knowing the material in a richer way than simply hearing the instructor provide directions on one occasion.

Practical issues can develop around the use of technological innovations in learning. Faculty are often overwhelmed with responsibilities, and the mastery of new technologies for novel uses can curb the desire to embrace learner centered epistemologies. In a case study involving the use of wikis for peer knowledge construction, Lim, So, and Tan (2010) discuss the alteration of classroom practices to adopt digital technologies in active learning:

> Transitory issues where design of socio-techno-spatial relationship is concerned would require learners to shift their dependence from instructor to peers. Learners need to be educated that learning is in the process of construction itself and not just the end product. The challenge then becomes how to facilitate the process of construction for productive and meaningful learning. Conversely, instructors would need to be equipped with sound pedagogical principles for the design of collaborative teaching and learning interactions. Translating this to the institutional level, this could imply an increase in manpower support and financial investment.
>
> (p. 209)

Lim et al. find that students using a course wiki tended to focus on policing grammar or agreeing with fellow student contributions to the wiki rather than on higher order levels of thinking and involvement. They suggest a cultural shift in the practice of engaging with technologies for collaborative learning:

> A possible way to redesign the socio-technical spatial relationships would be to create greater interdependence between the social practices and the use of technologies. Besides simply having learners' [sic] work in the public domain, instructors could invite experts in the field to the wikis or blogs created for comments and feedback. The presence of a larger audience, besides the instructors, could influence social practices to use technology more purposefully for meaningful interaction. In reciprocal ways, learners' work could add value in the real-world thereby empowering learners for knowledge construction. For such practices to occur, therein requires a shift in cultural beliefs that learning is about having learners use technology for knowledge construction as opposed to instructors using technology for knowledge transmission. Instructors could perhaps educate themselves by participating in teacher communities to learn what others are doing. They could perhaps begin with adaptation of current practices before transiting to innovative design of pedagogical practices.
>
> (p. 214)

These suggestions could include such strategies as using a scaffolding technique (discussed in greater detail in the chapter on taxonomies) whereby instructors guide students through knowledge acquisition and subsequently step back to allow the student to learn how to learn. Both instructors and students of media and communication have opportunities to use their skills as effective communicators across various media to adapt to an environment of collaborative knowledge construction. Singer (2008) promotes the use of blogs as a means to boost students' communicative skills and to emphasize the conversational, collaborative, reflective, and fluid nature of knowledge construction as an educational process. She notes that blogs can be "tools for individual empowerment as well as engagement with a topic and with other students. Blogs generally can provide users with a strong sense of community, agency, or both" (p. 12). For our students who seek media industry employment, the idea of using technology for the purposes of constructing knowledge as a community is particularly valuable, and educators can model those techniques for learners. For example, Delwiche (2006) found that the use of massively multiplayer online games (MMOs) in undergraduate communication courses was effective in bridging the context of game play to professional communicative contexts. MMOs can serve as "living, breathing textbooks that provide students with first-hand exposure to critical theory and professional practice" (p. 161) as students can map their gaming experiences onto professional domains.

William Walter (June, 2011), at the University of Florida, constructed a game called MAddE World for his Argument and Persuasion course. The game involves experimentation and play in a virtual universe with avatars, but its purpose is to sharpen students' persuasive writing skills. Students join teams and participate in quests in order to submit collective position statements on various topics and to debate these positions online. Each student's avatar develops in accordance with the team's performance in these engagements in argumentation.

Here is the basic context of the game:

> In this semester's game, we enter into a virtual world where two Cabals (secret organizations) are competing for the domination of intellectual pursuits of their society. These two organizations are in philosophical opposition. The Cabal of Mad Scientists believes that the universe exists only in a material sense, and therefore is capable of being understood through empirical investigation and reasoning. The Cabal of Madde Humanists believes in a universal, transcendental force that is approachable only through a realization of being and "tapping into" the essence of humanity.
>
> As a new character enters this virtual universe, they must choose an alignment to a Cabal and establish a separate identity for the game and form a team of like-minded characters. Students will create characters based on their own personal interest and academic field, and speak as this character through their research and writing. Based on the quality and improvement of thought and writing, characters will gain experience points and rewards that can be used in the ongoing narrative detailing the struggle between the scientists and humanists.

The students conduct raids and assaults on other teams and characters in order to gain loot and accumulate "experience points," which comprise part of each student's final grade. The assaults consist of arguments constructed around topics of their choice. Because Walter's teaching philosophy focuses on helping students to find their own voice, the game is a personalized means for students to experiment with establishing their own positions on a number of topics. His game can help to alleviate the cut-and-paste mindset that characterizes online learning activities by creating an opportunity for students to construct their own learning. They can assemble sources and frameworks to forge a unique learning experience for the groups within the game and for the students as a class group.

William Walter (June, 2011) uses the game construct in an attempt to draw students into learning in a familiar, fun format while still engaging them with standard assignments—what he calls "desire versus demand." Students are rewarded for "finding their voice through their desires" by writing arguments but also through the role playing and character development. Walter advises the students to be creative in the game experience, and in past courses the students have delved into the game so deeply that the amount of work can be overwhelming for Walter. But students eventually grasped the "desire versus demand" format and shifted from submitting traditional position papers to submitting original illustrations, images, and even an extended poem as an argument.

He finds that the game captivates students' desires to interact with peers while providing a structure from which to accomplish the goals of the course:

> I wanted to tap into the natural desire to write and to show students what writing wasn't. I believe that the indoctrination of certain pedagogical

> models from elementary school on to high school kills students' belief in their own writing; it kills their confidence. They start to look at writing as an anxious experience as opposed to one that is communicative and involving. So my goal was to break that mindset and hopefully teach them some new tactics. I also aim for multimedia texts or cross-media texts, so I use comic books because the arguments are there and uncovering them is half the fun. Ultimately, in the online gaming portion of the course, the students actually do their own research to support their arguments.

Walter reports that many students who've taken his argumentation course say they've never been so excited to write. The students learn to question their own assumptions and to become open to alternative ideas. He adds, "any kind of online format really does liberate the student because of the detachment that occurs in telepresence. I think that's the greatest advantage—the disconnect from the institutional practices. You are removing students from those practices—literally taking out that institutional space and the influences of that space. Walking into a classroom automatically frames a certain mindset, and having this online gaming forum observed but not intervened with always has a liberating effect."

He acknowledges the drawbacks of certain technologies in the learner-centered curriculum, however. In their edited volume on digital pedagogy, Beetham and Sharpe (2007) conclude that students will accept more responsibility for their own learning in an educational environment of shifts from information to communication, from inactive to interactive engagement, and from individual learning to socially contextual learning. Walter sees some difficulties in motivating students' desires in a technologically experimental, active-learning forum, noting:

> You have to incentivize student behavior by requiring them to post on one another's comments in order to build a community—to engage with what others are learning. We are in a transition phase between analog and digital and as with Ulmer's term "electracy," it hasn't solidified enough. There are not enough rigid rules and so you have to take the risk. Sometimes I'm a bit disappointed in the outcome. I try to stay in tune with what students are using, but right now Facebook is the only thing that's universally accessible with students and it's just too restrictive. It has its own social rules which restrict to a certain degree the breakaway from traditional writing modes that they're used to.

In an attempt to use technologies to accomplish his goals and to encourage students to be self-determined and committed to participating in online learning communities, Walter holds office hours via Skype. He can accommodate multiple students in a "collective chat space" where they can discuss projects or problems and interact with each other. The use of the technological interface can allay student reticence to meet the professor in office hours to provide a safe, meaningful, collaborative space for students to explore course topics further (and sometimes to depart from course topics).

Tom Johnson (June, 2012), professor of Journalism at the University of Texas at Austin regularly uses social media in his classes. In his Journalism History class, he created a Facebook group containing a photo album with major historical figures, documents and other terms for a "hall of fame or hall of shame." Students can vote on whether the figures belong in the hall of fame or shame. He posts discussion questions and class videos, and students use Facebook to ask their colleagues questions or to post their own questions. Johnson contends that the biggest danger for him is too great a reliance on technology. He sends graded assignments through other means so as not to penalize students without Facebook accounts. Students may not always accept the use of social media for educational purposes when they are inured to using them for entertainment, but these technologies are increasingly part of their general identities, and they will adapt to their educational uses.

How Not to Use Technology

Technology cannot fix bad teaching. Good teaching involves a sense of purpose. Good teaching requires authenticity, clear communication, interest in course material, and the ability to motivate students to find value in the material. Objectives for student learning drive pedagogical techniques, and technology may aid in the service of those objectives. Students do not always expect technological wizardry, but they do expect instructor expertise and caring. According to Roberts (2005), they expect a classroom setting that integrates lecture with interactive activities, and they consider course management software and PowerPoint to be standard tools of the classroom. However, too much emphasis on collaborative learning through technology may seem aimless. The goals and requirements of a course must be reflected in the choices of technologies used in that course. As Dustin Morrow (July, 2011), professor in the Department of Theater and Film at Portland State University, argues, "It is important that students understand that mastering technology comes only with practice and that understanding technology is just one small step toward becoming a good media creator. Knowing how an Avid operates doesn't make one an editor, just as a knowledge of Photoshop doesn't make one a graphic designer."

Faculty must consider whether there are ways in which using technology can limit creativity. For example, the linear nature of PowerPoint presentation software may handicap the instructor who wishes to explore issues from multiple perspectives simultaneously. Can technological discourses be overpowering? Faculty are bombarded with entreaties to prepare students for citizenship in a digital culture. Institutions push technological developments as solutions for overburdened faculty, administrators, and students. But, technological solutions should be embraced voluntarily without being imposed. Educational benefits rather than profit or convenience or external pressures—such as globalization or the knowledge economy—should dictate the uses of technology. Often, technologies such as course management software may ease administrative communication with students and serve as a central repository for course materials, but they can require a significant time investment.

Terry Harpold (June, 2011 & May, 2014) of the University of Florida provides some suggestions for instructors using technology. He alerts faculty about what to expect from students and what to expect from themselves. His experiences stem from his use of a class wiki, but his advice is broadly applicable:

> 1) Don't assume that, because your students spend hours each day tweeting, Facebooking, and WWW-browsing, they grasp the genuine potential of writing and reading in the digital field. Be prepared for their initial resistance to, then later (and possibly excessive) enthusiasm in response to, being required to *do* really new kinds of classwork. Their behaviors and personae online *are* being shaped by the new media, but they are in general little aware of how this is happening—most of them have a naive understanding of their writing, reading and reasoning practices while online; very few of them have engaged seriously with the robust body of critical thought on these subjects.
>
> They have at best a sort of intuitive, fuzzy grasp of what my colleague Greg Ulmer calls "electracy"—a competence in modes of expression and reasoning that are specific to digital media, comparable to those associated with "literacy" and print. But they usually don't *know* what it means to be an electrate subject. Because they still measure their class work in relation to best practices of print they may, for example, consider the paratactic and polylineal forms of expression that new media facilitate to be weak or improper forms, and elements to be expunged from their writing. Or, conversely, they may be so thrilled to be allowed to work in "messy" and "undisciplined" ways that they will resist the idea that these new forms of writing and revision can be *rigorously performed*. Shifting their habits of writing from hierarchically-defined, possessive-individualist modes to more intertwingled, collaborative modes doesn't mean slipping into a lazy, go-with-the-crowd folksonomy. It requires actually thinking and acting in social forms that remain in some very deep ways always conflictual and unstable. *That's* where the generativity of those forms comes from.
>
> 2) Don't assume that, because you've spent a good deal of time reading the critical theory and reflecting on its applications to the classroom you'll be ready for the dynamic that will emerge in such an environment. You *will* be surprised, pleasantly and unpleasantly, by students' engagement with medially-specific traits of readings, discussions, and revisions. And that's ultimately beneficial to your pedagogical training. Things will happen in threads of the wiki for which you were not prepared. I don't just mean that you'll have to mediate and possibly shut down flame wars and discussions that become misdirected because students are lacking in the phatic

information that tends, in a physical classroom, to keep tempers and digressions under control. There is always some of that, though I've found that students after a time can pretty well learn new protocols and rules of behavior and that the signal-to-noise ratio will return to balance after an initial period of break-in and some periodic flare-ups.

A good way to head off such problems is to insist from the beginning that every communication in the wiki is a committed piece of writing, even if it's just a fragment, even if it's intended as an aside or joke. Because everything written into the wiki is permanently preserved—though it may of course be edited and thus made to disappear from current versions of wiki pages—every misstep, as it were, is preserved and can potentially be seen by wiki participants. Once you make that clear, students are much less likely to misbehave than you might at first worry. Another thing I insist on from the start is that students cannot "txt" their contributions to the wiki—they have to contribute complete, grammatically-correct and correctly-spelled words and sentences. I'm not trying to discourage informality and invention, but I tell them that what we do in the wiki is just as serious and disciplined a practice of composition and revision as any writing they might do for a take-home midterm or a final paper.

My informal rule in these matters is that *everything that happens in the wiki is productive of something*—new understanding, new misunderstandings, new collaboration, new conflicts: new signifiers are generated, to which the classroom history is bound, around which it is oriented. And this creates new opportunities for reflection, engagement, for thinking not only about the conditions of teaching and discussion, but also for addressing the unique productivity of these media. The problem of the signal-to-noise ratio to which I alluded before only seems a problem if you think of "noise" as something always to be expunged from the exchange. It may be evidence of a potentially productive disturbance in the dialogue.

Professor Harpold's words provide caution for the instructor to expect some unanticipated outcomes when employing technologies in teaching, but those outcomes can be surprisingly rewarding. Students are often interested in experimenting with new modalities for learning, and a wise approach to using technology in teaching can thwart potential negatives arising from the unanticipated outcomes.

William Walter (June, 2011), the creator of the MAddE World virtual environment, also provides some advice for instructors in the use of technology in teaching.

Bringing technology into the classroom does not necessarily improve the quality of the teaching. Just because it's progressive doesn't mean it's better—it's a PowerPoint problem. With regard to my teaching philosophy, PowerPoint undermines my purpose because it re-appropriates a lot

> of experimental resources that you can use into the institutional space. So I think that's counter-productive. All I really need is a chalkboard.
>
> Nevertheless, don't be afraid to step into unfamiliar territory. You don't need to be the master of the technology that you're using or even really FEEL like you are because students will pick up on that and think that whatever you're doing is the "right" way to do things. This is especially with lectures—because it's a language of invention, you need to make sure that you're not too locked into what you believe the internet should be. I wasn't using Tumblr, but I knew a lot of people who did, and so I stepped into that just as unfamiliar as my students were. You should always warm up—test it out, but don't feel like you have to be the expert on the resource that you're using. Know about what it can and cannot do but encourage students to find that out for themselves. Otherwise they're just going to play to what they think your expectations are. That defeats the purpose. Some people just might not feel comfortable not being the authority. I understand that anxiety, but I believe that if you're going to destabilize a classroom you have to destabilize too. You have to go ahead and admit—"I'm figuring this out too." That allows students a lot more flexibility because there's no pressure to do it "right." Instead, it's play. It encourages a more playful attitude. When you do find something that you like, like Skype, it's OK to stick with that. If a resource works reuse it. You always should check yourself and make sure that your familiarity with and your use of the resource doesn't become something locked down and solid. I remind myself that just because a student is doing something that I've never seen before or I don't necessarily think is the best way to use the technology, they're experimenting with it and that's what's important.
>
> You have to find the ways to motivate the students. I found this social game play to be effective, but that's not the only thing to do. You have to make some sort of personal incentive. It's difficult, but be creative. Experiment. Don't be afraid to fail. If you're a good enough teacher, even your failures will have some sort of value. That's really daunting to a lot of teachers. It's a challenge that most people don't want to put the effort into because it's hard work. You cannot reach students without taking risks. Otherwise you'll just be miserable. You can always open a bar!

His successes with the MAddE World game and with using Skype for office hours are testaments to Walter's convictions. While instructors may be reluctant to experiment too wildly with technology, those experiments can result in some innovative pedagogy. For the media and communication educator, such experimentation is usually rewarded as our students expect an inventive, modern curriculum. Our students may demonstrate a greater sophistication with the use, the purposes, and the cultural relevance of various technologies, and instructors must therefore show substantive reasons for using technology for instructional purposes.

Issues of Copyright and Fair Use in Teaching with Technology in the United States

We use digital media in our teaching—both inside and outside of the classroom. We also create with them. Course materials and classroom activities might include mashups, blogs, video games, YouTube videos, audio remixes, scholarly documents, news archives, Tumblr entries, slideshows, music, or documentary films. Communication and media faculty have a dual responsibility with regard to understanding intellectual property (IP) law—we must protect our own IP creations (and those of our students) as well as respect IP copyrighted by others. The ability to use copyrighted materials in limited ways is protected by the legal doctrine of *fair use*. The purpose of fair use is to ensure that copyright restrictions do not imperil the free flow of information and creativity. Fair use is meant to serve the public good. Fair use is crucial to freedom of expression and social discourse in education. Educators are protected from copyright lawsuits when they rely on the principles of fair use.

Section 110 of the Copyright Act (Title 17 of the United States Code) allows exemptions for classroom instructors to use copyrighted material, without penalty of infringement, for the purposes of teaching and criticism within the classroom. However, communication/media instructors tend to use digital media in transformative ways in the classroom, and students often use digital means to create their own transformative works—a form of participatory culture. This creative process usually occurs through the use of tools of technology and is therefore addressed in this chapter. Section 110 states in part,

> Notwithstanding the provisions of section 106, the following are not infringements of copyright: (1) performance or display of a work by instructors or pupils in the course of face-to-face teaching activities of a nonprofit educational institution, in a classroom or similar place devoted to instruction, unless, in the case of a motion picture or other audiovisual work, the performance, or the display of individual images, is given by means of a copy that was not lawfully made under this title, and that the person responsible for the performance knew or had reason to believe was not lawfully made.
>
> (Copyright Law of the United States, p. 24)

Fair use of copyrighted material, explained in Section 107 of the Copyright Act, is the notion that the public may use copyrighted works, without permission or penalty of infringement, in a manner that does not inhibit the copyright holder's market for that material. Educational use is a fair use. With regard to face-to-face teaching in the classroom, the use of copyrighted works for educational purposes is permissible. With regard to online learning or distance education, the TEACH Act (The Technology, Education and Copyright Harmonization Act of 2002) created a set of revisions to the Copyright Act, explaining the procedures for the display of copyrighted works within nonprofit educational institutions. The Act, codified in Section 110(2) of the Copyright Act, sanctions the digital transmission of copyrighted works by nonprofit educational institutions provided specific conditions—centered on providing students with notice of copyright and education about copyright law—are met. The TEACH Act is an alternative to fair use or licensing but has limited usefulness due to its restrictive definitions of what constitutes an educational institution, digital rights management requirements, and time limits on access to class materials.

In the case *Cambridge University Press et al. v. Becker et al.*,[2] Georgia State University was sued by three publishers—Cambridge University Press, SAGE Publications, and Oxford University Press—over copyright infringement involving materials on electronic course reserves. The publishers alleged that the university violated copyright provisions by allowing access to digitized material without permission or license. The university claimed fair use, citing the increasingly popular use of e-reserve materials under provision of limited access (usually per semester). Ultimately Georgia State prevailed but with a few caveats that are important for instructors and administrators to comprehend. (Note that as of fall 2013, the publishers announced an appeal, but the case was listed as ongoing in the 11th Circuit Court.) The case distinguishes between permissible and exploitive copying by standardizing the amount of permissible copying under fair use as either 10% or a single chapter (Howard, 2012). A ruling of standardization is unusual in fair use cases, and it places libraries and faculty into a rigid structure of proportionality. Another aspect of this case involves the potential harm to the market of the copyrighted works. In this case, the judge acknowledged that the publisher plaintiffs had different licensing schemes for copyrighted works that created a convoluted set of problems for universities seeking permission to use these works fairly. For the purposes of understanding what this verdict means for instructors wondering about fair use of copyrighted material, it illustrates the principle that while educational uses are fair uses, there are some basic practices to follow to ensure lawsuit-free teaching with technology.

A fair use is one in which the use is transformative, provides credit to the originator, and is proportional. A transformative use puts copyrighted material into a new context or repurposes it for a new audience. To comment on a work itself—via parody or quoting—is nearly always considered a transformative use. Including film clips in a classroom discussion of aesthetic practices is a transformative use. Creating a class wiki about Internet memes that incorporates YouTube videos is a transformative use. Developing a library of prelicensed or public domain music samples for students to use in remixes is a transformative use. In these instances, providing credit to the original creator demonstrates a knowledge of fair use as well as a respect for the creator's hard work. And limiting the proportion of the material used to that which is appropriate to the *purpose* of the use keeps the use fair. To aid scholars and others in understanding the principles of fair use, Patricia Aufderheide and Peter Jaszi have created a series of best practices for fair use.[3] In their book

Reclaiming Fair Use (2011), they note some common ways to think about fair use practices. First, *comment and critique* requires quoting of the copyrighted material. This function is a staple of media and communication curricula engaged in analysis of mediated materials. It is also used extensively by documentary filmmakers (who are often educators) to create works of social, cultural, or political critique. Second, *illustration* requires that copyrighted material is referenced in other contexts. For example, a class exercise asking students to devise ethical solutions to specific photojournalistic situations might require the use of news photos as a reference point. Third, an *incidental or accidental* use might occur when copyrighted material is unintentionally captured in the process of creating something for the purpose of teaching, scholarship, comment, critique, or research. For example, a video podcast of a lecture inadvertently includes copyrighted images on student clothing or copyrighted ringtones on phones that erupt during the lecture. In these incidental cases, the educator should be certain that the copyrighted material is not central to the podcast/lecture and is not so vast that it may become a central focus.

As noted in the Society for Cinema and Media Studies' (SCMS) code of best practices (2007),

> The field of film and media studies in the United States was shaped by the legal principle of fair use—the ability of educators, critics, and others to teach, study, and write about media without having to ask copyright holders for permission every time their works are used. Educational and critical uses of media, such as those employed by film and media educators, are woven into the fabric of a free, democratic society, and lead directly to the continued health and creative vibrancy of both commercial and non-commercial film and media.
>
> (p. 1)

The SCMS code stresses the common practice of screening media content for students in face-to-face meetings as a primary form of fair use. As long as copies of the media content are lawfully made—by purchasing, renting, reproducing, or borrowing—the use is fair for educational purposes. Even unlawfully made copies may be considered under the fair use exception if the instructor is using the material for the purposes of teaching. The code also notes that "It is often necessary for educators to copy excerpts from films, television shows, and other media and include them in compilations or presentations for illustrative purposes. The ability to copy, excerpt and edit, capture stills, and manipulate images and sounds in this way enhances film and media educators' ability to analyze, critique, and teach media. The community of film and media educators believes that such practices qualify as fair uses of copyrighted works" (SCMS, pp. 4–5). Students are permitted these same freedoms under fair use as long as they do not distribute them for commercial objectives. Faculty may also incorporate copyrighted materials into curriculum materials such as PowerPoint lectures, podcasts, web sites, courseware, or videos as long as the proportion is congruent with the educational objective and attribution is provided for the quoted material.

Similarly, the code of best practices in fair use for online video (Center for Media and Social Impact, 2008) acknowledges that cultural practices embracing mashups and amateur video have expanded the educator's repertoire from which to draw in understanding new forms of cultural production. In general, fair uses of online video material—and other media texts—are ones that do not serve as substitutes for the original material during the process of critique or comment. Media and communication instructors and students must be aware that transformation is a key element to fair uses for educational purposes. For example, when creating videos (mashups, remixes, or original videos) for online distribution, the use of any copyrighted material must significantly alter its context or meaning in order to stay within the safe harbor of fair use. If a song is used in its entirety just to elicit a mood or when elements of copyrighted works are assembled to recreate the notoriety or appeal of the original, fair use does not apply (Center for Media and Social Impact, 2008).

Many faculty use online courseware and worry about the limits of fair use protections for materials they post. Some of the intrinsic features of online courseware such as password protection and the expiration of access to materials help instructors to use copyrighted works fairly. Instructors cannot create online "course packs" without paying royalties, but materials can be made available in ways similar to that of the "analog classroom." E-reserves are similar to paper reserves because of their limited availability. Linking to online resources is a fair use while posting works in their entirety to be copied by students is less so. Additionally, Table 3.1, the "video clip decision tree" found at the end of this section, provides a graphic guideline to those interested in fair uses of video clips for educational purposes. Created by Allan Gyorke and others at the Pennsylvania State University, the graphic is a quick reference to the "anti-circumvention" of technological copy protections on DVDs and other copyrighted works as outlined in the Digital Millennium Copyright Act. Educators are permitted, through the tenets of fair use, to disable the copy protection on video (or audio) materials when that circumvention fulfills a fair educational use. This means that small excerpts of video may be incorporated into new works for the purposes of criticism/comment as long as there is no other reasonable means by which to obtain the video.

These principles of fair use are flexible, and instructors must keep in mind that there are no set guidelines. But the fair use of mediated content is visible across educational institutions. One of the most essential lessons we can communicate to students is the importance of free expression and the creation of culture. Student production and distribution of mediated artifacts may cultivate deep understanding of communicative practices and processes. Recent social discourse about copyright piracy has likened any unlicensed use of copyrighted works to "theft." Institutional responses to copyright piracy have tended toward alarm, and educators' misunderstanding about their legal rights has thus intensified. Educators, however, have long recognized that culture builds upon itself through

TABLE 3.1 Decision Tree: Media, Anti-circumvention, TEACH and Fair Use

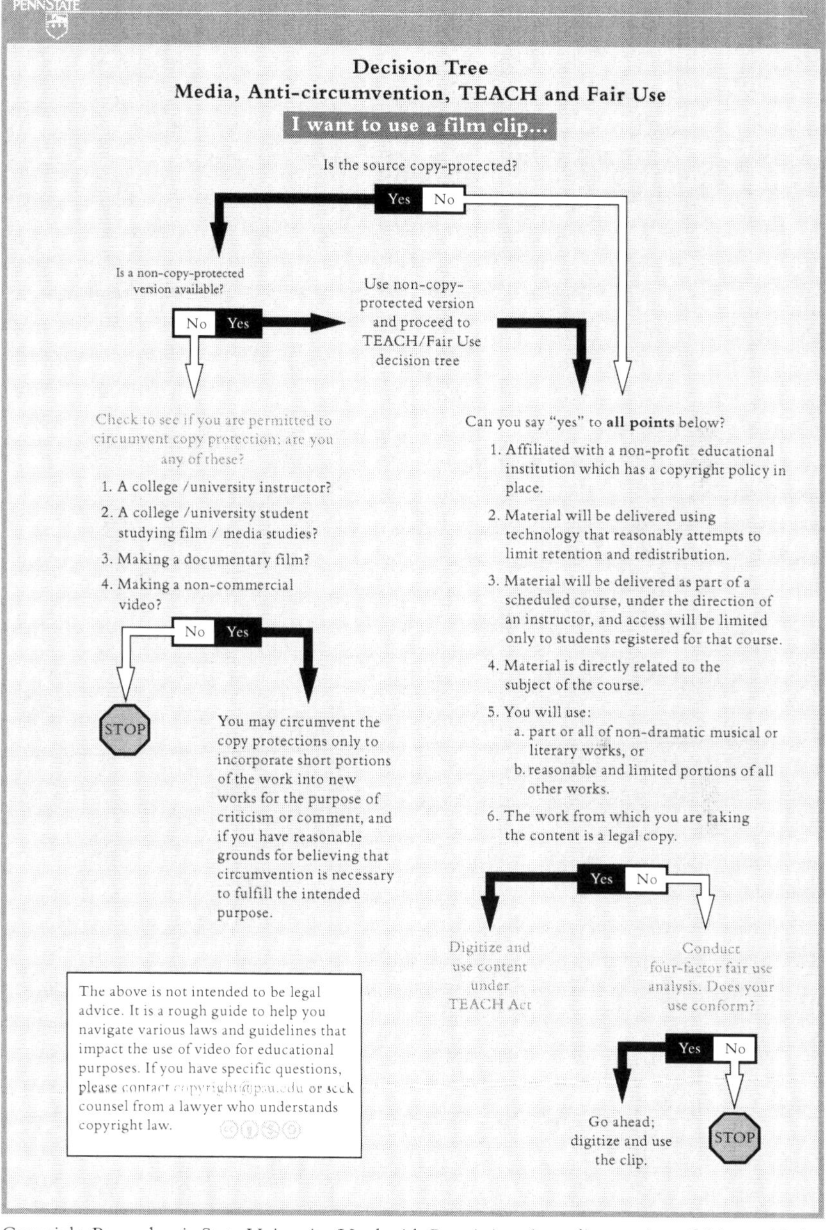

Copyright Pennsylvania State University. Used with Permission. An online version of this graphic is also available at http://copyright.psu.edu/2010/09/video-clip-decision-tree.html.

a rich trove of material both copyright protected and in the public domain. Fair use of copyrighted works is a right enjoyed by all citizens that recognize the pedagogical value inherent in mediated artifacts as objects of study. Ultimately, fair use figures into the academic identity of any communication instructor who teaches with technology.

Conclusion

Through its self-reflective nature, learning may represent a transformation of consciousness for students. Mediated technologies themselves also transform consciousness, according to Marshall McLuhan's (1964) dictates on the image as knowledge, the cultural exchange of information, and the notion of the global village. Digital culture is a relatively new phenomenon, and the study of mediated communication itself is slippery since the object of study transforms so frequently. Interesting questions are being raised around digital media that have implications in the communication classroom. What does it mean to live in a "culture of documentation"? What political imperatives govern the aesthetic choices of newer media and of mediated information in general? What will be the impact of non-neutral networks? Will the Internet become a collection of walled-off domains governed by corporations? Will national web systems become the norm? Believing with Carey (1989) that communication is culture, technology is of central concern in the growth and maintenance of world cultures; education is one means for that growth and maintenance. Education is inextricably linked to the role of technology as it relates to the global economy, and communication faculty are bound to examine this notion critically with students.

Faculty must consider institutional practices and the culture of higher education in general when adopting educational technologies. Technological tools offer range, flexibility, and adaptability in originating and delivering course content. But pedagogical implications of technology involve an examination of social values. Beetham and Sharpe (2007) speaking about online learning, note that "[j]ust as the impact of technology is changing how knowledge is valued in our society, so it is changing how we value different kinds of learning and achievement and different models of the learning organization. Some values, such as the values of the marketplace and the values of the traditional academic institution, are brought into conflict by the effects of technology" (p. 6).

This provides communication educators an opportunity to help students be capable participants in discourses about technology in ways that enable them to negotiate multiple perspectives on the use of and critique of technology. Students need to reflect on the cultural importance of technology in their educations and in their lives. Sharpe, Beetham, DeFreitas, and Conole (2010) remind us that "as we move towards more immersive environments, with more integrated social software capabilities, we see play and discovery becoming the means by which learners approach key concepts. While technology will offer learners the potential to create and share knowledge in ways we can only imagine, it is up to us now to make their learning creative, challenging and open-ended" (p. 11). This quote reminds educators that teaching matters. Dazzling students with technology will not mask inadequacies in teaching. The goals and the learning objectives of the course as well as the instructor's philosophy of teaching will dictate technological practices. Prior to making decisions about particular technologies, consider how they will support learning activities. Consider how a particular technology can enhance understanding of concepts central to communication and media studies. Consider how a particular technology may serve to equalize classrooms full of diverse students with different backgrounds, experiences, and learning styles. Consider how contemporary faculty might teach about media responsibly without incorporating the use of and the analysis of technological artifacts into the curriculum.

Our identities as communication faculty require at least a minimal facility with technology, from both a critical perspective and a perspective of practice. Experimentation with so-called digital literacies and participatory culture helps instructors to enact their own identities and different subject positions with regard to different technological tools. Faculty can probe their own relationships with knowledge. In the contemporary culture of citizen journalism, remix, and YouTube, instructors cannot expect to be the sole providers of knowledge. At the same time, instructors are obligated to engage with technology as part of their lives within the academy. Educators must use technology in concert with pedagogical goals and academic identities. While some of those uses may be dictated by institutional constraints, we understand the value of using technologies thoughtfully and with purpose. This means consistency with our teaching philosophy, our course goals, and the deployment of technology.

Note: For an in-depth guide to the legal ramifications of YouTube video removals, see the Electronic Frontier Foundation's *Guide to YouTube Removals* at https://www.eff.org/issues/intellectual-property/guide-to-youtube-removals.

Notes

1 See Gee, J. P. (2004). *Situated language and learning: A critique of traditional schooling.* New York, NY: Routledge.
2 Also known as *Cambridge University Press et al. v. Patton et al.*
3 The codes of best practices are available at the Center for Media and Social Impact at http://www.cmsimpact.org/fair-use.

References

Amiel, T., & Reeves, T. C. (2008). Design-based research and educational technology: Rethinking technology and the research agenda. *Educational Technology & Society, 11*(4), 29–40.

Aufderheide, P., & Jaszi, P. (2011). *Reclaiming fair use: How to put balance back in copyright.* Chicago, IL: University of Chicago Press.

Bates, A. W., & Poole, G. (2003). *Effective teaching with technology in higher education.* San Francisco, CA: Jossey-Bass.

Beetham, H., & Oliver, M. (2010). The changing practices of knowledge and learning. In R. Sharpe, H. Beetham, & S. DeFreitas (Eds.), *Rethinking learning for a digital age* (pp. 155–169). New York, NY: Routledge.

Beetham, H., & Sharpe, R. (2007). *Rethinking pedagogy for a digital age.* London, UK: Routledge.
Boon, S., & Sinclair, C. (2009). A world I don't inhabit: Disquiet and identity in Second Life and Facebook. *Educational Media International, 46*(2), 99–110.
Boyer, D. (2011). The institutional transformation of universities in the era of digital information. In B. Zelizer (Ed.), *Making the university matter* (pp. 177–185). New York, NY: Routledge.
Bradwell, P. (2009). *The edgeless university: Why higher education must embrace technology.* London, UK: Demos. http://www.demos.co.uk/publications/the-edgeless-university
Carey, J. (1989). *Communication as culture: Essays on media and society.* Boston, MA: Unwin Hyman.
Center for Media and Social Impact. (2008). Code of Best Practices in Fair Use for Online Video. http://www.cmsimpact.org/fair-use/related-materials/codes/code-best-practices-fair-use-online-video
Copyright Law of the United States. http://www.copyright.gov/title17/92chap1.pdf
Delwiche, A. (2006). Massively multiplayer online games (MMOs) in the new media classroom. *Educational Technology & Society, 9*(3), 160–172.
Dewey, J. (1916). *Democracy and education: An introduction to the philosophy of education.* New York, NY: Macmillan.
Gee, J. P. (2004). *Situated language and learning: A critique of traditional schooling.* New York, NY: Routledge.
Howard, J. (2012, May 13). Long-awaited ruling in copyright case mostly favors Georgia State U. *Chronicle of Higher Education.* http://chronicle.com/article/Long-Awaited-Ruling-in/131859/
Jenkins, H. (2002). Interactive audiences? In D. Harries (Ed.), *The new media book* (pp. 157–170). London, UK: British Film Institute.
Jenkins, H., Purushotma, R., Weigel, M., Clinton, K., & Robison, A. J. (2006). *Confronting the challenges of participatory culture: Media education for the 21st century.* Cambridge, MA: MIT. http://digitallearning.macfound.org/atf/cf/%7B7E45C7E0-A3E0-4B89-AC9C-E807E1B0AE4E%7D/JENKINS_WHITE_PAPER.PDF
Lim, W-Y., So, H-J., & Tan, S-C. (2010). eLearning 2.0 and new literacies: Are social practices lagging behind? *Interactive Learning Environments, 18*(3), 203–218.
Mayer, R. E. (2001). *Multimedia learning.* Cambridge, U.K.: Cambridge University Press.
McLuhan, M. (1964). *Understanding media: The extensions of man.* New York, NY: McGraw-Hill.
Oblinger, D. G., & Oblinger, J. L. (2005). Is it age or IT: First steps toward understanding the net generation. In D. G. Oblinger & J. L. Oblinger (Eds.), *Educating the net generation* (pp. 2.1–2.20). Educause. http://net.educause.edu/ir/library/pdf/pub7101b.pdf
Quinlan, O. (2011, June 25). Which first—Social media or social constructivism? http://www.oliverquinlan.com/blog/2011/06/25/which-first-social-media-or-social-constructivism/
Richardson, W. (2006). *Blogs, wikis, podcasts, and other powerful web tools for classrooms.* Thousand Oaks, CA: Sage.
Roberts, G. (2005). Technology and learning expectations of the net generation. In D. G. Oblinger & J. L. Oblinger (Eds.), *Educating the net generation* (pp. 3.1–3.7). Educause. http://net.educause.edu/ir/library/pdf/pub7101c.pdf
SCMS (Society for Cinema and Media Studies). Statement of Best Practices for Fair Use in Teaching for Film and Media Educators (2007). http://www.digital.lib.pdx.edu/resources/SCMSBestPracticesforFairUseinTeaching-Final.pdf
Sharpe, R., Beetham, H., DeFreitas, S., & Conole, G. (2010). An introduction to rethinking learning for a digital age. In R. Sharpe, H. Beetham, & S. DeFreitas (Eds.), *Rethinking learning for a digital age* (pp. 1–12). New York, NY: Routledge.

Singer, J. B. (2008). Posting for points: Edublogs in the JMC curriculum. *Journalism & Mass Communication Educator, 63*(1), 10–27.

Traxler, J. (2012). Educators go over the garden wall. *Interactive Learning Environments, 20*(3), 199–201.

Turkle, S. (2011). *Alone together.* New York, NY: Basic Books.

Turney, C. S. M., Robinson, D., Lee, M., & Soutar, A. (2009). Using technology to direct learning in higher education: The way forward? *Active Learning in Higher Education, 10*(1), 71–83. DOI: 10.1177/1469787408100196

Young, J. R. (2008, May 30). Frustrated with corporate course-management systems, some professors go 'edupunk.' *Chronicle of Higher Education.* http://chronicle.com/blogs/wiredcampus/frustrated-with-corporate-course-management-systems-some-professors-go-edupunk/3977

4

CATEGORIZING THINKING, ORGANIZING LEARNING

For John Dewey, thinking is a rendering of our experiences that enables us to have intention and to act. Dewey's (1916) concept of *reflective thought* signifies an active and deliberate consideration of beliefs, evidence for these beliefs, and the consequences of these beliefs. In the contemporary academy, many instructors enact Dewey's ideas by espousing critical thinking and reflection. We want our students to be empowered by knowledge. We also want to provide them with experiences that aid in their knowledge construction. From a practical standpoint, the objectives we want to achieve in the classroom emanate from our philosophies of teaching, which inform our individual goals for each course. The substance of course goals can be derived from understanding the various domains of thinking. These domains apply regardless of an individual instructor's orientation or philosophy because they provide common ground for thinking about learning. In a larger sense, our research and creative perspectives also flow from our pedagogical philosophies and our outlook on education in general. Together, these philosophies, perspectives, goals, and ideas form the core of our academic identity.

The next four chapters of this book concern two major threads: how we teach and what we want students to take into the world with them. Both of these threads have an abstract nature ("hierarchies" of thinking; designing goals; ways of learning) and a concrete nature (tools of assessment; writing goals; constructing courses). These chapters center on ideas about goals, learning styles, categories of thinking, assessment, and instructional design as they pertain to communication and media studies. Beginning with the abstract nature of these endeavors, this chapter outlines a means for ordering thinking and learning for our students. The next chapter discusses the specifics of constructing goals and measures of assessment for individual courses.

Many university instructors of mediated communication tend to focus on engaging the cognitive aspects of student learning. Because students are taught as both critical scholars of media and as practitioners in media/communication professions, learning strategies must involve skill dimensions and affective dimensions (particularly ethics) in addition to cognitive dimensions. This chapter explores all of these dimensions of learning to provide various alternatives for engaging students more deeply in the process of learning.

In a discipline that is so broad, instructors may have difficulty distilling certain content areas into intelligible objectives. As Calhoun (2011) notes, "communication is heterogeneous not just in the mix of fields it embraces, but in the organizational and curricular models it has produced for itself" (p. 1481). But all fields are heterogeneous, he claims, and what matters is the connection among the parts—in the case of media studies, how media connect to cultural evolution, social inequity, and organizational structure (Calhoun, 2011). Faculty can make those connections more obvious to students by composing goals and objectives that address the process of learning—and the learner, too—as a whole, acknowledging the importance of affective, cognitive, and skill learning domains.

Organizing Learning

Bloom's taxonomy is a categorical system of cognitive activities presented in a hierarchy of escalating complexity (Bloom, Engelhart, Furst, Hill, & Krathwohl, 1954). Understanding that it may be difficult to classify educational objectives as biologists classify living things, Bloom et al. devised the taxonomy to encourage the sharing of ideas among faculty about testing and to stimulate "research on examining and on the relations between examining and education" (p. 4). Despite being critiqued for its bureaucratic origination (Paul, 1992), Bloom's system is useful for instructors to organize their ideas about learning objectives. It also allows students to grasp instructor expectations. It is a shared language about learning goals. The six levels of Bloom's original taxonomy are *knowledge, comprehension, application, analysis, synthesis,* and *evaluation*, beginning with the fundamental and concrete and moving toward the abstract. This taxonomy crystallizes for the instructor a basic plan to include learning goals beyond mere recollection. It stresses the application of knowledge and the extrapolation of situations in which knowledge might be used. It also helps the instructor to design evaluation mechanisms and to construct learning activities or experiences. In sum, the taxonomy was created to classify "the intended behavior of students—the ways in which individuals are to act, think, or feel as the result of participating in some unit of instruction" (Bloom et al., 1954, p. 12). It emphasizes the change in students as they move through the educational process. Bloom's taxonomy is meant to apply across curricula, institutions, and educational philosophies.

From a perspective embracing critical thinking as foundational in education, Richard Paul (1992) critiques Bloom's taxonomy on the basis that, in part, it confuses knowledge with recall. He argues that memorized statements do not constitute knowledge and that the achievement of knowledge presupposes the mastery of the other categories of the taxonomy. One of the taxonomy's original coauthors, David Krathwohl (2002), updated the categorization to these six hierarchical levels: *remember, understand, apply, analyze, evaluate,* and *create*. The updated

TABLE 4.1 The Cognitive Processes Dimension—Categories, Cognitive Processes (and Alternative Names)

Lower order thinking skills		→		*Higher order thinking skills*	
remember	**understand**	**apply**	**analyze**	**evaluate**	**create**
recognizing	interpreting	executing	differentiating	checking	generating
• identifying	• clarifying	• carrying out	• discriminating	• coordinating	• hypothesizing
recalling	• paraphrasing	implementing	• distinguishing	• detecting	planning
• retrieving	• representing	• using	• focusing	• monitoring	• designing
	• translating		• selecting	• testing	producing
	exemplifying		organizing	critiquing	• constructing
	• illustrating		• fiding coherence	• judging	
	• instantiating		• integrating		
	classifying		• outlining		
	• categorizing		• parsing		
	• subsuming		• structuring		
	summarizing		attributing		
	• abstracting		• deconstructing		
	• generalizing				
	inferring				
	• concluding				
	• extrapolating				
	• interpolating				
	• predicting				
	comparing				
	• contrasting				
	• mapping				
	• matching				
	explaining				
	• constructing models				

Adapted from Anderson and Krathwohl (2001, pp. 67–68). Credit: Rex Heer, Center for Excellence in Learning and Teaching, Iowa State University. Used with permission.

categorization seen in Table 4.1 is clear, and it provides a foundation for new models of discipline-specific educational objectives.

Adding to Bloom's taxonomy for a media/communication context, I suggest an overlay of cognitive dimensions for general competence in a media studies/communication curriculum. Although this arrangement is also based on cognitive complexity, it demonstrates more fluidity between objectives as they overlap on occasion. The arrangement (see Table 4.2) attempts to move the student through an understanding of foundational communication principles, the application of these principles to create meaning, the analysis of messages, contexts, structures, and audiences, and the creation of new communicative forms. The purpose of creating a taxonomy of media/communication objectives mirrors Bloom's original purposes:

TABLE 4.2 Objectives for Media & Communication Studies Based on Bloom's Taxonomy

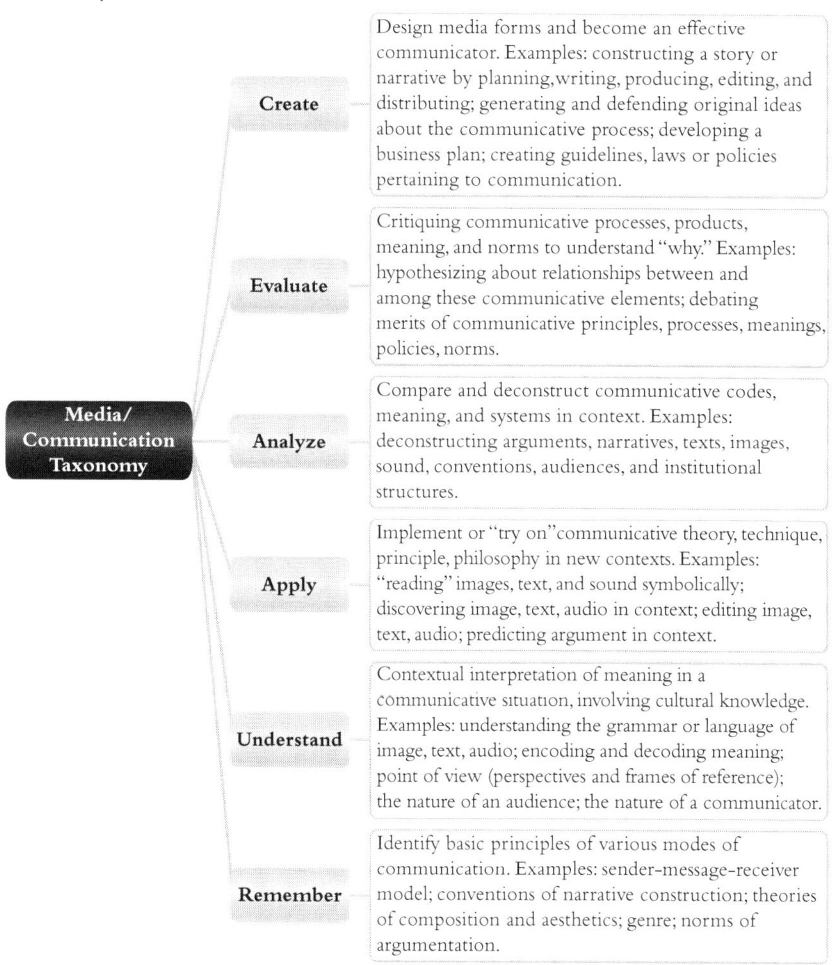

to allow for the organization of learning goals, the construction of learning activities, and the design of assessment devices for media and communication faculty.

This taxonomy is designed to provide broad cognitive objectives for our students while simultaneously reminding us that, following Dewey (1916), knowledge creation is a process that evolves from experience. Students who are provided opportunities to play with concepts, ideas, principles, and norms are not only working toward being successful communicators but also understanding critical concepts such as power relationships, meaning negotiation, diversity, and autonomy. The *remember* objective requires students to be able to identify basic concepts or principles through recall, but it also requires that students be able to recognize and know discipline-specific terms, conventions, processes, theories, and structures. The *understand* objective requires students to grasp the appropriate context of meaning, i.e., students translate, categorize, and extrapolate the communication-specific terms, conventions, processes, theories, and structures into new examples, paraphrases, or analogies. Students are able to explain the meaning of these phenomena to others. The *apply* objective requires students to be able to use principles, theories, conventions, or ideas in hypothetical situations or to solve problems. Applied knowledge refers to the implementation of learned material in products such as models, presentations, and simulated events. The *analyze* objective requires students to relate principles, codes, conventions, meanings, or systems to each other and to a whole. It obliges students to be able to break down principles into constituent portions in order to realize structure and organization, and to identify cause and effect. The *evaluate* objective is about reflecting on integrated knowledge of communicative concepts, principles, structures, or meanings in order to make judgments about their value against particular criteria or standards. The emphasis in media and communication is not just on appraising quality and authenticity but on thinking about why these judgments are made and what they mean. Lastly, the *create* objective asks students to forge new forms from constituent elements. For media and communication students, the objective is about becoming a successful communicator.

The taxonomy should help instructors to create course objectives that address lower-order as well as higher-order levels of thinking in concert with instructor teaching philosophy. Course assignments and activities flow from the objectives. As an example, suppose you are teaching a course in media law. Presume that your teaching philosophy is best defined as a mixture of critical and constructivist in that your interests lie in using critical inquiry to question the politics of knowledge. How might you construct your media law class so that students grasp the fundamental principles of media law but also learn to challenge assumptions about the context, meaning, construction, and application of the law? You can use basic knowledge of laws pertaining to expression (the First Amendment in the United States), privacy, and intellectual property to analyze hypothetical cases involving digital technologies. How and why do existing laws relate to the hypothetical situation? What laws do not apply to the situation? Why are privacy rights surrounding digital technologies usually characterized in terms of organizational rights as opposed to individual rights? What new ways of examining digital privacy rights might be productive? Which stakeholders stand to gain or lose with regard to these new perspectives? How do these hypothetical cases relate to other social structures? Other economic structures? Ideological debates? Moral imperatives? What new policies might your students design as a result of their inquiry? How might these new policies be enacted in a variety of contexts? Working collaboratively and individually, a course in media law can be devised to explore all of these areas through carefully planned learning activities, assignments, or exams.

Bloom's taxonomy also contains *affective* and *skill* dimensions in addition to its *cognitive* dimensions. The affective and skill dimensions will be explored below. Other means of organizing cognitive learning, often based on constructivist pedagogical philosophies, are useful for media and communication courses. One of these is *instructional scaffolding*. Based on principles of cognitive psychology, instructional scaffolding seeks to support a learner through tools or processes or strategies (Wood, Bruner, & Ross, 1978). Scaffolding does not use specific categories of learning but instead relies on the student's progression through levels of cognitive development that enable problem solving. Using Vygotsky's (1978) conceptualization of apprenticeship whereby a mentor guides a novice through the learning process, instructional scaffolding serves as a framework that is eventually removed as the learner becomes more proficient. The mentor or instructor selects a learning task to be mastered and then devises strategies that are suitable for the learners. The scaffolds may be structured as activities designed for skill acquisition or they may be dynamic and creative, for example, when addressing higher-level cognitive abilities where successive tasks are not suitable (Wood et al., 1978). Essentially, scaffolding denotes any learning activities whereby the instructor uses techniques or procedures to aid students. Scaffolding activities are oriented toward the development of conceptual and practical knowledge. Examples of cognitive scaffolding include the use of questions, modeling, diagramming, collaborating, or planning.

For media and communication students, lower-order cognitive scaffolding activities could include exercises in coding web pages or shooting video to acquire basic skills. The instructor demonstrates the techniques to the students who must then partner with another student to explain and demonstrate the technique back to one another. During class time, students work with one another and with the instructor, who provides expert feedback on the acquisition of basic skills. Students may use technical tutorials, individual experimentation, or group collaboration to be able eventually to construct web sites or shoot video on their own. Once the foundational scaffolding falls away with every student having acquired those basic web development or video capabilities, the instructor can focus on developing a new scaffold for higher-order cognitive development. For example, the students must produce their own web or video projects, in the proper context, with expert guidance from the instructor. The students must identify the roles each participant will play in the production, the intended audience for the final product, the meanings they wish to convey, and an overall critique of both the production itself and the production process. The instructor consults throughout the procedure, playing an increasingly invisible role as the students contend with and attain higher-order cognitive abilities.

Writing is straightforwardly taught through scaffolding. Instructors can create models illustrating techniques of argument or genre, and students then complete exercises to imitate the model or improve an incomplete or flawed example. Similarly, critical examination of media texts can be taught through a scaffold. The instructor models where and how to select a text for analysis. Students then select texts and write summaries of their texts to be shared with a partner. For a semiotic analysis, the instructor diagrams an analysis using a sample text so that students may model the technique. Students have already mastered, using the skill acquisition scaffold technique described above, the terminology of semiotics. Using their own texts, students identify symbols, signs, icons, referents, and so forth to construct a basic formulation of what the text might mean. With guidance from the instructor, students work in pairs or groups to articulate the possible meanings of various elements of the texts. They evaluate and justify these meanings and potentially rework the text to create alternative meanings through collaboration and presentation.

These scaffolding examples are offered to demonstrate the range of tactics that can provide opportunities for students to engage with thinking processes in novel and active ways. Scaffolding techniques require instructors to guide students without solving problems for students. The goal is for students to become responsible in constructing knowledge dynamically rather than consuming knowledge passively.

There are alternatives to Bloom's cognitive taxonomy, including the SOLO (Structure of Observed Learning Outcomes) by Biggs and Collis (1982) as well as Fink's (2003) non-hierarchical taxonomy. Like Bloom's taxonomy, the SOLO taxonomy represents increasingly complex levels of understanding of a particular subject. In the *prestructural* level, students are exposed to disconnected pieces of information. In the *unistructural* level, students make rudimentary connections without truly comprehending their significance. In the *multistructural* level, students make more sophisticated connections but lack the grasp of meta-connections and overall substance. In the *relational* level students understand the relation of parts to the whole. In the *extended abstract* level, students relate the material to other concepts within the topic and beyond it. The SOLO taxonomy focuses on cognitive processes but does not include a critical component.

Fink's (2003) taxonomy of significant learning attempts to broaden the sphere of cognitive learning to include more affective dimensions. *Foundational knowledge* encompasses understanding and remembering ideas and information. *Application* involves critical, creative, and practical thinking, as well as supplementary skill sets such as management of projects or effective communication.

Integration consists of making connections among ideas, people, or areas of life. *Human dimension* is about understanding and interacting with others. Students realize the social or personal implications of learning. *Caring* involves the discovery of students' feelings, interests, and values pertaining to course material. It provides the motivational energy to learn. *Learning how to learn* encompasses the ability for long-term, self-directed learning. Both the SOLO and Fink taxonomies are useful in rounding out Bloom's taxonomy and providing media and communication instructors a comprehensive means for organizing congruent objectives, goals, classroom activities, and assessment procedures in any course.

In order to address what Bloom et al. (1954) regarded as a holistic form of education, the taxonomy included affective (feeling) and psychomotor (skill) dimensions as well as the cognitive. Working together, the three aspects of the taxonomy are meant to help educators "gain a perspective on the emphasis given to certain behaviors by a particular set of educational plans" (p. 2). The affective taxonomy includes objectives describing the way students react emotionally. Affective goals are directed toward the awareness and development of interests, values, attitudes, and motivations. The five levels of the affective domain begin with *receiving*, which reflects the student's ability to hear and pay attention. *Responding* shows a more active type of attention in which students react to a stimulus. The student who successfully achieves this objective demonstrates a willingness and motivation to respond. *Valuing* reflects a student's ability to confer value onto the learning material. At this level, students internalize a set of ideals and express a degree of commitment to those ideals through observable behaviors. *Organizing* refers to the student's facility with incorporating disparate values and ideas into her/his own system of ideals. The student compares values, resolves any inconsistencies, and synthesizes them into a whole philosophy. *Characterizing* refers to the adoption of a value structure that becomes internalized so it characterizes the student's behavior. Examples include self-reliance, teamwork, commitment to ethical principles and codes, and open-mindedness. Media and communication instructors may find value in Bloom's affective domain since it captures the notion that students may embrace what's being taught on an emotional level. It provides a vocabulary for instructors to express expectations of true appreciation for the ideas explored within a course.

Bloom's psychomotor dimensions are less well developed than the cognitive and affective elements, but other scholars (Simpson, 1972; Dave, 1970; Harrow, 1972) have built upon the original taxonomy to create skill dimensions. Simpson's (1972) skill dimensions are *perception* (using sensory cues to direct motor actions); *set* (physical, mental, and emotional readiness to act); *guided response* (initial stages in learning a complex skill; imitation and trial and error); *mechanism* (intermediary stages where proficiency of movement is demonstrated); *complex overt response* (performance of complex motor skills involving complicated movements); *adaptation* (skills are strong and movements can be adapted to particular requirements);

origination (the ability to create new movement patterns congruent with specific conditions). Using the skill domains, media and communication instructors may construct objectives that focus on habituation of desired skills. For example, proficiency with nonverbal communication or other presentation skills, image or sound editing software, or encoding and decoding information into graphic forms may be desirable.

Digital Culture and Learning Systems

Another classification for learning that combines cognitive, active, and skill dimensions is the notion of *connectivism*, created by George Siemens (2005). Building on the broader learning theories of cognitivism, behaviorism, and constructivism, Siemens expands learning theory to account for technological evolution. Connectivism is a model of collaborative learning positing that technological tools shape our thinking, that cognitive information processing can now be buoyed by technology, and that knowing where to find information is paramount. The tenets of connectivism are:

- Learning and knowledge rest in diversity of opinions.
- Learning is a process of connecting specialized nodes or information sources.
- Learning may reside in non-human appliances.
- Capacity to know more is more critical than what is currently known.
- Nurturing and maintaining connections is needed to facilitate continual learning.
- Ability to see connections between fields, ideas, and concepts is a core skill.
- Currency (accurate, up-to-date knowledge) is the intent of all connectivist learning activities.
- Decision-making is itself a learning process. Choosing what to learn and the meaning of incoming information is seen through the lens of a shifting reality. While there is a right answer now, it may be wrong tomorrow due to alterations in the information climate affecting the decision. (Siemens, 2005, n.p.)

Connectivism is, according to Siemens, a form of constructive, active learning in which learners generate knowledge through efforts to understand their experiences—but that those experiences must be connected with experiences of others in order for learning to occur in an environment of rapidly shifting technological development. Learning occurs in knowledge flows between individuals and organizations, according to connectivism: "The starting point of connectivism is the individual. Personal knowledge is comprised of a network, which feeds into organizations and institutions, which in turn feed back into the network, and then continue to provide learning to the individual. This cycle of knowledge development (personal to network to organization) allows learners to remain current in their field through the connections they have formed" (Siemens, 2005, n.p.).

Essentially, connectivism treats learning as a communal activity enabled by digital technologies. While this construct is technologically deterministic, it can apply to the media/communication classroom since students often access global networks via digital devices during class or in other learning contexts. Similarly, the participatory culture (Jenkins, 2002) of informal, digitally mediated collaboration is an environment that evokes the tenets of connectivism. Students work together, formally and informally, to craft and share their own media, with values focused on nurturing connection, timeliness of knowledge, decision making, and the desire to know more.

Indeed, Jenkins et al. (2006) propose an array of learning skills for the digital environment that suggest a harmony between participatory culture and connectivism. These skills include the ability to experiment, to construct models of real-world practices, to pool resources with others in the pursuit of a learning goal, to synthesize and disseminate information, to navigate information flows across multiple media, and to negotiate meaning across divergent communities. This range of learning skills enables students to explore their creativity in ways that pertain to the contemporary academic environment's emphasis on active learning. Through the collaborative learning experience, students respond to their peers' input and feedback and are able to reflect on their own contribution. Potentially, then, students develop the ability to experiment and to take risks as learners. Moreover, this skill set can activate higher orders of cognitive and affective learning domains. Not only are students expected to evaluate and create within the requirements of this skill set, but they also learn, through working collaboratively, to respect others' values and to potentially reconsider their own. To encourage student engagement and a deeper, more thorough level of understanding, instructors need to design authentic objectives for students that span learning domains.

Because many students have grown up in a digital culture and are "digital natives," Greg Ulmer's (2003) concept of *electracy* is related to connectivism and participatory culture. Electracy is a form of literacy that maximizes the communicative kind of "literacy" or skill and facility necessary to exploit the full communicative promise of multimedia, social media, or virtual realms. This means that electracy promotes the ways of logic and communication indigenous to newer media. In a shifting culture engulfed in media, electracy constitutes the social, ideological, and institutional phenomena attending this shift. Pedagogy based in the notion of electracy emphasizes aesthetics, creativity, and collective knowledge-building—it is derived from the examination of epistemologies and ontology arising from networked culture. Electrate pedagogy resides in techniques emphasizing creativity and discovery rather than verification (Ulmer, 2003). So, students could author a video game to illustrate a concept or idea for a research project. Or, they might examine the evolution of an idea through an exhibition of visual images illustrating that evolution. Along with connectivism, electracy offers a means to categorize learning domains in ways that account for contemporary digital realities within the academy.

Ulmer argues that "Electrate learning is structured like creativity, and does not replace the pedagogy of verification that structures most literate education, but supplements it with the structure of discovery" (Memmott, n.d., p. 3). For Ulmer, electrate pedagogy is about experimentation with popular culture or avant-garde texts and digital media to employ creative tactics—imagination and visual aesthetics—in learning.

Beyond Categories

These taxonomies and learning domains[1] are offered to guide the creation of objectives and goals and to ensure consistent assessment of those objectives. The overall value of Bloom's taxonomy is found in its comprehensiveness and clarity. It creates a basic grammar for instructors to write specific and consistent learning objectives. The chapters that follow on goal-setting, assessment, learning styles, and course construction use Bloom's taxonomy as a foundation. Educators must provide an environment in which students have opportunities to develop higher-order cognitive, affective, and skill objectives. Bloom's taxonomy allows educators to reflect on the structure and delivery of individual courses and curricula in an attempt to make explicit our overarching learning goals. Do we offer sufficient learning opportunities for students to analyze, evaluate, create, organize, characterize, adapt, and originate? How are those higher order dimensions represented in particular areas of media studies and communication? Have we moved beyond the notion that learning is the mere acquisition of information? Using active learning techniques, might students then attain a richer, deeper learning experience that improves their critical abilities, increases their capacity to apply knowledge to new situations, and foments a drive for lifelong learning?

Beyond the cognitive levels of remembering and understanding, media and communication instructors must demonstrate and reinforce the connections that evaluating and creating have to fundamental communicative processes and concepts. For example, students need to absorb the conventions of narrative construction and be able to interpret meaning according to context in order to make value judgments about media and to create new media. Once students appreciate the fundamentals, they understand how and why those fundamentals persist throughout the study of communication. When they are able to make connections between those fundamentals and their relevance in complex communicative processes, students can use analytical abilities and affective skills to create new media forms with confidence and elegance.

The complex cognitive and affective levels of Bloom's taxonomy represent Dewey's (1916) ideas about reflective thinking—being able to consider a subject carefully in order to understand the meanings and implications of that subject and to internalize the values or ideals that accompany such understanding. Faculty who are cognizant of the merits of these various taxonomies can challenge students to think reflectively about course content in terms of their own perspectives and experiences. Students might then confront their own previously unknow assumptions or feelings to undergo true learning and growth.

Note

1 See also the discussion of "the Four Pillars of Learning" found in UNESCO's International Commission on Education for the Twenty-first Century report at http://www.unesco.org/delors/delors_e.pdf. The four pillars are "learning to know," "learning to do," "learning to live together," and "learning to be."

References

Anderson, L.W. (Ed.), Krathwohl, D.R. (Ed.), Airasian, P.W., Cruikshank, K.A., Mayer, R.E., Pintrich, P.R., Raths, J., & Wittrock, M.C. (2001). *A taxonomy for learning, teaching, and assessing: A revision of Bloom's taxonomy of educational objectives* (Complete edition). New York: Longman.

Biggs, J. B., & Collis, K. (1982). *Evaluating the quality of learning: The SOLO taxonomy*. New York, NY: Academic Press.

Bloom, B. S., Engelhart, M. D., Furst, E. J., Hill, W. H., & Krathwohl, D. R. (1954). *Taxonomy of educational objectives: The classification of educational goals*. New York, NY: Longman.

Calhoun, C. (2011). Communication as social science (and more). *International Journal of Communication, 5*, 1479–1496.

Dave, R. H. (1970). Psychomotor levels. In R. J. Armstrong (Ed.), *Developing and writing behavioral objectives*. Tucson, AZ: Educational Innovators Press.

Dewey, J. (1916). *Democracy and education: An introduction to the philosophy of education*. New York, NY: Macmillan.

Fink, L. D. (2003). *Creating significant learning experiences: An integrated approach to designing college courses*. San Francisco, CA: Jossey-Bass.

Harrow, A. (1972). *A taxonomy of psychomotor domain: A guide for developing behavioral objectives*. New York, NY: David McKay.

Jenkins, H. (2002). Interactive audiences? In D. Harries (Ed.), *The new media book* (pp. 157–170). London, UK: British Film Institute.

Krathwohl, D.W. (2002). A revision of Bloom's taxonomy: An overview. *Theory into Practice, 41*(4), 212–218.

Memmott, T. (n.d.). *Toward electracy: A conversation with Greg Ulmer*. http://beehive.temporalimage.com/content_apps34/ulmer/0.html

Paul, R. (1992). *Critical thinking: What every person needs to survive in a rapidly changing world*. Rohnert Park, CA: Foundation for Critical Thinking.

Siemens, G. (2005). Connectivism: A learning theory for the digital age. *eLearnSpace*. http://www.elearnspace.org/Articles/connectivism.htm

Simpson, E. J. (1972). *The classification of educational objectives in the psychomotor domain*. Washington, DC: Gryphon House.

Ulmer, G. (2003). *Internet invention: From literacy to electracy*. New York, NY: Longman.

Vygotsky, L. S. (1978). *Mind in society: The development of higher psychological processes*. Cambridge, MA: Harvard University Press.

Wood, D. J., Bruner, J. S., & Ross, G. (1978). The role of tutoring in problem solving. *Journal of Child Psychiatry and Psychology, 17*(2), 89–100.

AND ASSESSMENT FOR AND COMMUNICATION COURSES

In his address to the 2012 meeting of the International Communication Association, Larry Gross said,

> As recognized in the classic rhetorical tradition of Western education, communication is the fundamental human trait and the basis of all culture. The forms and media of communication are the nervous system that links the components of our national and increasingly global political, economic and social networks.
> (Gross, 2012, p. 924)

Gross is highlighting the importance of communication's place in higher education as it contributes to an educated public and to a general understanding of cultural change. Setting curricular goals for such an all-encompassing enterprise can be demanding. Another scholar of communication, Jo Sprague (1990), reiterates a belief of Neil Postman's that universities

> should serve a thermostatic function, constantly changing and adapting to emphasize whatever society seems to be ignoring at a given time. Educational goals should reflect the needs of society, the nature of students, the content of our discipline, and the teachers' own values.
> (p. 35)

Sprague is imploring communication instructors to consider important questions about our goals for our students, the nature of education, and the place of communication in the academy. Not only is our field broad and foundational, but it shapes and is shaped by global information flows, networking trends, shifts in cultural and political values, organizational cultures, social inequalities, and nearly every quotidian feature of the contemporary world. In addition, faculty must respond to institutional mandates as well as contemporary realities in media industries. All of these are external factors that help to shape our courses as we create learning goals. Internal factors influencing the creation of learning goals include our teaching philosophies, our understanding of learning domains, our subject expertise, and our identities within the academy.

With recognition of these factors, this chapter addresses the process of establishing educational goals and learning objectives for courses in media and communication. It may seem arduous to bother with goal setting—like writing an outline for an article or composing a shot list for a video—but taking time to contemplate instructional goals will save time, streamline course design, determine your course activities, and ensure a richer, more focused classroom experience for students and instructors.

Moreover, the ability to create assignments that work in concert with learning goals is an important means of creating a lasting classroom experience for students. Because of the need to educate students as media professionals and as media consumers, assessment in the mediated communication curriculum must address theoretical and practical dimensions of pedagogy. Additionally, evaluating assignments and examinations is an important skill in an era of increased accountability in classrooms. Accordingly, this chapter also explores the basics for creating assessment devices.

Course Goals and General Pedagogical Philosophy

To design courses, instructors often begin thinking about specific learning activities, course projects, or course materials before thinking about the end product—what students will take from the course. To create a course that has long-term value for students, faculty must consider several elements that contribute to the goal-setting process. First, what general approach toward education suits your purposes? Sprague (1990) outlines four commonly held perspectives about education as transmitting cultural knowledge, developing students' intellectual skills, providing students with career skills, and reshaping the values of society. In applying these general perspectives respectively to communication, Sprague notes (along with Carey, 1989) that communication is central to the creation and maintenance of culture and is thus paramount in understanding all aspects of culture; that communication skills are vital building blocks for other knowledge; that communication skills are indispensable career skills; and that communication is inherently linked to social reality and is thus value-laden (Sprague, 1990). Alternative ways of characterizing general approaches to education might stress conflicting positions for media and communication education, i.e., does your orientation emphasize social critique or social stability, idealism or realism, abstractness or concreteness, regulation or emancipation, interventionism or protectionism, or some combination of these? These overarching perspectives remind us why we teach media and communication, and they are central to our identities within the academy.

A second element to consider in the goal-setting process is your specific pedagogical philosophy. As argued in chapter 1, the teaching philosophy guides course activities and practices. What is important about the particular courses you teach? What is the purpose of your course within the larger curriculum? What is the educator's role? What material should be included or excluded from your instructional repertoire? What characteristics of the communication discipline oblige certain pedagogical approaches? More detail about specific teaching philosophies and goal setting will be explored below, but these questions provide a starting point for creating goals that echo your pedagogical philosophy.

A third element important to the goal-setting process is student expectations. Who are the students at your institution? What prior knowledge do they possess? What can you expect from them given the particular course(s) you teach? Do your students have experience with active learning activities as well as the lecture format? Courses that are designed to be performative or skill-oriented often generate different student expectations than courses that are more conceptual in nature. Students taking a web design course may expect to work in group settings where students enrolled in a communication theory course may not. How will those expectations influence the construction of course goals? For example, if your students enroll in your course with vocational aims, will you include a critical component addressing the changes in creative industries brought about by political economic forces? How will your perspective on student expectations influence your goals?

Fourth, what ways of learning will you pinpoint in each course you teach? Using Bloom's taxonomy (Bloom, Engelhart, Furst, Hill, & Krathwohl, 1954), for example, the goals you construct for analysis and evaluation in a course on gender and the media will differ from the goals you construct for those categories in a course on basic audio production. Will you choose to integrate affective learning domains into your course goals through Bloom's affective dimensions or Fink's (2003) "human" or "caring" dimensions?[1] How much importance will you place on the development of students' open-mindedness or ethical sensibilities? Will your course include an emphasis on psychomotor dimensions of learning such as public speaking techniques or mechanical skills with photo editing software? Using a taxonomy of learning dimensions will not only facilitate the formation of course goals but will ensure that those goals address students' intellectual progression—actual learning—rather than just the course subject areas. Specific techniques for developing concrete goals are outlined below. It is crucial to remember that the goals or objectives you write for your course will inspire your teaching methods and means of assessment. As you continue to teach, you may refine your teaching philosophy and consequently your goals, so the process of goal setting is ultimately a dynamic one.

Antagonisms in Goal Setting

Generally, our goals in media and communication involve sculpting competent (if not elegant) communicators. Our ability to achieve this overarching goal is influenced not only by our personal philosophies but also by some institutional, situational, or political factors. When media and communication are cast in the curriculum as a dichotomy between professionalism and liberal studies, faculty struggle to forge goals that address industry concerns while simultaneously educating the whole student. Faculty may experience conflicting proclivities toward their roles in industry and the academy, while students experience conflicts between their roles as media producers and users. Can our course goals be divorced from cultural politics? Do we want them to be? Mediated communication is a site for the negotiation of meaning, and with its central role in culture, it serves as host to critical social debates. While students may enroll in courses with visions of technical proficiency, it is incumbent upon faculty to produce students who can engage in those social debates thoughtfully. The media are social structures through which we live and thus they require deep study. Our teaching goals must reflect the cultural relevance of communication in all its forms.

At the same time, our pedagogical goals are influenced by institutional conditions. University budgeting, fund-raising efforts, faculty hiring practices, political mandates, institutional efficiency models, and technological mandates all shape the way media and communication curricula develop and transform over time. These conditions may result in larger class sizes, fewer faculty hires, a decrease in operating budgets for media facilities, departmental reorganization or reduction, or lack of support for research. At smaller colleges, these factors can result in the dissolution of media and communication programs altogether. Departments may become dependent upon professional connections to meet budget shortfalls. All of these conditions affect curricular arrangements and, ultimately, individual course goals. Students and faculty may feel disconnected from a curriculum that stresses vocational proficiency goals without a larger context of cultural critique or a curriculum that emphasizes a humanistic approach toward the study of media while relegating production to an afterthought. From a practical standpoint, we want our courses to be successful and meaningful for our students. The tensions between our ideals and institutional factors may be difficult to attenuate, but having a well-developed teaching philosophy and academic identity will strengthen our ability to create successful course goals.

Lastly, elements of situation affect goal setting. Fink (2003) cites a number of situational factors dealing with context, expectations, teaching/learning characteristics, and subject matter that influence the design of course goals. The contextual factors Fink notes are class size, course level, method of course delivery, and duration of class time. Expectational factors include societal needs, professional accreditation requirements, or institutional curricular needs. Teaching and learning characteristics include the instructor's prior knowledge and experience with the subject and with teaching itself, and students' learning styles, life situations, demographics, and prior experiences with the subject. Subject matter factors are more amorphous and include the emphasis on cognitive or affective or psychomotor skills, general disciplinary epistemology, and the stability of the field. For example, larger paradigmatic shifts within media and communication studies have centered on, most recently, globalization and technology. Designing goals that incorporate material into our courses about technology and globalization enhances their relevance and significance for students.

Overall, the antagonisms involved in goal setting serve to help us sharpen our priorities in creating course goals. Faculty teaching media and communication face the challenge created by students' assumptions that the media can be easily understood. Because all of them use media and many of them create their own media, students often presume that they grasp the totality of valuable knowledge about media. The goals we design for our courses must address the fundamental nature of media and communication in order to compel students to think about how meaning is created and maintained.

General Goals for Communication That Accommodate Evolving Relationships between Media Creators and Media Consumers

As the distinction between media consumers and media producers becomes more thin, our course goals evolve to reflect this shift. The shift is evident in the friction between critique and celebration of mediated content or processes or structures. Creating goals that honor the dynamic between producer/consumer without acquiescing to celebratory impulses requires a recognition of how theory informs every aspect of both understanding and creating media. Faculty must make students aware of theory so that students will become intelligent producers for media-savvy, contemporary audiences. This is what Dewey (1916) means by cultivating reflexive habits of thinking. For Dewey, the process of education equals the goal of education—to learn to think deliberately about beliefs and actions and to formulate judgments about them. As Giroux (1989) envisions this goal, students learn to be thoughtful about their communicative practices through an engagement with theory. Merely "being in the trenches" without reflection means that content producers (students or faculty) cannot explain their own actions in ways that inform others. Without theory and without reflection, there is no connection between communicative traditions and an understanding of *why* those traditions develop and continue.

Echoing Giroux's thinking, Sholle and Denski (1994) seek goals for teaching media and communication that emphasize reflection as well as technique:

> The application of critical theory to the media production classroom begins with the recognition that teaching television production is fundamentally a political act. All such instruction involves empowering students to (each from his or her own perspective) represent the world through images, with the further realization that none of these representations is neutral.
>
> (p. 137)

These representations are culturally derived, and students must be thoughtful about culture and communication to become educated in the ways that most contemporary faculty deem necessary. Faculty can create a deep thoughtfulness about culture and communication through Jenkins' (2006) notion of participatory culture in which a culturally conscious, community-aware, collaborative means of experimentation with media respects the ethos of the fused producer/consumer but does so reflectively. How students arrive at a completed project—the process—is as important in acquiring reflexivity as is the project itself.

Thus, media/communication education is not about teaching students to package content as a commodity to be sold. It is about understanding that communication is a fundamental human activity that conveys meaning and culture. It is about making communicative activity explicit—how do we create and understand symbols, how do we structure messages, how do we collectively generate social discourses, and how do media institutions interact with social institutions? For Sholle and Denski (1994), students will therefore acquire:

> (1) knowledge of the sorts of choices available in encoding processes; (2) knowledge of effects or influences these choices hold over decoding processes; (3) the analytical ability to recognize and deal with these choices wisely, both as creators of messages and as respondents. ... Communication studies within the liberal arts must understand communication not as a job track, but as a key agent of social relations deserving of intellectual attention, including scientific and philosophical inquiry.
>
> (p. 141)

The ideas, images, and perceptions of contemporary culture are propagated through mediated communication. Thus, not only do analytic efforts in educating students about production biases address the critique/celebration rift, but they also contend with the blurred lines between producers and consumers. For example, Luthra's (2007) goals for courses on critical media studies and international communication reflect her emphasis on justice and equality in ways that address institutional power imbalances. She seeks to engage her students by "start[ing] them on a quest for solutions to pressing problems of global inequities and the interlocking oppressions of race, class, gender, nation, ability, and heterosexuality that result from these inequities. ... A still greater challenge in International Communication is to convey the importance of moving towards more sustainable, humane, multicultural and cosmopolitan futures, with empathic communication across borders being a first step in this direction" (p. 204). Luthra's goals are directed toward a global understanding of the social, political, and economic realities that have historically shaped media systems. In this vein, educators might ask macro questions that foster the design of goals that reflect contemporary shifts in the nature of media and communication. What is the role of the media in forming the sociopolitical agenda? How do media institutions and products serve as important storytellers in any culture? In what ways do media define what comprises knowledge? How might students be encouraged to contribute their own voices to the larger media culture? The larger goals discussed above illuminate communication as a field that can "change not just what people know, or even what they can do, but who they are" (Sprague, 1990, p. 23).

The Process of Goal Setting

The first step in constructing course goals is to identify *what* students will take away from your course and connecting those objectives with your pedagogical philosophy. If, for example, you want your students to evaluate television advertising in terms of gender identity stereotyping because you subscribe to a feminist/critical teaching philosophy, your course objective might read: "students will critique television advertisements and make judgments about their gender identity claims." If your goal is similar but your teaching philosophy is postmodern, your course objective might emphasize the students' subject position in evaluating advertising. The resulting course objective might read: "students will situate television advertisements within various social perspectives according to stated and unstated claims they make about gender identity." From a constructivist philosophical perspective, a similar goal might be accompanied by a course objective reading: "students will create a podcast responding to group interpretations of constructions of gender identity in television advertisements." The language of course objectives is straightforward and oriented toward action, i.e., what your students should be able *to do* as a result of attending your course.

Littlejohn's (2002) core communication theories—those that center on general conceptions shared by all types of communication—are useful origins for thinking about larger goals. Core communication theory is about (1) the process of developing messages; (2) interpretation and generation of meaning; (3) message structure and organization; (4) interactional dynamics, the joint creation of discourse and meaning; and (5) institutional and societal dynamics (p. 15). Most, if not all, of the goals and objectives instructors create for students can be derived from these core theories. Your goals serve as a storyline for your course—logistical links that create a narrative foundation. These core theories can be the underpinning of that storyline in communication/media courses.

Using the broader goals you have developed for your students, you will subsequently create course objectives that suggest specific course activities and specific assessments. Illustrating this technique, Kim Bissell (August, 2011), Director of the Institute for Communication and Information Research in the College of Communication and Information Sciences at the University of Alabama, describes her process of setting goals for her courses:

> I try to think about where I want [my students] to be at the end of the semester and then back it up from there. If I want my PhD students to have a completed research paper by the end of the semester, I have to design the class and schedule assignments in a way that facilitates them getting to that goal. If it's an undergrad course, I try to think about the concepts or conceptual knowledge I want them to have, and then I attempt to work in the topics of discussion and assignments in a way that takes them step-by-step to that level. My goals are a direct extension of my beliefs about teaching. I set high standards and thus, I have high expectations and goals for them. So, my end-game (the point I want them to reach by the end of the semester)

reflects those high standards. And, in the end, they usually wind up doing more than they ever expected they could do.

Thinking of course objectives as the *products* of a course, instructors may avoid outdated models of teaching as the mere imparting of information and learning as the mere reiteration of that information (Freire's banking model[2]). To write course goals, use Bloom's taxonomy to construct each objective in terms of the outcomes you envision for your students. Objectives, sometimes described as *learning outcomes*, may emphasize different levels of competency with knowledge, performance, or mind-set. For the media and communication instructor, this may include objectives focused on incorporating diverse voices into narrative video or audio productions. In addition, instructors may consider goals aiming for the development of resourcefulness, tolerance, and versatility. In the communication classroom, this type of objective might focus on a critique of the policies and norms surrounding copyright law and public culture. According to Toohey (1999), effective learning goals should adhere to several characteristics. First, "learning objectives need to represent real goals" (p. 150). This means that goals represent significant change as a result of engaging with course content. Second, "learning objectives must place academic skills or personal learning in the context of the particular subject matter in hand" (p. 150). Goals should therefore be narrow enough to apply to communication and media studies. Third, learning objectives should include "a description of the kind of performances by which achievement will be judged" (p. 150). Thus, course activities or assignments should align with goals. Fourth, "learning objectives should allow for either mastery or progress, depending on the nature of the learning" (p. 150). This refers to an emphasis on the process of developing knowledge and understanding. Last, "learning objectives should be memorable and limited in number" (p. 151). Too many goals or amorphous ones can confuse the learning process.

Your instructional goals, derived from your basic pedagogical philosophy, will guide your class activities, course assessments, and the larger success of your course. As an example, using Bloom's taxonomy for an "analysis" goal, you ask students to deconstruct cultural assumptions about the purpose of news. Is it to transmit cultural values? Is it to provide an account of the day's events in a neutral context? You must determine how your class activities will coalesce around this goal. You could ask students to bring news items to class and work together to scrutinize the function of the news item and compare results with other students. With a critical philosophical orientation, you may ask students to concentrate their efforts on examining the links between knowledge elites and power as represented in news items. With a constructivist orientation, you may seek an analysis of historical news narratives that may be evident in current news stories. A multicultural orientation might emphasize marginalized voices and perspectives within the news items in terms of political or cultural power.

Branching from this "analysis" goal, a course objective seeking to address Fink's "caring dimension" might ask students to examine their own biases about the purpose of news. Students could write blogs or journals in which they address notions of social responsibility and ethics as well as examine their own assumptions about the function of news. Writing useful course objectives that can create a lasting impact on student beliefs, knowledge, or action involves making logical connections between your pedagogical philosophy, course content, and concrete ideas about student outcomes. What basic concepts should students remember and understand? How should students learn to think? For example, does your course content emphasize practical, problem solving thinking in accordance with learning techniques such as editing? Or does your course content emphasize creative thinking that might encourage students to construct their own knowledge about, for example, putting together a documentary film? How should students connect course material with ideas and events in their own lives? How should students engage with course material in future contexts as professionals or as citizens? How should students think about their own values or beliefs when engaging with course material? Once you have determined the key learning goals for your course, write your objectives with concrete language. Fink (2003) has created a list of verbs to use in writing learning goals, and many such lists based on Bloom's taxonomy exist online. Briefly, some *remembering* verbs include recognize, define, identify; *understanding* verbs include describe, identify, classify, interpret; *application* verbs include illustrate, calculate, solve; *analyzing* verbs include debate, investigate, uncover, test; *evaluating* verbs include justify, question, judge, critique; *creating* verbs include design, formulate, plan, generate.

Here are a few specific examples of objectives from a course called *Technology and Culture*. The philosophical perspective tends toward an amalgamation of the critical and the constructivist. Following Bloom's taxonomy, a remembering goal is "to identify and describe social, political, cultural influences of and on new communication technologies." An analysis goal is "to investigate a range of cultural artifacts which represent and reflect the interaction of new communication technologies and the traditional cultural forms." An evaluate goal is "to critique predictions surrounding new technologies based on knowledge of the impact of past technologies." Following Fink, a *learning how to learn goal* is "discover strategies to continue building a fuller understanding of your role in the interplay between communication technologies and contemporary culture." Course activities addressing these goals include in-class group exercises, in-class individual writing assignments that are shared and not graded, lecture and discussion, a take-home exam, creative projects, graded "reaction papers," and in-class debates. These individual goals could easily accommodate a multicultural pedagogical standpoint by incorporating course activities and assessments that examine technology as agents of marginalization, liberation, or cultural difference.

Howard Rheingold's (2012) syllabus for Social Media Literacies contains detailed course objectives that speak to Fink's "learn how to learn" objective and to Bloom's taxonomy of affective goals—particularly valuing and organizing. Some also stress George Siemens's (2005) connectivism notion of collaborative learning. Selected objectives include:

- Cultivate an ability to discern, analyze, and manage the way they deploy their attention.
- Understand and practice appropriate online behavior.
- Learn the modes, consequences, some of the responsibilities and dangers of different kinds of digital participation, from curation to blogging.
- Distinguish the characteristics and methods, advantages and pitfalls, of virtual communities, smart mobs, collective intelligence, crowdsourcing, social production, collaborative consumption, and wiki collaboration.
- Recognize the ways the structure and dynamics of networks affect the behaviors of populations, the elements of applying of social network analysis to online culture, the dynamics of social capital online, the steps necessary to cultivate personal learning networks.
- Become familiar with competing perspectives on social media practices and their effects; learn how to make analytic arguments regarding key debates around the use of social media.

The values of participatory culture are clear in Rheingold's objectives. Students work collaboratively to create a reflective process of experimentation and networking. Often the objectives focusing on Bloom's "create" dimension are challenging to construct because of the complex behaviors associated with creating. For the media and communication instructor, many *creating* objectives revolve around images and audio and text in ways that privilege not just the creator but the receiver of generated messages. These objectives may stress a facility with formulating new ideas, the flexibility to generate a range of ideas, and the ability to design original concepts. A course objective for constructing some type of narrative may, depending on your teaching philosophy, accentuate aesthetics, multiple viewpoints, value judgments, collaborative work, dominant perspectives, or self-reflexivity.

This is a good point to remind ourselves that the goals we construct for courses provide an opportunity to practice Dewey's (1916) reflexive habits of mind. As we construct the storyline for our courses through goals and objectives, we make judgments about what's intrinsically valuable. We ask ourselves questions about how our goals may or may not reflect empowerment or cultural capital or collaborative thinking or social justice or problem solving or critical deliberation or skill development or empathy. We create opportunities for us and for our students to render choices about how to live in the world. Communication is a ubiquitous, fundamental life process in which we must engage. The challenge for relevant goal construction, then, according to Sprague (1990), is to realize that

> Communication is not just another content area for students to master or even just another academic skill. Nor is ours a subject that is new to students. We must recognize that when we say we are going to teach

> people to communicate, we are "teaching" them something they have been doing rather successfully for most of their lives. The ways that they presently communicate are closely tied to their individual attitudes, values, and self-concepts.
>
> (p. 23)

Thus, to be relevant in a contemporary context, communication/media faculty must tie our subject matter to other concerns that mold students' lives.

Connecting Course Goals with Assessment and Course Design

Once you have determined what you want students to gain from your course, you will connect specific objectives to an overall design for the course that includes learning activities and assessments. The alignment of goals with assessment provides an avenue for determining the efficacy of course objectives. If you have thoughtfully created course objectives that emphasize multiple learning domains (whether using Bloom's taxonomy or another system), your assessment measures should correlate to those objectives so your course will be successful. If you cannot connect a course goal or specific objective to an assessment or activity, the goal or objective must be reconsidered. For example, if a larger goal of your course is to have students recognize the aspects of visual media that address audiences according to predetermined characterizations of race, gender, sexuality, nationality, or socioeconomic status, but you have no assessment plan for this goal, it may not be truly integral to your course.

Maria Simone (August, 2012), Associate Professor at Rowan University, articulates how her goals and her teaching philosophy are intertwined.

> In addition to the goals that are specific to the content curriculum of a given course, all of the courses I teach have general learning objectives that I believe draw directly from my teaching philosophy. It emphasizes these values:
>
> - enthusiasm (my own and the students' for the topic)
> - respect for diversity and voice
> - challenge (encouraging students to work hard, to work at their potential, to be critical and reflective)
> - support (mostly my support of students as they work to achieve their goals)
> - knowledge (respect for learning, realizing that learning and gaining knowledge is an ongoing process)

The general learning objectives that I list for all of my courses are:

- Challenge assumptions (your own and others'), resisting the temptation to stick with habits of thought
- Upon challenging said assumptions, think critically about which ideas you wish to retain and which you wish to reject

> - Assert and support claims with reliable and credible evidence
> - Develop the ability to read critically and assess claims
> - Strengthen oral and written communication across different styles and contexts
> - Identify, explain and apply research strategies for both primary and secondary research
>
> The values of my teaching philosophy infuse my understanding of these learning objectives. They also infuse the teaching strategies I use in the classroom as well as my assessment techniques.

Professor Simone thoughtfully aligns her course objectives with assessments in these ways.

> My approach to learning assessment is multi-faceted. I provide both formal and informal opportunities for assessment, as well as a variety of different types of assignments. … An example of an informal mode of assessment: For each reading, students answer questions about the reading—ranging from basic comprehension to reflection. They email me those answers before class begins. This is like a quiz, but it allows students to work through the questions as they read and identify problem areas that they can then discuss in the class. I call them "participation preparation activities." This activity relates directly to my philosophical values of support, challenge and knowledge, and my goals of critical thinking/reflection and assessing claims.
>
> I also use a wiki assignment. Students are responsible for developing content in a wiki space related to the class in ways including class notes, glossary, recommended research sources, discussions, links, or career paths. Their responsibilities rotate each week, and by the end of the semester, we have a clearinghouse of information related to the course content. This assignment aligns with my teaching philosophy values of enthusiasm, diversity and voice, challenge, support, and knowledge. It aligns with general course goals of critical thinking, challenging assumptions, assessing claims, strengthening written communication in different styles and contexts, and practicing secondary research skills.

Professor Simone's clear identification of course goals allows her to consider how alterations in classroom experiences or assignments may influence the achievement of her objectives. This is an informed approach to course development that permits consistency with her pedagogical philosophical perspective.

William Walter (June, 2011), a writing instructor at the University of Florida, exhibits a postmodern ethos in his courses that is about challenging established notions of educational hierarchies. In his *Argument and Persuasion* course, the overarching goal as stated in his syllabus reads in part:

> This is, first and foremost, a writing course. The ultimate goal is for students to further their own abilities as writers through critical thought, rhetoric and persuasion, and the expression of complex ideas in a straightforward and accurate manner. To this end, the course has been designed around the subject of epistemology, theories of knowledge, as a means of facilitating thought, producing knowledge, and clarifying an understanding of "truth."

To link the "ultimate goal" to assessment in a manner consistent with his teaching philosophy, he provides this assignment:

> Using everything you have learned in class and the techniques from the major assignments, write a paper that makes an argument about the empiricism-transcendentalism issue. You will be expected to draw on sources on both sides of the fence, using their ideas as support for your argument or as tools to expose the problems with the opposing side and trim away the extraneous chicanery to the useful nugget of the idea, which should ideally be synthesized into your own worldview.

The assignment emphasizes how students can create new meaning from reconstructing old arguments. Creating new meaning and synthesizing new ideas into one's worldview is a means toward "clarifying an understanding of 'truth.'" Professor Walter works to show students what an accomplished goal looks like by modeling critical persuasion, having them practice persuasive argumentation with each other, and providing feedback consistently during the process of knowledge production. Students are more likely to meet course goals if they comprehend how they can be met.

Dustin Morrow (July, 2011), professor in the Department of Theater and Film at Portland State University, sets up his courses to align goals and assignments transparently: "From the very beginning of a class students should be aware of what I'm expecting from them. Grading should never be an ambush. From the outset, students should comprehend my approach to the assignments as the person who will be evaluating their work." Similarly, Jarice Hanson (July, 2011), Professor of Communication at the University of Massachusetts at Amherst, illustrates her alignment of goals and assignments by alerting students about how her course fits into the larger departmental curriculum.

> Some general goals include familiarizing students with literature they haven't read before; analyzing broader criticism, using examples from media, to separate reasoned critique from opinion; and helping them understand their role in the media environment. But I also have specific goals related to course material and the social and professional lives of my students.

> I try to see where my course fits with the rest of the curriculum, and I try to help students see that each course is valuable in its own way, but that it is only one part of a larger picture. I encourage them to develop their own projects or paper topics, but I try to align the goals of the course with the self-reflection they have to demonstrate in their papers or projects.

These are broad ways in which faculty can bear in mind goals for student learning in order to structure assignments and course activities accordingly. Aligning goals to assessments is not, however, an inflexible means of learning. Unanticipated learning outcomes are to be expected, as individual students bring their own viewpoints to the learning environment and perhaps choose to emphasize particular aspects of the course objectives. In addition, collaborative learning environments may generate unforeseen outcomes as students work together to create new knowledge and new ideas. Some instructors may even allow students to help in constructing course goals and assessments.

To increase the unity between course goals and assessments, instructors can construct objectives attentively with disciplinary, institutional, and student characteristics in mind. Inventing a course with goals geared toward higher order cognitive levels of learning (e.g., Bloom's *analysis, evaluation*, and *creation* dimensions) with assessment tools that stress basic factual understanding produces a discordant, confusing learning environment that may lead students to question the value of the course. In the above example of the *Technology and Culture* course, a multiple choice exam assessing fundamental concepts will not serve the "evaluation" goal of "critiquing predictions surrounding new technologies based on knowledge of the impact of past technologies," but an essay considering potential impacts of social media on corporate surveillance techniques will. Also, Professor Simone's above comments demonstrate how her wiki content development assignment can advance her goal of "challenging assumptions" in accordance with her philosophy that stresses a respect for the learning process and critical/reflective approaches. Ultimately, there should be a sound fit between your learning goals for your students and the assignments you construct. This soundness will also be reflected in your course design, covered in more depth in the following chapter. It will also be reflected in your identity within the academy as a media/communication instructor. Because our classrooms represent tiny universes of our own research, theoretical positions, and academic experiences, our course goals signify how we represent ourselves to learners as well as to colleagues and to the public.

Assessing Learning In Communication/Media Studies

Across the academy, educational assessment is recognized to be an industry unto itself with standardized testing mechanisms, courseware packages, institutional labor (assessment "offices" within universities, corporate training seminars), commercial publishing, and accrediting bodies. The industry is a socially constructed, context-independent practice that is informed by intrinsic politics and power relations (see, in particular, Filer, 2000). Although assessment is often seen as an empirical measure of educational productivity as well as student achievement, implicit in assessment measures are cultural and institutional values and imperatives. It may be regarded as a form of disciplinary control in the Foucauldian sense. Because formal judgments of students, faculty, curricula, and institutions are unavoidable realities, faculty must be cognizant of the politics of assessment in order to seek assessment tools and processes that are equitable and contextually situated and that promote enduring learning.

As noted, the ability to create assignments that work in concert with learning goals is a driving force in lifelong learning. Our students are educated as communication/media professionals, consumers, and creators, and thus assessment must encompass theoretical and practical aspects. How do faculty know if students have learned? How do faculty delve into conceptual communication issues as opposed to merely covering material? How can faculty support student development in meaningful ways? Assessment directs learning, and it demonstrates the values and purpose of the overall curriculum. Students grasp what is important about a course based on what is assessed. This section of the chapter explores the basics of creating assessment devices, including grading rubrics, with thought toward the conceptual and applied dimensions of the communication curriculum. Assessment refers to both the methods used to gauge student learning for grading/judgment purposes as well as the means to determine whether students are meeting the learning objectives we set for them. It is about improving student learning and instructor performance. Beyond graded assignments, assessment includes feedback that is informal, student centered, and goal oriented. This next section argues for the development of a consistency among teaching philosophy, course goals, and course assessments.

Philosophies of Assessment in the Mediated Communication Course

In her exploration of feminist pedagogy, Rakow (2001) notes the challenge inherent in creating a pedagogy that is fully consistent with one's research agenda and philosophical stance.

> The trials and tribulations of a feminist and otherwise critical scholar in the classroom do not begin and end with the textbook, but include other texts as well: the text that students bring to the classroom about who and what makes a good class; the text of received knowledge about media and institutions that the curriculum of our programs reproduce; the texts about gender and race our students bring with them from their own experience and the "common sense" of their cultural groups.
>
> (p. 381)

She recognizes that a critical philosophy, while it aims to challenge preconceived notions of knowledge, question hierarchical authority, and privilege local knowledge, must still adhere to the practicalities of both internal and external assessment. Various accrediting bodies acknowledge student learning assessment as a necessary criterion for compliance. Rakow (2001) cites criteria for core values and competencies from the Accrediting Council on Education in Journalism and Mass Communication (dealing with communication and diversity, ethics, institutional practices, etc.) as grist for establishing goals and assessments consistent with critical feminism. She illustrates the idea that effective teaching calls for assessments that mirror course goals, grounded in one's pedagogical philosophy and in one's authentic academic identity.

For faculty with a critical orientation, course goals may address social justice, individual emancipation through an analytical engagement with one's personal history, an inquiry into social institutional power, and the cultivation of one's personal voice. Assessments aimed at measuring or qualitatively gauging such goals often emphasize higher orders of cognitive thinking. Assessments of this nature might involve the creation of a public information campaign aimed at media justice issues or the writing of personal essays that reflect on exposure to racist, homophobic, sexist, or ageist propaganda. Another assessment might involve the development of a business plan for an independent media production company that prioritizes social responsibility. However, a basic understanding of oppressive conditions, power relations, inequality, and injustice may form a foundation for more sophisticated thinking and can be assessed with tools for measurement (including multiple choice exam questions and general classroom interaction). Students could be asked to identify, for example, homophobic imagery and language within a mediated text (a lower-order assessment in Bloom's taxonomy) and subsequently create alternative imagery and language that reveals these homophobic notions to promote respect for all sexual identities (higher-order assessment in Bloom's taxonomy).

Because critical pedagogy encourages skepticism with regard to knowledge hierarchies, assessment by its nature inherently conflicts with this goal. Nevertheless, we must make grading decisions about students. The reflexive quality of critical philosophy permits the instructor and the students to contemplate the production and reproduction of power relationships and the privileging of the narratives of assessment in the higher educational environment. It might consider institutional, societal, faculty, and student agendas. It might offer spaces for the negotiation of meaning and knowledge. It might consider interpretive assessments that rely on a wider range of possibilities than just objective, right/wrong judgments. The ultimate value of assessments from a critical pedagogical perspective is that students have opportunities to act within the public as well as educational spheres as they develop their own voices.

A constructivist approach to assessment within media/communication courses should allow for collaborative learning structures where students question and debate the process of knowledge construction within multiple contexts. Constructivism involves building knowledge through experience rather than merely acting upon received knowledge. Assessments may attempt to measure students' skill in building knowledge by observing cumulative outcomes or by gauging their facility with new situations. Overall, a constructivist approach enables faculty to estimate students' abilities to create new knowledge. A sample assessment might be for students to create a remix video in which the goal is to transform the bits and pieces into a larger statement about the nature of communication in contemporary culture. They might critique accepted perspectives on communication from textbooks and work together to construct and refine their own statements about the place of social media or traditional mass media within contemporary institutional structures. How might their evaluations of prior knowledge contribute to a more sophisticated perspective on the process and nature of communication? How does their experimentation with remix create a pathway for understanding the communicative process? How does the language and form of remix affect the interpretation of its content? Such an assessment serves the creating, analyzing, and evaluating goals within Bloom's taxonomy and provides opportunities for students to make sense of knowledge in contextually bound ways.

Because constructivist-inspired pedagogy encourages instructors to design learning *experiences* for students, case studies make useful constructivist assessments. Such an assessment could involve the understanding, analysis, and evaluation of specific advertising or public relations campaigns and the design of new campaigns. A case study might examine editing practices over time across digital media forms to reflect upon their impact on cultural meaning and students' own knowledge and identity construction. Students might then work together to create alternative editing practices that represent their own perspectives. Another potential constructivist-inspired assessment could require students, working collaboratively, to devise a distribution strategy for a media artist's work. For example, the group might create an audio recording, pursue copyright clearance for any samples in the recording, create a social media presence for the artist(s), strategize live performance schedules, and pursue any marketing avenues. All of these potential assessments enable students to pool their talents in order to solve communication problems or create new meaning or examine their own perspectives within a new context. All of these potential assessments work for multiple levels of Bloom's taxonomy and other learning indices. In the end, constructivist-inspired assessments provide a means for students to build new knowledge through experimenting, collaborating, questioning, and reevaluating.

Multicultural assessments within communication/media courses might examine cultural differences, multiple perspectives, and cultural meaning to privilege the experiences of traditionally marginalized groups. Informal as well as formal assessments can be devised that engage with cultural difference and equal value. Mediated discourses arising from arrangements of gender, sexuality, race, class, age, or religion present ample opportunity for examination. On a profound level (in terms of Bloom's taxonomy, Fink's non-hierarchical system, and other means of organizing learning) assessments can encourage student discomfort as a site for learning. Some students have reported uneasiness during classroom discussions of privilege, social dominance, and race- or gender-based inequality (Brooks & Ward, 2007). Nevertheless, personal discomfort may lead to important personal revelations. A formal or informal assessment might ask students to rewrite, from an alternative cultural perspective, a mediated text that reflects a dominant cultural perspective. For example, students can recast a standard pop song into an alternative genre, reflecting minority cultural perspectives. Through a multicultural pedagogy, students can reflect upon the role of communication in individual identity formation, in social privilege, or in cultural divisions. Assessments from a multicultural pedagogical perspective provide opportunities for students to engage with concepts of social equality, esteem for all cultures, and socioeconomic justice for marginalized groups.

Postmodern assessments center on students' abilities to question received knowledge. Creating assignments that challenge the epistemological grounding of the educational system is uniquely complicated. For communication instructors, this challenge may mean the interrogation of mediated representations or excluded perspectives within communication. An assessment from a postmodern pedagogical perspective could require students to debate the merits of privacy law in an environment of social media. Students could be for or against the ethical, moral, and legal dimensions of privacy. Such an assessment engages the analysis and evaluation areas of Bloom's taxonomy but also encourages the creation of new or alternative views.

William Walter, a University of Florida writing instructor, uses an online role playing game he created to teach writing and the citizenship of "new media" in his *Writing Through Media* course. His assignments ask students to consent to a postmodern methodology. One assignment is designed to help students discover their own voice through writing by posting to the class "media stream" about:

> The issue you care about. The thing that irks you. The thing that's wrong with the world that you can't quite put your finger on. Do not be mistaken (this is no simple argument!), this isn't a diatribe. It's not a rant. It's an exploration of yourself and the social issue that you, on a very profound level, have yet to fully resolve or contend with. Take (and manipulate) the images and ideas around you and become the channel, the medium, for the rest of the world. Try and convey the world as-you-see-it in a stream of consciousness, all targeted around some particular target. Start small … and explore that issue, building a larger and larger impression as you explore connections and relations that might implicate a greater social issue (i.e. some people have no consideration of the world outside immediate presence). Pick the target and follow where it leads you. Feel free to zig and zag, but never lose sight of that target. It is the guiding star of your e-genda [an agenda for the electronic age].

The assignment requires students to use their own experiences and their own reflections upon them to begin considering larger social narratives. Another assignment builds upon this "media stream" to examine personal views on discourses surrounding the notion of "career" in contemporary culture.

> Using … Tumblr, design a page (additional to your Media Stream) that targets "an event in a field of knowledge" within your disciplinary interests; select an invention, discovery, innovation, or breakthrough that particularly strikes a feeling with you. Even if you can't name that feeling yet, it is ripe with potential for self-exploration, and should be considered valuable. Document and detail this "event" as you see it, not only focusing on "the facts of the matter," but including associations, related events, and anything that you feel "just about sums up" your relation to the invention. Splice these associations together on your Tumblr page to generate your self-image.

Building on this identity-seeking exercise, other assignments focus on discourses within other social institutions, including this one on entertainment:

> Think back to the days before you "grew up" and came to college. What movies come to mind? What TV shows? Select your most prominent media-memory, and build your third Tumblr page as a shrine to it. … Divide the page in three parts (any creative way you can):
>
> 1. Present your memory of the story (in your eyes, not in Wikipedia's plot summary). Try and capture that memory with poetic detail. What is it that you see in your mind's eye?
> 2. Find that story and revisit it. Watch again, especially focusing on the scene(s) from your memory, and record what you notice that's new, and what you've misremembered.
> 3. Connect the past and present with your personal life. What family memories are attached to the text? What is related to what you misremembered? Superimpose this (family) narrative on top of the two (remembered, revisited) narratives, binding them together. This isn't an explanation, it's a weaving.
>
> There are no limits or guidelines to how you organize these sections. Do what makes sense. Find the layout and inlet that best suits your sense of connection. The goal is to weave the popular memory (cultural text) with the personal experience (relations to text). We hope to reveal something through this. What that something is … well, that's entirely up to you.

These assessments oblige students to be comfortable with a non-traditional approach to course activities and grading. Professor Walter notes that the students tended to write with subjective voices and that he had to "reinforce the idea that this is more for your professional writing style." He adds:

> That's been the difficult thing in these experimental models; it is so flexible and I do encourage alternative tactics. But when they get to these assignments it is difficult to get them to realize that these are two different forms of writing. As much as desire should drive writing, unfortunately, you have to conform to certain tropes. That was the most difficult thing to deal with. Toward the end of the semester I felt like they had a fairly good grasp of the difference. I had students who said they'd never been this excited to write in their lives.

Professor Walter uses his postmodern approach to soothe the students' anxiety about writing, but acknowledges the challenges to non-traditional approaches to assessing communication.

> My goal was to … teach them some new tactics. … I'm not opposed to these tiered grade systems because the students can target. But I don't have an answer for exactly what I WANT them to write. That's why this course is designed to separate the traditional writing practices, too—this desire-oriented participatory system where their grade is based on their natural writing style and testing what they can do. [I] didn't evaluate anything based on whether popular culture or the sciences agrees with you. It was more like—that seems like a pretty good orientation. I may not agree with you but you did it pretty well. The traditional papers try to repeat what I said in class, but what I say in class is just an example and not to be regurgitated. Students generally assume that if you teach from something that must be THE thing to emulate. … students are less creative thinkers, but that's my motivation to do these courses—I'm almost desperate to unlock a little creativity … figuring out how to approach life from a position that is not locked down.

For Professor Walter, his assessments reflect his teaching philosophy in ways that query prevailing knowledge structures. He demonstrates that a consistency between pedagogical philosophy and assessments aids faculty in making course goals transparent to students and in realizing those goals. Moreover, the teaching philosophy echoes one's academic identity and hence helps faculty choose teaching practices that contribute to the achievement of specific course objectives.

Constructing Assignments and Exams in Accordance with Course Goals

As observed in the introduction to this book, media/communication curricula are multidimensional and include the performance of communication, the creation of media, and an engagement with media as an object of study. If our task is to build discipline-based learning environments in which students grasp the epistemology of the field, assessments—emanating from course goals—must connect with communication as a central facet of everyday life. What elements represent expertise in the field of media/communication? How do our assessment techniques address contemporary standards of proficiency? What are those standards? How does the research community help create or respond to those standards, particularly in light of social demands for accountability? Assessments can be tools for continued learning and reflection rather than a mere appraisal of what students have learned.

The purpose of all assessments, whether formal or informal, should be explained so students are clear about how assignments, exams, or course activities align with overall goals. Instructors dedicated to course goals that emphasize, for instance, the creation of narratives in new media platforms, want assessments enabling the creative process as opposed to basic dimensions of learning that, for example, multiple-choice exams might gauge. To create assessments that encourage continued learning, based in concrete course objectives, rather than simply appraising what students have learned already, Wiggins (1998) recommends standards for assessing contextually based learning objectives. These standards are context-specific if they:

1. *[Are] realistic.* The task or tasks replicate the ways in which a person's knowledge and abilities are "tested" in real-world situations.
2. *Require judgment and innovation.* The student has to use knowledge and skills wisely and effectively to solve unstructured problems … and the solution involves more than following a set routine or procedure. …
3. *Ask the student to do the subject.* Instead of reciting, restating, or replicating through demonstration [course subject matter], the student has to carry out exploration and work within the discipline. …
4. *Replicate or simulate the contexts in which adults are "tested" in the workplace, in civic life, and in personal life.* Contexts involve specific situations that have particular constraints, purposes, and audiences. Typical school tests are contextless. Students need to experience what it is like to do tasks in workplace and other real-life contexts, which tend to be messy and murky. In other words, genuine tasks require good judgment. …
5. *Assess the student's ability to use a repertoire of knowledge and skill efficiently and effectively to negotiate a complex task.* Most conventional test items are isolated elements of performance …
6. *Allow appropriate opportunities for students to rehearse, practice, consult resources, and get feedback on and refine performances and products.* Although there is a role for the conventional "secure" test that keeps questions secret and keeps resource materials from students until during the test, that testing must coexist with educative assessment if students are to improve performance. … (pp. 22, 24)

The point of such assessments is to align with course goals in ways that are meaningful to students throughout their lives. These assessments are what Fink (2003) refers to as "forward-looking," and they coalesce with Bloom's higher-order cognitive as well as affective learning domains. For media/communication students, such assessments have obvious practical utility, but they also provide opportunities for students to engage deeply with media as objects of study rather than merely as consumers.[3]

Within communication and other disciplines, multiple-choice exams have been scrutinized as part of a larger focus on assessment as a matter of higher educational policy and procedure. Within the academy, there is renewed pressure to accentuate critical and creative thinking as basic learning objectives. Multiple-choice and other objective exam questions are useful in assessing the remembering and understanding dimensions of Bloom's taxonomy, often in the form of recognition or recall of communication concepts or facts or possibly in the form of how communicative concepts or approaches apply to a given condition. Although there are techniques for ensuring that higher-order cognition is assessed via objective examinations, many such exam questions measure students' memorization or regurgitation skills and may have limited usefulness in a communication context. However, curricular circumstances sometimes necessitate the use of objective exams, such as large, basic conceptual courses with hundreds of students or inventories of prior student knowledge in lower-division production courses. If a course objective seeks higher-order cognition, a multiple-choice item can present a scenario or graphic with questions aimed at application, analysis, or evaluation. For example, a magazine image of a beer advertisement using appeals based on race, gender, sexuality, age, or class may be shown, accompanied by a series of multiple-choice questions in which students are asked to evaluate the nature of the claims in terms of stereotypes or to analyze the advertisement on the basis of political economic theory.

Other tactics may be used in multiple-choice exams to reduce the quantization of scores and enhance higher-order thinking. Space can be provided for students to explain their answers, with partial credit being given for wrong but well-reasoned answers without a large increase in grading time. Alternatively, students may be permitted to work collaboratively on multiple-choice exams after they've taken the exam individually. Scores can be weighted differently for the two components, with the individual score weighing more. Student discussion during the collaborative portion is focused and can serve as an additional layer of assessment for learning. These techniques are useful in, for example, an introductory media aesthetics course where you might want your students to deconstruct conventional wisdom about camera angles or the function of sound in video production or basic web design aesthetics. Or these techniques could be used in a media law class to critique the sociopolitical norms surrounding the dynamic nature of copyright law in the United States. These assessments of complex evaluative and analytic skills can work in circumstances where learning objectives are cognitively sophisticated but objective assessments may be necessary.

Written exams or quizzes present a broad range of possibilities for assessing cognitive, affective, and even skill-oriented goals. In addition to carefully constructed multiple-choice or other objective questions, short answer or essay questions add a qualitative component to assessments and reduce possibilities for guessing. Both short answer and essay questions take time to grade, but creating a model answer with essential points to cover reduces the burden. These types of questions facilitate student creativity, problem-solving skills, and analytical abilities. A short answer question for a media law exam that seeks to assess students' ability to connect legal principles with everyday media experiences might ask, "Explain why hate speech is protected by the First Amendment to the U.S. Constitution." An essay question seeking to assess evaluative abilities might be, "Take a position and *either* attack or defend the following statement: *Nothing to hide = nothing to fear* as it pertains to surveillance, privacy, and ethics." These questions allow students to craft original answers demonstrating higher-order thinking. When constructing short answer and essay questions, you should clearly explain the task students are to do in order to minimize the possibilities for extraneous writing. Take-home exams, collaborative exams, and comprehensive research papers can be used to assess higher-order thinking on a deeper, more intricate level.

Engleberg (2007) proposes "written and video scenarios" for a fundamentals of communication course. She argues that these types of assessments are more meaningful for students; they address objectives directly, are student centered, and provide opportunities for longer-term retention and saliency. They also have the advantage of demonstrating context, so higher-order thinking skills are employed. In Engelberg's example of a written scenario on transactional communication, she presents a dialogue following a car breakdown in a parking lot. Mrs. Johnson calls her husband for help, and he replies that he will arrive shortly. Mrs. Johnson responds that she is "in front of the drug store." Mr. Johnson arrives at the parking lot to find that his wife is not there. Assuming that she was able to start the car and leave, he begins to drive away but calls his wife just to be sure. The dialogue and representative exam questions follow.

"Why didn't you wait for me or call me back?" he asks.
"I *am* waiting for you," she says.
"Where? *In* the store?"
"No. Right in front of the store!"
"Well I don't see you—or the car."
"Are you blind? I'm standing right here and I don't see *you*."
"Where is here?"
"Right in front of the drug store."
"Drug store? You said *rug* store."

Multiple Choice Questions:

1. Mr. Johnson failed to ________________ Mrs. Johnson's phone message about her location. Which answer fills in the blank?
   a. accurately encode
   b. accurately decode*
   c. adapt to
   d. appreciate
   e. empathize with
2. How could Mr. and Mrs. Johnson have improved their communication? They should have ...
   a. minimized the amount of noise in the communication process.
   b. adjusted to the context in which the communication took place.
   c. selected a better channel for communication.
   d. provided feedback to one another to clarify the message.*
   e. improved their choice of language. ...

Short Essay Question: Select and explain two communication strategies that could have been used to avoid the misunderstanding between Mr. and Mrs. Johnson. (Engleberg, 2007, pp. 8–9)

As Engleberg (2007) notes, this type of scenario requires some effort to create, but it engages various domains of Bloom's taxonomy. She also describes a similar scenario assessment in which a video is shown to students who answer a variety of questions. Video scenarios can also be used for class discussion or written paper assignments. These scenarios are rich in context and they convey a sense of a holistic communicative environment.

As seen throughout this chapter, the diversity of lines of inquiry in media/communication curricula permit instructors much ingenuity in creating assessments. A course goal stated earlier in this chapter, from a feminist/critical pedagogical orientation, was "students will critique television advertisements and make judgments about their gender identity claims." A formal assessment of this objective could require students to select a particular advertisement and write a detailed discourse analysis of the advertisement, focusing on gender stereotyping. Another formal assessment could require students to create, either collaboratively or individually, an advertisement that responds critically to the original ad, making its own gender identity claims. Another formal assessment, working on a less profound level, could involve a series of essay or short answer exam questions in which students respond to a given advertisement. An informal assessment of this objective could use break-out groups within class in which students analyze and critique a set of advertisements, sharing their group insights with the class as a whole. A formal assessment of the course objective "understand and demonstrate basic elements of video editing" could require students to work collaboratively or individually to edit a piece of video. An informal assessment could use class discussion to explore the aesthetic rationale behind basic editing principles. While an exam might be able to assess basic understanding of video editing, only a skill-based assessment will be able to ascertain students' demonstration abilities.

Assessments can help gauge instructor effectiveness in achieving course objectives. If students are not meeting objectives, the instructor can use formal and informal assessments to determine whether problems lie in teaching methods, poor assignment or exam construction, lack of student motivation, or the objectives themselves. For assessments to measure authentic learning of course objectives, they must be comprehensive, valid (aligned with goals), and context-specific (meaningful within the area of study).

Informal assessments give students opportunities to practice the material, to exercise their judgment about it, or to delve into their own ideas about it in ways that allow instructor or peer feedback. Non-graded assessments enable instructor flexibility and creativity, and students usually enjoy exploration of ideas and interaction with peers and faculty in class. Here are a few ideas for informal assessments.[4]

- Pose a question and ask students to write about it for a few minutes. Students then trade papers and write responses to their peers' statements. Papers can be traded again, time permitting. These are discussed briefly in class and turned in for no grade. The instructor reads through them after class and may comment on them in the next class period.
- Have students create journals, wiki sites, portfolios, etc., as a means for interrogating and constructing their own identity within the field. They can reflect on their own practices within communication—and perhaps assess their own performance or thinking or skills.
- Give students an individual, ungraded "quiz" on some aspect of the material that will be covered that day. Collect the quizzes, look them over, and have students break into small groups. Give back the quizzes and ask students to revise answers collectively. They may reflect on their own understanding of the material as they learn from their peers.

This type of learning process is not impeded by the specter of a grade, and students often find these assessments engaging. They are a means, too, for instructors to gain qualitative data about students' perceptions, viewpoints, and experiences within the course. Additionally, peer critique and self critique of the communication process (writing, speaking, editing, etc.) help students work on their own communicative process—a metacommunicative learning practice. These assessments can motivate students to learn more in accordance with course goals. They also allow instructors to clarify, in subsequent classes, any ambiguous points or problematic concepts.

Here is an in-class, group exercise I created for the *Technology and Culture* course for a unit investigating art and technology.

Group Discussion: Digital Art/Technology

In groups of 4–5, answer the following questions about your digital art form. Your group's technology is Digital Painting (Photoshop). We will discuss your answers as a whole class following your 20-minute group consultation.

1. How has digital technology changed this art form from its original, non-digital form?
2. Is this art form as "authentic" as the non-digital art form from which it is derived? Why or why not?
3. Here is our course-created definition of art: "The use of skill and imagination in the creation of aesthetic objects, environments, or experiences that can be shared with others." Does your digital art form increase opportunities for artistic expression? Why or why not?
4. What does the popularity (or lack of popularity) of digital art in our society mean for our consideration of technology and culture? Consider your thoughts about technology and the human spirit.

The purpose of the exercise is to facilitate deeper learning about a controversial subject. I also wanted to create a peer-learning situation, but from a structured position so that the conversations would have some direction. I interacted with each group as the students discussed their technologies (others included music sampling (remix), digitized filmmaking, and electronic music). I provided feedback to help guide their discussions toward learning objectives when necessary. When the students came back together as a whole class, the resulting conversation was freewheeling, but informed by the breakout discussions. It was more multifaceted and meaningful than a simple whole-class initial dialogue, and the students and I had fun. Every student in the class participated in the conversation.

Because informal, ungraded assessments in class include students' lived experiences, interactions among students and the instructor, and immediate feedback, they tend to be more contextually interesting for students. These assessment situations are flexible and sometimes perilous as students and instructors reveal and refine their perspectives and identities. Classroom assessment situations often provide the most direct pathways to course goals, particularly in communication courses. They are effective means for probing the affective learning domains as well as cognitive and skill domains. Rather than simply auditing what students have learned, informal assessments can move students to learn (see example in Box 1).

Box 1. An informal assessment from Nancy Morris (August, 2013), Professor of Media Studies at Temple University, on media globalization

This is an informal assessment for graduate students but it could work with any small group or as group work in a large course. It serves as a "wrap-up" exercise for the end of a unit or of the course. I had amassed news articles related to class topics, and I distributed the articles to the students. Each student got three miscellaneous articles, and they were asked to spend a few minutes reading them and then reporting to the class how the articles related to course topics. The articles were quite varied—one was just the daily TV guide from the newspaper, an article about Hilary Clinton in China, one about an upcoming museum exhibit on 60s fashion, etc. We went around the room in three rounds, each student briefly summarizing the article and discussing how it related to semester topics. A few times they said, "I'm not sure about this one. It's about x,y,z, but ..." and then their classmates interjected on how the topics related. I told them that I did this as a way for them to see how the topics we had been discussing thread through so much of our lives and culture, and said that I hope they would leave the class with this awareness and some tools for interpreting it all. It worked well.

Grading and Rubrics

Because communication/media learning objectives involve performance, creation, and reflection, grading can be a complex endeavor. Grading informs classroom interactions, the culture of a course, and relationships between faculty and students. Learning objectives form the foundation of course grading and should be clearly communicated to students. Similarly, grading criteria should be transparent so that the instructor can determine whether students are achieving learning objectives. Grading is a means to communicate to faculty how well students learn so that instructors can alter teaching strategies to refocus learning objectives. Rubin (1990) argues that evaluation should be based on achievement and learning rather than subjective measures such as effort, work habits, or attitudes. She notes, "teachers need to justify to students their grading systems so students see achievement of assignments, rather than investment of time, as the relevant outcome" (pp. 398–399) and that consistent evaluation standards create systems of equal opportunity for success. Thus, grading practices should not involve power relations or bias. Instructors do not assign grades; students earn grades.

Walvoord and Anderson (2009) outline the multiple functions of grading:

> *Evaluation.* The grading process should produce a valid, fair, and trustworthy judgment about the quality of each student's work.

> *Communication.* The grade itself is a communication to the student, as well as to employers, graduate schools, and others. The grading process also spurs communication between faculty and students, among faculty colleagues, and between institutions and their constituents.
> *Motivation.* Grading affects how students study, what they focus on, how much time they spend, and how involved they become in the course. Thus, it is a powerful part of the motivational structure of the course.
> *Organization.* A grade on a test or assignment helps to mark transitions, bring closure, and focus effort for both students and teachers.
> *Faculty and student reflection.* The grading process can yield rich information about what students are learning collectively and can serve as the first step in systematic assessment and information-driven teaching.
>
> (p. 2)

Although these functions do not indicate the institutional and political imperatives that require the assignment of grades, they provide a baseline from which to think about formal assessment. Feedback between faculty and students can be more meaningful when faculty provide quality judgments about student work. In order to do this, grading standards and criteria must be clearly articulated to the students. Since grading standards differ between disciplines and between faculty within the same discipline, equitable judgments cannot be made without clear criteria. Grading criteria are derived from the course learning objectives.

For example, in the *Technology and Culture* course, one learning objective is "to articulate ideas about the relationship between communication technologies and culture." The larger goal is to develop habits of mind in which students consider political, economic, artistic, and philosophical claims about technology and its role in human communication. In a writing assignment for this goal, grading criteria are provided in a holistic format.

Reaction Paper on Art and Technology

Walter Benjamin (1968) argues in *The Work of Art in the Age of Mechanical Reproduction* that truly radical art uses technology to cut through "accepted" notions of reality to challenge authority. Using Benjamin's article as well as additional course readings, assess whether

1. Benjamin's argument holds true in contemporary American society
2. There is a role for the 'authentic' in an age of digital design and manufacture

Include a consideration of Benjamin's concept of the "aura" of a work of art. To strengthen your arguments, consider including examples from other sources or from your own personal experience.

This assignment is worth 15 percent of your grade, and should be answered in 2–4 pages. You will be graded on the following criteria:

- Answering the question: have you addressed the questions thoroughly and coherently?
- Application of relevant class material: are course concepts and readings deployed when they are relevant? When course concepts and readings are included, are they used correctly? Does the use of course concepts and readings demonstrate that the writer understands them?
- Clarity of thought: is your use of evidence clearly expressed?
- Organization: is your answer logically and clearly presented?
- Thoroughness of analysis: is your answer complete and have you considered the supporting evidence acutely rather than providing a superficial analysis?
- General grammatical correctness: is your answer free of spelling and grammatical and syntax errors that may obscure clarity? Are sentences well formed? Are words chosen carefully? Bibliography must be in APA format.

Walvoord and Anderson (2009) note that grading criteria can be provided to students through grade descriptions, checklists, or rubrics. Grade descriptions indicate requirements for a particular grade, e.g., "An 'A' paper states and defends a logical argument using evidence supported by course materials and includes no more than three grammar or syntax errors." Checklists contain no scale but instead consist of a list of items the evaluator requires, such as "all arguments are clearly stated, logically employed, and supported by evidence from course materials" or "web sites must follow principles of good design as articulated in course materials and must contain working links." Rubrics deploy a scale to describe the necessary components of student work. Most rubrics assess three to seven components and provide some type of gradation of quality to indicate to students the precise criteria needed to obtain points. A rubric for a website design assignment might include components like navigation/links, layout, color/fonts/graphics, content, grammar, copyright/documentation. Each component would be worth a specific number of points, and point values are determined by criteria provided for each component. Walvoord and Anderson (2009) and Fink (2003) provide examples of rubrics for multiple disciplines, and the Iowa State University ISUComm program maintains a series of communication oriented rubrics at http://isucomm.iastate.edu/commrubrics.

Using rubrics with scales allows instructors to tally points that are translated into an overall grade for an assignment. Using the more holistic formats (checklist, grade descriptions) requires instructors to develop an interior sensibility about A, B, C, or D work. Ultimately, grading, like other elements of teaching, is a personally determined matter. Bean (1996) shows how that determination works by quoting Cornell English professor Harry Shaw's guidelines for deciding upon letter grades for written essays:

> **How I Assign Letter Grades**
> In grading "thesis papers" ... I ask myself the following set of questions:
>
> 1. Does the paper have a thesis?
> 2. Does the thesis address itself to an appropriate question or topic?
> 3. Is the paper free from long stretches of quotations and summaries that exist only for their own sakes and remain unanalyzed?
> 4. Can the writer produce complete sentences?
> 5. Is the paper free from basic grammatical errors?
>
> If the answer to any of these questions is "no," I give the paper some kind of C. If the answer to most of the questions is "no," its grade will be even lower.
>
> For papers which have emerged unscathed thus far, I add the following questions:
>
> 1. How thoughtful is the paper? Does it show real originality?
> 2. How adequate is the thesis? Does it respond to its question or topic in a full and interesting way? Does it have an appropriate degree of complexity?
> 3. How well organized is the paper? Does it stick to the point? Does every paragraph contain a clear topic sentence? If not, is another kind of organizing principle at work? Are the transitions well made? Does it have a real conclusion, not simply a stopping place?
> 4. Is the style efficient, not wordy or unclear?
> 5. Does the writing betray any special elegance?
> 6. Above all, can I hear a lively, intelligent, interesting human voice speaking to me (or to another audience, if that's what the writer intends) as I read the paper?
>
> Depending on my answers to such questions, I give the paper some kind of A or some kind of B [pp.149–150].
>
> (as quoted in Bean, 1996, p. 264)

These criteria acknowledge a level of subjectivity that is the prerogative of an instructor who has developed that interior sensibility about student work from immersion in the teaching and learning enterprise. An instructor's disciplinary expertise, honed through involvement in learning, teaching, and scholarship, informs an internal understanding of evaluating student work. However, one of the chief rationales for the use of rubrics is that they increase the objectivity of grading due to their specificity. According to Walvoord and Anderson (2009), rubrics increase the consistency and fairness of grading, increase efficiency in the grading process, and allow instructors to pinpoint weaknesses in student work to alter teaching strategies (p. 44). Similarly, Spandel (2006) mounts a defense of rubrics in which she extols their unique value for writing assignments:

> They give us direction and a basis for conversation. They cause us to go deep inside performance and question our traditional beliefs about what we define as proficient. They keep us honest, for when we put our thinking on paper, there is no longer a place to hide. Best of all, they serve as a guide to revision, giving student writers an insider's view of what makes writing work.
>
> (p. 19)

She emphasizes the need for precision in rubrics that can serve to model good work for students. Rubrics should encourage students to develop a voice while helping them to gain from the insight and wisdom of the instructor (Spandel, 2006). Andrade (2005) favors rubrics for their descriptions of shortcomings in student work as well as the desired components. She notes that rubrics can be used in teaching rather than just grading when they are co-created with students or used for peer assessment. Rubrics may help instructors clarify their learning objectives, align instructional activities toward those objectives, and produce feedback that judges progress toward achievement of goals (Andrade, 2005). Rubrics may also help to increase the quality of student work due to detailed explanations of criteria as well as opportunities for reflective thinking (Spandel, 2006; Andrade, 2005). Lattuca (2005) acknowledges the subjectivity inherent in grading, but claims that a rubric "alleviates student and instructor fears about the subjective nature of grading and banishes concerns about grading on a curve, that is, assessing students relative to one another rather than against a predetermined standard of performance" (p. 249). Expert judgment should be the key element in grading since disciplinary knowledge permits instructors to convey the attributes of proficiency (Lattuca, 2005).

Yet, some scholars argue that rubrics may not be useful in certain circumstances. All assessment is subjective to some extent. Kim Bissell (August, 2011), Director of the Institute for Communication & Information Research, College of Communication & Information Sciences at the University of Alabama, cautions instructors about overreliance on grading rubrics:

> I used to use grading rubrics for the skills courses that I taught (photojournalism and design) but I found that it is almost a cop-out, at least for me, in terms of giving them sufficient feedback to improve their work. The

> undergrad courses I teach are magazine design courses, so I can give each student a grade on the use of type, color, white space, etc., but if I don't tell them how or why they could have done something differently, they won't improve. So, I shifted to typing them up long notes about each of their submitted assignments. It allowed me to tell them specifically how the page/s could be improved, and it allowed them better understanding of the grade they had received.

Because we cannot deny the intrinsic subjective nature of human judgment (Andrade, 2005; Kohn, 2006), we must account for it. Even with disciplinary standards and specific grading criteria, what constitutes "good" work in communication/media studies is confounded by how broad and interdisciplinary the field is. Peer assessments with rubrics can go awry, with students not grasping how to judge one another's work or simply making callous comments (Andrade, 2005). And while efficiency may not be enough of a rationale for using scoring rubrics according to Kohn (2006), the larger problem is that rubrics provoke students to focus on a list of elements to include in the assignment rather than on actual learning. Kohn argues that the use of scoring rubrics often produces higher grades but less sharp or thoughtful work. Thus, learning goals may be thwarted when students focus too much on "achieving" a particular grade. Kohn states that "quality is more than the sum of its rubricized parts" and that "studies have shown that too much attention to the quality of one's performance is associated with more superficial thinking, less interest in whatever one is doing, less perseverance in the face of failure, and a tendency to attribute the outcome to innate ability and other factors though to be beyond one's control" (p. 14).

Rubrics can be useful for scoring assignments, such as a speech or a basic video editing assignment, in which the instructor is likely to write similar comments many times. They are perhaps less useful for assignments where complex, personalized feedback is necessary for true communication about learning objectives. Stevens and Levi (2004) provide a guide to help determine whether a scoring rubric is valuable:

> **Do You Need a Rubric?**
>
> How do you know if you need a rubric? One sure sign is if you check off more than three items from the following list:
>
> - You are getting carpal tunnel syndrome from writing the same comments on almost every student paper.
> - It's 3 A.M. The stack of papers on your desk is fast approaching the ceiling. You're already 4 weeks behind in your grading, and it's clear that you won't be finishing it tonight either.
> - Students often complain that they cannot read the notes you labored so long to produce.

- You have graded all your papers and worry that the last ones were graded slightly differently from the first ones.
- You want students to complete a complex assignment that integrates all the work over the term and are not sure how to communicate all the varied expectations easily and clearly.
- You want students to develop the ability to reflect on ill-structured problems but you aren't sure how to clearly communicate that to them.
- You give a carefully planned assignment that you never used before and to your surprise, it takes the whole class period to explain it to students.
- You give a long narrative description of the assignment in the syllabus, but the students continually ask two to three questions per class about your expectations.
- You are spending long periods of time on the phone with the Writing Center or other tutorial services because the students you sent there are unable to explain the assignments or expectations clearly.
- You work with your colleagues and collaborate on designing the same assignments for program courses, yet you wonder if your grading scales are different.
- You've sometimes been disappointed by whole assignments because all or most of your class turned out to be unaware of academic expectations so basic that you neglected to mention them (e.g., the need for citations or page numbers).
- You have worked very hard to explain the complex end-of-term paper; yet students are starting to regard you as an enemy out to trick them with incomprehensible assignments.
- You're starting to wonder if they're right.

(pp. 4–5)

Regardless of whether or not you choose to use a grading rubric for a particular assignment, feedback is essential to the learning process. It serves as a dialogue between instructor and student about not just learning objectives but also means for improvement and the communication of disciplinary values and norms. Instructor feedback should note performance on learning goals, but it should also mention points of unexpected brilliance or originality or utter lack of comprehension. It should be done gently and respectfully but honestly. It should be encouraging and manageable for both student and instructor. It should interconnect with specific learning objectives for the course. Walvoord and Anderson (2009) suggest that feedback should help students grow, and so the question, "what does this learner need from me at this time?" (p. 130) guides the feedback. Moreover, feedback is not limited to assessments by an instructor. Self-assessments and peer assessments provide opportunities for reflective thinking, and assessments from external faculty or from communication professionals may help students realize learning objectives focusing on lifelong learning or applied skills.

Terry Harpold (June, 2011 & May, 2014), at the University of Florida's English department, shares observations about providing feedback in his "Hypermedia" writing course.

> I kick off the course with a simple exercise, asking each of the students to compose a wiki page that describes … the historical trace of what she's read, what she likes to read, what she aims to have read. This usually gets things rolling, as students write about their reading histories, peer into other students' reading histories, link up the emerging nodes, comments and critiques, etc. in an emergent discussion of what is worth reading and reading again. This becomes an ongoing, increasingly brambly exchange that often leads students to take up new texts or return to old favorites, and reminds us all of the extent to which our situation of reading is intimately individual and at the same time binds us to large and diverse communities. Usually, these branches of the wiki remain among the most active as the semester progresses, as students add in new pages and comments and emend old ones. And I participate in the bramble, writing about my reading during the semester—above all, my pleasure reading, as one of the goals of the exercise is to remind students that they *can* engage in pleasure reading, even when they have piles of assigned texts to read.
>
> *All* class writing is in the wiki, and many of the texts we read are uploaded to, and read within, the wiki. Students have to compose long and short wiki entries on readings, sometimes as individuals, sometimes in teams. In every case, they are free to emend their entries, and others are free to do so as well. That takes some getting used to—a lot of students don't want anyone else revising their work—but when they grasp that this is a basic condition of the course and see that it can be productive in unanticipated ways, they embrace it.
>
> Also visible in the wiki are my comments on student work—up to a point. The administrator of a wiki has the ability to limit access to pages to only selected individuals. For every student and workgroup in the course, there are secret branches of the wiki that only they and I can access. It's on those pages that I record things like grades and comments that should only be read by those individuals. This requires that I think carefully about how to parse or split up comments into private and public channels, so it's extra work. But it has several clear advantages. If multiple students get some fact of the discussion wrong, or commit some infelicity of writing, I can create a single node for that event, and just link every subsequent instance of the error to that node, and not have to write the same complaint or advice on student papers over and over.
>
> More significant, if students can review other students' papers they can better appreciate what's working and not working well in their own writing, and will aspire, I've found, to write stronger papers because they understand that their work is visible to others. Dated assignments usually have two due dates: a first date by which the initial draft must be posted to the wiki, and a second by which final draft is due. Between those dates, students

> can see what others have done, and can edit/emend their contributions accordingly. I encourage them to cite other students' wiki pages, created for that assignment and earlier assignments, to link to and incorporate those pages into their writing, as appropriate—in much the way that we all write professionally, building an argument in relation to a body of new and established scholarship. (One of the mantras of the course is that scholarship is a *social* activity.) On the final due date, I lock down a version of each student's writing assignment (that's the one I grade), but another version remains open to further revisions by anyone in the course.
>
> I do limit the visibility of their work: the course wiki is not open to the internet. No one outside can edit or even read it. I've found that students are more willing to deal with exposure of their work-in-progress if they understand that it is visible only to a specific cohort of like-minded collaborators, and not to anyone with Google access.

Harpold's approach demonstrates the usefulness of peer feedback in the learning process in ways that inspire students to do their best work. He seeks collaborative learning opportunities for his students, but he is careful to emphasize a critical approach to thinking. Because he seeks to nurture the critical voice in student writing, his peer feedback assessment strategy is one that helps students develop that voice in a way that motivates them to want to succeed. Bean (1996) reinforces this idea, arguing that peer feedback, based on clear criteria from the instructor, can impel drastic improvements in student work:

> It is satisfying indeed to see how well many undergraduates can write when they are engaged in their projects and follow the stages of the writing process through multiple drafts and peer reviews. By setting high standards, by encouraging multiple drafts, by refusing to be the first human being to read a student's paper—in short, by expecting excellence—instructors can feel justified in applying rigorous criteria.
>
> (p. 264)

Earlier in this section I wrote that Foucault's (1977) notion of disciplinary power—in which subjects who are monitored ultimately discipline themselves by modifying their behavior—may be observed in the institutional values that characterize educational assessment. Students' behaviors are based upon their experiences in the learning environment, and students who are expected merely to perform on exams and to act passively as receivers of knowledge will occupy that disciplined position. If educational goals within communication seek to develop students as active learners, assessments (both formal and informal) should emphasize the feedback process so that students can ameliorate patterns originated through passive learning experiences. If we choose to transform learning environments into spaces of active learning where communication students are inquisitors of culture rather than just cultural users, assessment tactics must include descriptive feedback. Students of media and communication, who create, observe, and interact with multiple media forms from multiple theoretical positions, must be encouraged to pursue knowledge as enduring learners rather than as mere products of the higher education system.

Ultimately, our goals seek to educate the whole person and perhaps to help students find work that fulfills them in their lives as citizens or individuals. As a faculty member, your academic identity enmeshes with your pedagogical philosophy to determine your larger teaching goals, your individual course goals, and your assessment procedures. These goals and procedures flow together to create, for you, a seamless integration of teaching and research and creative activity.

If the creation of our goals and assessments is the product of cultural and disciplinary cultures as well as our own specific interests, we might return to Larry Gross's (2012) International Communication Association speech for some insight into the challenges that speak to how we create goals in the contemporary academy:

> Communication scholars draw upon a wealth of disparate theoretical and empirical strands in order to clarify such questions of societal import, illuminate new paths of research, and explore solutions to pressing problems. Communication scholars, individually and collectively, need to assert our centrality to any cogent and credible account of the contemporary world, and thus, our centrality in the education of the citizens of the 21st century. (p. 924)

Students broaden their perspectives through immersion in the environment of higher education. They explore new ideas and habits of mind, they share experiences with one another, and they grow. Thoughtful assessment processes can support learning in ways that complement students' lived experiences, resulting in more engaged, interested student populations. While the goals of higher education may be increasingly tied to a market orientation (job training), this larger social goal can be translated into a learning goal whereby we help students find a meaningful place in the world.

Appendix A

Marin/Treatment Assignment for Scriptwriting Course

Kristine Weatherston (August, 2013), Department of Media Studies and Production, Temple University

[Author note: Professor Weatherston's assignment is aimed at a course learning objective seeking to integrate theory and practice of narrative and dramatic structure. This assignment is based on student engagement with Louis Marin's *Sublime Poussin*, which outlines the theory and practice of reading paintings through textual and iconographic scrutiny using the work of Nicolas Poussin as a foundation.]

1. Read the Louis Marin chapter excerpts from *Sublime Poussin*.
2. Go to the Philadelphia Museum of Art.
   a. **Locate a painting in the museum that strikes you in some way**. There is no right or wrong painting to choose—from Renaissance, to Impressionist, to modern art—the choice is completely yours. The museum is home to over 227,000 works of art.
   b. **Spend quality, uninterrupted time with this work of art**. Observe the painting, study its properties and formal qualities, and **take notes** on how the work of art makes you feel. What is the painting trying to tell you?
      i. I recommend at least 30 minutes to 1 hour, sitting and standing within various proximities of the painting. Any less time is insufficient.
   c. A good idea for observation is to think about how you might shoot and/or edit a **master shot sequence** in video/tv/film—i.e., moving your body and point of view from wide to medium to close up, and back again as if you are a camera.
   d. **The more time you engage with the artwork and remain in its presence, the greater the amount of information and breadth of detail will be revealed to you**—brush strokes, colors, blending, shapes, shadows, textures, lines, depth, light, tone, meaning, temporal and spatial relationships, genre, story, characters, historical context, symbols, significance, etc.... and the materiality of the work matters! Is it oil on canvas, or wax on wood? Size? Shape? Frame style?
   e. **Shoot your own photos of the artwork**. Patrons are allowed to shoot images of the artwork in the museum without a flash. You will need these photos for later reference and for your presentation. Shoot a lot of photos from various angles/composition/POV.
3. Write a 3–5 page original treatment for a screenplay based on your observations
   a. Apply what you know about writing treatments and Marin's methodology for observing art.
   b. Use your notes and images to develop an original, visual, compelling narrative that would theoretically be further developed for the screen.
   c. Write this story in the form of a treatment for the screen—using present tense, little to no dialogue, and writing action driven scenes/sequences that show character development, dramatic need, and plot/narrative structure.
4. Create a 5–7 minute presentation
   a. Create a dynamic 5–7 minute presentation, using your images and other supporting visuals.
   b. Presentations must include visuals—your images of the art (and other supporting materials you deem necessary) will help show your original story to the class.

   c. **Do not read from your treatment**—rather, share your short story with the idea that you are "pitching" a screenplay to a room full of creatives and executives.
5. Consider these final thoughts/suggestions:
   a. No need to be too literal. If you are drawn to a Degas painting such as *The Ballet Class* which features a ballerina, you do not have to tell a story about a ballerina or ballet, or tell a story about dancing set in the same time period as the painting. You may want to use ideas like ballet, youth, femininity, etc., as metaphors for new themes and ideas to explore and delve into in the context/genre of your own original story told for the screen.
   b. You can also be totally literal. This is your story. Anything goes.
   c. Do not cheat and find an image in a book or online and merely observe from a remediated space. You will not experience the artwork fully nor will you experience the purpose of the assignment. **You will only cheat yourself**.
   d. Again, any painting, from any period, is preferred. But if you find that a sculpture, mask, piece of armor, textile, glass, print, or other form of artwork speaks more to your aesthetic and narrative senses, then this is perfectly acceptable too. What matters is the story that you are inspired to write based on your execution of Marin's methodology, i.e., your own physical and emotional connections to the artwork and what the art speaks to you through your in-person observations.
   e. You are not required to engage in any further outside research for this assignment. But if you choose to do so for the story and/or presentation, I suggest researching the artwork/other material *after* your observation.
   f. This assignment may be further developed and expanded for your Final Long-Short Screenplay for this course.

Notes

1 Fink's *human dimension* encourages student interaction with others so that they realize the social implications of learning. *Caring* motivates students to learn by helping them discover their feelings, interests, and values about course material.
2 In Freire's "banking model," students are vessels who receive deposits of knowledge from educators rather than co-creators of knowledge.
3 For an extended example of this type of formal assessment, see Appendix A for an assignment for a script writing course.
4 There are many sources for learning activities that assess student learning in an informal manner. One such general text is Mel Silberman's *Active Learning: 101 Strategies to Teach Any Subject* (Pearson, 1996).

References

Andrade, H. G. (2005). Teaching with rubrics: The good, the bad, and the ugly. *College Teaching, 53*(1), 27–30.

Bean, J. C. (1996). *Engaging ideas: The professor's guide to integrating writing, critical thinking, and active learning in the classroom*. San Francisco, CA: Jossey-Bass.

Benjamin, W. (1968). "The work of art in the age of mechanical reproduction" in *Illuminations* (pp. 217–251). New York: Schocken Books.

Bloom, B. S., Engelhart, M. D., Furst, E. J., Hill, W. H., & Krathwohl, D. R. (1954). *Taxonomy of educational objectives: The classification of educational goals*. New York, NY: Longman.

Brooks, D. E., & Ward, C. J. (2007). Assessing students' engagement with pedagogies of diversity. *Journalism & Mass Communication Educator, 62*(3), 244–262.

Carey, J. (1989). *Communication as culture: Essays on media and society*. Boston, MA: Unwin Hyman.

Dewey, J. (1916). *Democracy and education: An introduction to the philosophy of education*. New York, NY: Macmillan.

Engleberg, I. (2007). Using written and video scenarios to assess student learning outcomes in the basic communication course. *Conference Papers, National Communication Association*, pp. 1–15.

Filer, A. (2000). *Assessment: Social practice and social product*. London, UK: RoutledgeFalmer.

Fink, L. D. (2003). *Creating significant learning experiences: An integrated approach to designing college courses*. San Francisco, CA: Jossey-Bass.

Foucault, M. (1977). *Discipline and punish: Birth of the prison* (A. Sheridan, Trans.). New York, NY: Pantheon.

Giroux, H. A. (1989). Schooling as a form of cultural politics: Toward a pedagogy of and for difference. In H. A. Giroux & P. L. McLaren (Eds.), *Critical pedagogy, the state, and cultural struggle* (pp. 125–151). Albany, NY: State University of New York Press.

Gross, L. (2012). Fastening our seatbelts: Turning crisis into opportunity. *Journal of Communication, 62*(6), 919–931. doi:10.1111/j.1460-2466.2012.01679.x

Kohn, A. (2006). Speaking my mind: The trouble with rubrics. *The English Journal, 95*(4), 12–15.

Lattuca, L. R. (2005). Making learning visible: Student and peer evaluation. *Journalism & Mass Communication Educator, 60*(3), 247–251.

Littlejohn, S. W. (2002). *Theories of human communication*. Belmont, CA: Wadsworth.

Luthra, R. (2007). Media education toward a more equitable world. In A. Nowak, S. Abel, & K. Ross (Eds.), *Rethinking media education: Critical pedagogy and identity politics* (pp. 203–215). Cresskill, NJ: Hampton.

Rakow, L. F. (2001). Teaching against the text. *Feminist Media Studies, 1*(3), 381–383.

Rheingold, H. (2012). Syllabus: Social media literacies. http://mitpress.mit.edu/sites/default/files/titles/content/9780262017459_Net_Smart_College_Syllabus.pdf

Rubin, R. B. (1990). Evaluating the product. In J. A. Daly, G. W. Friedrich, & A. L. Vangelisti (Eds.), *Teaching communication: Theory, research, and methods* (pp. 379–401). Hillsdale, NJ: LEA.

Sholle, D., & Denski, S. (1994). *Media education and the (re)production of culture*. Westport, CT: Bergin & Garvey.

Siemens, G. (2005). Connectivism: A learning theory for the digital age. *eLearnSpace*. http://www.elearnspace.org/Articles/connectivism.htm

Spandel, V. (2006). In defense of rubrics. *English Journal, 96*(1), 19–22.

Sprague, J. (1990). The goals of communication education. In J. A. Daly, G. W. Friedrich, & A. L. Vangelisti (Eds.), *Teaching communication: Theory, research, and methods* (pp. 19–38). Hillsdale, NJ: LEA.

Stevens, D. D., & Levi, A. J. (2004). *Introduction to rubrics*. Sterling, VA: Stylus Publishing.

Toohey, S. (1999). *Designing courses for higher education*. Buckingham, UK: Open University Press.

Walvoord, B. E., & Anderson, V. J. (2009). *Effective grading: A tool for learning and assessment in college*. San Francisco, CA: Jossey-Bass. Retrieved from http://lib.myilibrary.com?ID=235483

Wiggins, G. P. (1998). *Educative assessment: Designing assessments to inform and improve student performance*. San Francisco, CA: Jossey-Bass.

6 INSTRUCTIONAL DESIGN: MAPPING MEDIA/COMMUNICATION COURSES

What do we want our students to take away from our communication courses? What is the optimal way of learning? What is the role of the instructor? These questions guide course design, but other factors influence it. Our understanding of communication/media as an important field of study and our own educational experiences in communication/media courses are probably the chief influences on how we design courses. Disciplinary values and beliefs hold sway over our decision making. For example, courses in "media and society" or "public communication" or "basic video production" are mainstays in most curricula in the United States. We may accept or reject this convention, but we generally acknowledge it. Similarly, cultural discourse about mediated and communicative environments occupies space in our minds as educators. We tend to believe that our curricula must be responsive to public concerns about media as social institutions. Factors such as curricular trends, student abilities, technological imperatives, institutional politics and budgeting, departmental culture, and our own concepts of education affect the ways in which we design our courses. This chapter emphasizes communication course design that links ideas about pedagogical philosophy, learning objectives, and taxonomies of learning to provide agency for creating meaningful courses that promote student involvement.

Design and Philosophy

The first step in designing or mapping a course is to decide what primary educational values will ground the course. Because communication is endemic to human existence, any course will engage with students' awareness of themselves as communicators. Nevertheless, in most circumstances, we determine what to teach and how to teach it. We are mindful of the concerns enumerated above, but we possess the ability to choose fundamental course design principles. Should communication ethics be a requirement? Should students be required to honor diversity in their communication? How much will communicative skill factor into course goals? Should social responsibility be a part of a communication or journalism curriculum? The course design that emphasizes, for example, psychomotor learning over conceptual learning will necessarily be undertaken differently. Because your teaching philosophy informs your course goals, objectives, and assessments, the design of your course will mirror your educational values. For example, if your overall course goal is to develop a critical understanding of the interplay between technology and culture, your course organization should reflect themes that interrogate sociocultural imperatives that shape the development of new information/communication technologies in addition to the sociocultural influences of those technologies. The course might focus on a critical evaluation of the ways new communication technologies inform our notions of work, leisure, knowledge, art, identity, politics, and environment. The learning activities might include non-graded in-class reflective writing designed to help students formulate their own perspectives and sharpen their critical abilities. Consequently, the design of your course reflects your own pedagogical philosophy and the educational values you wish to explore with your students. Different philosophical approaches will dictate different organizational approaches.

Toohey (1999) identifies five approaches upon which university courses may be structured:

- Traditional or discipline-based
- Performance- or systems-based
- Cognitive
- Personal relevance/experiential
- Socially critical

(p. 48)

Each approach reflects particular assumptions about the way learning should best be organized and the list is not exhaustive. These approaches are considered within the context of learning goals and assessments (Toohey, 1999), but faculty should be mindful of pedagogical philosophy, external elements, and taxonomies that order thinking and learning. Toohey claims that "the most accurate picture of the educational values and beliefs inherent in a course is usually to be found not in the statement of goals but in the way time is allocated to different topics and learning activities and in the nature of the assessment" (p. 49). This statement indicates the importance of course design in creating a meaningful, lasting learning experience for students. Toohey's work does not consider course design approaches befitting some of the learning theories that have emerged in the 21st century, including general theories about learning in online/mobile media environments or about lifelong learning. Although Toohey's categories are incomplete, we can use them to consider some practical strategies for structuring knowledge with an eye toward our views of knowledge, the process of learning, goals, content, assessments, and resources.

Traditional or discipline-based approach. Disciplinary convention informs the commonsense organization of course material. Courses in web design may organize activities from the simple to the complex. Courses in communication history may follow a chronology or a cause/effect orientation. According to Toohey (1999), this approach is not centered on student interests or learning styles but instead rests on accumulated wisdom of experts and traditional arrangements of knowledge. The model of learning is one of Freire's (1970) banking or of fact transmission, and learning goals are broadly focused. These courses are effectively delivered as lectures. I would argue that disciplinary convention need not inform thematic structure in such rigid ways; rather, students may be encouraged, through more innovative goals, activities, and assessments, to be reflective in their engagement with knowledge of the discipline.

Performance- or systems-based approach. A systemic approach to course design involves a direct correlation between the course goals and evaluative assessments so that learning is applied—a means to an end (Toohey, 1999). Taxonomically, this approach favors the psychomotor or skill dimension as a way to organize learning. However, the systemic approach stresses accountability rather than creativity in that it upholds competencies as the measure of success and capacity for replication as an essential feature. Theory is seen as inextricably connected to action, and learning is skill-based or problem-based rather than conceptual or holistic. The learning process is fairly rote—the instructor matches expected outcomes with skills that are taught, and students are expected to follow the planned steps. Goals are performance-based and learning experiences are structured as a map to achieve those goals. Because the course content in this type of organizational approach is based on effective performance, industry standards may determine content. For example, a course in video editing is partially determined by current aesthetic trends or by software capabilities. Students need adequate facilities to demonstrate competencies. Although this systems approach may seem inflexible because of its rote nature, it may be epistemologically appropriate for prerequisite courses that require certain skill levels to be mastered before students proceed to the next sequential level. Toohey (1999) does caution, however, that the systemic approach is often more value-laden than it might appear: "On the surface it may appear to be 'value free,' but in practice it often translates into a position which conveys that values are not important. Consequently there is no place in the curriculum for examining ethical issues inherent in the way the profession interacts with society" (p. 55).

Cognitive approach. Course design highlights the development of the intellect—the ability to think logically, to reason acutely, and to cultivate habits of mind focused on precision, structure, and rigor. These habits of mind take form in the practice of "thinking, reasoning, understanding and meaning-making" (Toohey, 1999, p. 55). The cognitive approach has some constructivist leanings in that learning is about relationships among constellations of knowledge that are interpreted and evaluated. Knowledge is constructed by learners who are able to develop strong reasoning and analytical skills. The learning process is often evidence-based. As the students' cognitive abilities are refined and their knowledge is structured, learning strategies involve problem solving or knowledge application so that instructors can identify misapprehensions and challenge judgments. Because critical thinking is an ultimate learning goal, mastery of concepts and processes is emphasized. Hence, many communication and media courses can be organized around a problem-solving orientation or within a context of applying knowledge to real-world scenarios. For example, what are the most effective strategies for analyzing and rectifying a public relations crisis? How do current and historical interpretations of the First Amendment apply to issues arising from citizen journalism? How do the philosophies, politics, and economics surrounding the creation of new communication technologies intersect with our cultural values? Assessments in the cognitive approach, due to the emphasis on deep understanding, are therefore likely to be quite complex and involved. The cognitive approach can be integrated into active learning strategies and can succeed with multiple teaching philosophies.

Experiential approach. Toohey's (1999) experiential approach is based on notions of learning through experiences that have personal relevance for learners. Courses are often organized in accordance with life experiences as opposed to thematic units. Student needs are foremost, within a context of competencies that reflect professional, individual, and disciplinary needs. Learning is collaborative, and the instructor often acts in a guiding or facilitating role. Courses may be organized around some type of large, complex class project geared toward a specific objective. For example, a group of students might design a mobile web site and app for a particular client who contributes ideas to the project. Students are encouraged to take responsibility for their learning. In essence, this approach is modeled in Jenkins, Purushotma, Weigel, Clinton, and Robison's (2009) elaboration of participatory culture, in which students create cultural products in a collaborative environment. Within media studies, the experiential approach merges well with a constructivist philosophy in its emphasis on knowledge construction through experimentation with ideas, shared problem solving, reexamination of prior knowledge, and construction of new knowledge.

Socially critical approach. Social change through critical consciousness is the overall goal of this approach (Toohey, 1999). It seeks to question institutional elites as purveyors of the status quo. Existing social arrangements are thought to result in inequality and lack of opportunity for disadvantaged social groups. This perspective is about exposing and confronting prevailing ideologies of oppression rather than replicating them. Because knowledge is conditioned by circumstances of the economy, history, politics, and culture, a critical approach attempts to illuminate those circumstances and investigate how they interrelate to produce the conditions of social subjugation or inequality. For communication and media studies, this means an exploration of the connections between communication curricula and media institutions. It might also mean an exploration of *-isms* that are communicated culturally, such as sexism, racism, homophobia, ageism, etc. Course goals often center on the ability to recognize, develop, and defend one's own position about issues and processes. For communication students, this means questioning the interests of key groups, ideas, and audiences as well as examining the links between ideological assumptions and the ability of communication patterns to alter social reality. Course structure could therefore be modeled after major social dilemmas or focused on communication institutions or projects.

These approaches embody different philosophical views that inform the organization of course structure. As Toohey (1999) notes, each approach implicates a perspective on educational values but that many courses incorporate a respect for each approach within their organizational structures. For example, a course on Media and Society could communicate disciplinary knowledge through a focus on cognitive approaches to reasoned thinking about media and society, a critical examination of media institutions, and an emphasis on experiential learning and skill development through a type of creative project. The course might also accentuate questions of multiculturalism, identity, power, and personal voice through such creative projects. Ultimately, courses can be structured in ways that demonstrate the value of disciplinary traditions, performance-based knowledge, intellectual development, critical inquiry, and personally relevant learning.

Illustrating his broadly constructivist pedagogical philosophy, Dustin Morrow (July, 2011), professor in the Department of Theater and Film at Portland State University, discusses his ideas about flexibility in course design:

> Every course has a rhythm. Parts of any course (especially a media production course, which usually involves instruction in technology and the workshopping of ideas and works-in-progress) will move faster or slower than other parts, but one should be able to see the rhythm of a course to some degree even in the construction of the syllabus. There should be a constant moving forward—an always-measurable progression. It is the teacher's responsibility to pace a class correctly, and always be prepared to make adjustments—students shouldn't be straining to keep up, nor should they ever get too far ahead.
>
> On the other hand, the old adage that the worse the writer the greater the attachment to the writing, applies to teaching as well. The least stimulating classes I can remember taking in college were the ones in which the teacher held on to his/her syllabus with an iron fist. The exchange of ideas in a classroom is a living thing, a moving entity, and to some degree a teacher needs to let a class go where it needs to go, so long as it is ultimately progressing toward the goals of the course. Teaching is not just about imparting knowledge, it's about facilitating well-rounded experiences for students in which they learn from each other and from their own active participation in discussions, assignments, and the direction of the course.

For Professor Morrow, courses are organized around an ultimate purpose, but still remain malleable enough to accommodate reflexivity in the learning experience. Because our students are unable to escape their immersion in media environments, an organizational structure that allows for a broad grasp of how concepts and practices are integrated is appealing and necessary. Understanding our own philosophical proclivities is a valuable step in course organization—our philosophy clarifies our position within disciplinary and institutional culture, and it solidifies our decisions about teaching practices.

Design and Objectives

Having created course objectives and assessments (see chapter 5), you will next plan course content. For example, overall goals for a media law class might focus on evaluating the historical, legal, and ethical precedents that inform notions of free expression in the United States as well as critiquing current legal perspectives on copyright and privacy law. Accordingly, assessments might include an exam on the First Amendment and basic regulation as well as three position papers in which students respond to hypothetical situations corresponding to copyright law, privacy law, and the concept of free expression. A course organization plan suited to these goals and assessments would then include coverage of the First Amendment, regulation of mediated expression, copyright law, privacy law, and a recapitulation of larger concepts of free expression within a synthesizing context. The course goals, assessments, and topic structure work in conjunction to create meaningful learning experiences for students. Moreover, the class activities will follow from the course organization. If you design class activities carefully and transparently, students can easily link objectives and assessments in ways that illuminate the big picture for them. Your overall teaching strategy, then, is a combination of pedagogical philosophy, course goals, objectives, assessments, organization, and class activities. The mapping of course content may take several different types of forms that serve your learning goals.

As Ambrose, Bridges, DiPietro, Lovett, and Norman (2010) caution, we must be cognizant of our students' status as neophytes in our subject areas and organize learning accordingly: "As experts in our fields, we create and maintain, often unconsciously, a complex network that connects the important facts, concepts, procedures, and other elements within our domain" (p. 43). We rely on the deep, meaningful connections between concepts or principles that we've made over time, and we must trust our knowledge base to help structure learning in our courses so that it becomes significant to students. Ambrose et al. continue, arguing that

> teaching is a highly contextualized activity because it is shaped by the students we have, advancements in our respective fields, changes in technology, and so on. Therefore, our teaching must constantly adapt to changing

> parameters. Although this realization can be overwhelming for some, it can also help us reframe our approach to improving our teaching because it means that we need not expect a static perfection, but a developing mastery of teaching.
> (p. 218)

That mastery is reflected in the conceptualization of course structure. Fink (2003) claims that courses are structured in accordance with important "concepts, issues, topics or themes that constitute the subjects of the course" (p. 128). However, those criteria are not always evident; they are influenced by professional expertise, pedagogical philosophy, departmental curriculum, and other institutional or external factors. Ideally, course topics will build upon one another in a holistic pattern toward a course goal that students can identify. We want our students to be able to connect discrete chunks of knowledge together to create meaningful, lasting wholes. They should understand why they might want to take your course, what the intent of assignments or activities is, and how the course fits into the larger curriculum or discipline. This type of organizational transparency offers students a sense of investment in their own education.

Creating a course structure depends on several determinations, including the logical division of subject matter into elements (such as how those elements interrelate sequentially); how concepts and skills are presented to students to support course goals; and how learning activities are structured (Toohey, 1999). Thematic structure may take several forms that represent relationships in ways that promote reflective learning. Faculty often use chronology as a structuring principle, but material may be structured by cause/effect, comparison, hierarchy, form of expression (video, audio, web, prose, etc.), simple categories, whole/part, project-based, or other logical means for students to construct larger meanings. Some methods of organization may seem to come organically from the material, e.g., a course on organizational communication could be organized by site—workplace, home, community, school, etc. Ambrose et al. (2010) argue that the organization of knowledge for students should underscore the totality of a course subject to encourage deeper learning—an ability to apply and evaluate knowledge and to cultivate shrewd habits of mind. Often, the chronological structure of material contributes to a potential for students to memorize discrete facts rather than to create logical, functional, systemic wholes. Since thematic structure supports all course activities, objectives, and assessments, Ambrose et al. (2010) caution that instructors should be reflective about how the organization of course material corresponds to the means by which knowledge will be drawn upon. In other words, using an organizational strategy that works in concert with goals and assessments will streamline the process of designing a course and help students understand the course as a whole.

So, for example, if we want students to learn to conceptualize and execute a short narrative video on a musical artist, the syllabus and learning activities should be organized around the idea of storytelling. Learning to shoot and edit video are contiguous skills that occur in succession and can be taught this way—as a sequence. But the conceptual relationship between the elements of a story about a musical artist must be organized around a particular narrative structure (e.g., roots, rise to glory, professional success, challenges or setbacks). Thus, the production skills may be taught in a way that differs from the conceptual mode of storytelling. Students might think sequentially to remember steps in a process, such as learning to shoot and edit video, but sequential learning does not often provide a full picture of how things relate to one another in other ways. Also, if a step is missing, knowledge acquisition may be hampered. Limiting teaching and learning to a sequence of steps may result in a potential inability to apply knowledge in alternative contexts. It's also less creative because mere memorization of steps may impede students' ability to conceive of alternative processes beyond sequential steps. Much of contemporary storytelling involves non-linear narrative, and thus sequential steps may be an inadequate organizing principle. Moreover, some type of cross-referenced, interconnected organization beyond or outside a sequence shows students an especially full picture of knowledge of a subject—in this case, narrative storytelling. A type of thematic categorical organization tends to help students recognize interrelationships among various elements in a story. In this style of organization, narrative themes would be presented as categories with no sequence or linear progression. In our example, the instructor can provide students with common templates for storytelling (e.g., human vs. self or human vs. society or the hero's fall from grace) or with the aesthetic grammar associated with certain story themes (e.g., shooting and editing choices as elements of the story itself) or with theories used to configure thematic storytelling choices (e.g., Joseph Campbell's "hero's journey" or Aristotle's "catharsis"). As long as students are able to build associations between and among bits of information, they will develop more complex, nuanced knowledge structures.

Often when we structure our courses we forget that faculty possess disciplinary knowledge based on history, tradition, and common epistemologies. While students do not possess expert disciplinary knowledge, they can develop more sophisticated arrangements of knowledge when we underscore for them how expert disciplinary knowledge is organized and how its patterns relate to the goals and tasks of a course. A common course in communication/media studies is *Media and Society* or *Communication Studies*, and this course could be organized around multiple thematic structures based upon the instructor's command of disciplinary knowledge. It could be structured around problem-solving with regard to major communicative issues, theories of communication, media industries or networks, major ideas or themes characterizing the study of communication, media audiences or messages, or case studies. Faculty draw on these deep knowledge structures to help students make logical connections or to solve problems or to evaluate knowledge claims. Ambrose et al. (2010) and Fink (2003) advocate the use of organizational structures that allow students to make these logical connections through, for example, a cause/effect dimension, a problem-solving orientation, or an analysis of contrasting cases. Communication faculty can use specific organizing principles to teach, for instance, a cause/effect approach to the foundations of critical theory. Students could be exposed to the background of the Frankfurt School to help them understand not only the context of the theory itself, but how the theory might be applied in production contexts as they learn to generate media content. The cause/effect dimension would be: the Frankfurt School sociologists observed the atrocities—often undertaken in the name of scientific/technological progress—associated with the Nazi party rise to power; saw the efficacy of the Nazi propaganda machine; fled Europe during the rise of the Nazi occupation; and regrouped in New York to launch Marxist critiques of positivistic ideology and method as well as mass media and mass culture. When students see the cause/effect relationship of these elements, they can learn in more profound ways by linking these facts meaningfully, retaining more information, and creating deeper pathways to wisdom.

As described in previous chapters, making decisions about course structure begins with a complete accounting of your philosophical inclinations, your course objectives, and your course assessments. Once you have then identified the major concepts or topics for your course and the appropriate sequence for them, you will decide upon the learning activities that students will undertake. These strategies will be evident in your course syllabus, which, according to Nilson (2007), serves as a form of scholarship in and of itself.

> For any given course, your syllabi display your conception of how a field or sub-field is organized—or *should* be organized for the purpose of communicating it—and how students can best master its knowledge and skills. Your teaching philosophy is readable between the lines of your syllabus, as well as in parts of the text itself. The document, especially your assignments and class-time plans, is a window to your theories of teaching and learning, whether you see yourself as a knowledge-transmitter, a resource, a facilitator, a manager, an experience creator, or an activist.
>
> (p. 7)

Informing students of your organizational strategy helps ensure their understanding of the larger essence of what you want to communicate in the course. Instructors may choose to represent the organizational structure in a traditional, narrative style or in a graphic, visual style (see Nilson, 2007) on the syllabus. The representation of the course organization should be clear to students. For example, a class on fandom and culture might be structured around particular taste cultures, the negotiation of audiences as consumers and creators, legal issues surrounding remix or appropriation of culture, fandom and representation, and explorations of the impacts of fandom on politics, the economy, the law, and culture writ large. This organizational strategy represents a conceptual, holistic, categorical approach to structuring learning. Students should understand how the content builds upon itself to create this holistic comprehension of the nature of fandom and its cultural import within the scheme of communication/media studies. Providing students with explicit representations of your organizational principles will help them manage their learning—it's a roadmap your students use to understand the destination and how to plan for it. In the fandom and culture example, you might organize a unit of the course around the four legal principles of "fair use" in creating and disseminating transformative material, the current case law surrounding fair use, controversies involving fair use, and possible future directions of fair use in an era of participatory culture.

Ambrose et al. (2010) suggest tactics for helping students to organize learning in explicit yet flexible ways. These include: (1) Construct a concept map to accentuate the features around which you want students to structure their learning. (2) Coordinate your learning objectives with the tasks most appropriate to achieve your goals. For instance, provide students with an empty grid in which they specify arguments for and against the legal concept of fair use. (3) Communicate your thinking behind the organization of the course and remind students of this logic periodically. (4) Use notions of boundary or contrast to emphasize aspects of your organization. This entails presenting anomalous cases or contrasting elements to stress differences so that students develop deep knowledge structures or alternative means of knowledge organization. For example, immersing students in two contradictorily reasoned copyright case decisions involving fair use in the transformation of fan material can produce these deeper learning structures. (5) Overtly state the connections between course ideas so that students can see where new material relates to concepts already covered. (6) Ask students to conceptualize alternative knowledge structures and to create their own concept maps for instilling a deeper understanding of course material. In the fandom and culture example, students might try breaking down the stereotypes associated with various fan cultures or mapping concepts related to the politics of fandom in a globalized information economy. In the end, these tactics will help instructors and students to acquire a richer, more multifaceted organization of knowledge. Simultaneously, students will recognize the importance of what they're learning, be able to connect it to prior knowledge in profound ways, and apply knowledge in new contexts.

As communication/media educators, we are often challenged to construct courses that are multidisciplinary or that bind theoretical and skill-based content. This challenge may result in course organizations that may become so complex that they impede learning. Planning a sensible scope for the course will allow students to engage with material more deeply and actively. If we want our students to develop the ability to reflect upon their own experiences and fathom how their lives intersect with the culture at large, we must design courses that respect this viewpoint and incorporate it into course organization. Do we want to teach student creativity in, for example, production-oriented courses so that they do not churn out hackneyed art forms? Do we need to organize such production-oriented courses so that we teach alternative conceptualizations of some commonplace production techniques or aesthetic choices? In actuality, media production courses are often adapted to liberal educational outcomes without recognizing it. Edwards (2001) claims that "[t]hrough learning about and participating in the media production process, students develop critical thinking, leadership and management abilities, aesthetic sensibility, communication, and problem solving skills. … Many students are most proud of their mastery of technical craft, not acknowledging the various abilities and strategies they develop during the struggle to make a film or video that go beyond technical expertise" (p. 11). Perhaps an organizational structure that accounts for the commercial, technological, and ideological constraints upon their work while encouraging novel approaches toward creating media forms might be most useful for educating successful, thoughtful communicators.

To illustrate several different methods for organizing a course in magazine publishing within a journalism curriculum, Rhodes and Roessner (2009) interviewed instructors who used four modes of organization to structure their courses to optimize experiential learning. First, in the *prototype* model, students work to research and analyze a market, develop and present a business plan, and create a product prototype. Second, the *magazine launch* model requires students to release a finished project as they work in assorted staff roles to generate and finalize the magazine content. Third, the *existing magazine model: team development for content and product* model operates as a "real-world" situation in which a team of students conceptualize content for an existing publication (usually a student-oriented periodical). Students learn to juggle priorities, manage peers, and budget their time. Fourth, the *existing magazine model: team development with previously written copy to produce product* model has students focus on editing skills by using content written in a previous semester to produce a copy of a specific campus-wide publication. In all of these magazine publishing models, students learn via experience both new skill sets and new ways to conceptualize content creation.

Thus, various types of course organizational structures can work, in connection with objectives and assessments, to educate effective communicators. In total, these examples of course organization strategies illustrate the fact that communication is a fundamental human activity and is fundamentally about meaning. Students must be made to see that their communicative choices influence the encoding of messages as well as the process of decoding messages so that they can become responsible communicators. We do this by organizing our courses in meaningful ways.

Creating Meaningful Courses

If we want to produce adept communicators and enhance students' social capital, course design should reflect relevant approaches. If students value what they learn and can imbue it with personal significance, they are more likely to internalize learning. With course goals and assessments in mind, courses must be designed according to content as well as context. In a student-centered environment, for example, the content of the course is important, but it is supplemented by the course context in which students share experiences, collaborate, and act as co-creators of knowledge. The context of most communication/media classes is one of student as producer, consumer, and critic. It is also one of multidisciplinarity, global information flows, organizational cultures, and industry changes. It is ideally one of attention to social and political values and awareness of social justice issues.

As noted in the chapter on categorizing thinking, taxonomies organize how we make meaning. Faculty use taxonomies to construct learning goals and objectives and ultimately to order the knowledge structures of our courses. In general, the affective, cognitive, and skill learning domains (Bloom's taxonomy and others) provide structures through which we can inspire the student to grasp foundational communication principles, apply those principles to create meaning, investigate messages, contexts, structures, and audiences, and create original communicative forms. The domains provide structures through which we facilitate the development of student interest, principles, attitudes, motivations, and skills. The learning taxonomies provide specific signposts for meaningful course organizational design. For example, the chart from chapter 4 (Table 4.2) denotes a taxonomy for media/communication studies based on Bloom's taxonomy. In this scheme, the evaluative dimension of learning seeks to have students critique communication processes, products, meanings, and norms, to understand 'why.' Examples of that dimension included hypothesizing about relationships between and among those communicative elements or debating merits of communicative principles, processes, meanings, designs, norms, and policies. Students learning to evaluate the legalities of remix culture would therefore organize learning around the debate over the intentions of intellectual property law and the climate of individually produced media content. What are the norms surrounding remix practices? In what ways do current copyright policies and legal precedents seem inadequate? The structures you choose to organize learning create a storyline for the students. For that storyline to be meaningful, students must see themselves as part of the story. They must see how key tensions, ideas, and stakeholders can be engaged with deeply to raise new questions, to consolidate formerly discrete units of knowledge, and to create opportunities for choice about how to act or what to think.

Using Wayne's (2001) typology of ways to understand media production as a cultural practice, we can construct an extended example of how to structure courses to encourage significant learning experiences. He advocates self-consciousness in studying the production of culture so that students will be more critically reflective about their own production practices. Because we want our students to grasp media on a more sophisticated level than mere *consumption,* meaningful course design works toward reflexive, theoretical, and critical practitioners in Wayne's typology. Wayne's "reflexive practitioner" can question the production process, learn from successes and failures, and chronicle new ideas for future practice. Reflexive practice is about textual encoding. The "theoretical practitioner" understands how textual choice, meaning, and context work in concert to construct meaning. Theoretical practice is about understanding the message. The "critical practitioner" can articulate the power structures inherent in cultural production and representation.

Critical producers can situate content within a larger conversation about meaning and principle within texts. Critical practice is about consumption.

For Wayne (2001), media production courses that are structured with this typology can yield students who transcend the strictures of what's already known, theoretically and practically, about cultural production to innovate, to tell new stories, and to push boundaries. This creates a type of transformative learning that is experiential *and* theoretical. An understanding of the theory/practice dialectic, through Wayne's typology, helps students to quash the constraints of hegemonic knowledge constructions surrounding so many media processes and products. He uses the example of objective journalism standards as a dominant narrative within communication studies that is rarely critiqued. But the ability to recognize hegemonic processes and products—by being reflective—is central to obtaining a genuinely meaningful education. Wayne's (2001) model incorporates elements that allow students to craft personally relevant knowledge. His example is one way to structure learning significantly within a context of thoughtfulness about cultural production. Learning outcomes for such courses would stress the creation of novel media forms outside the parameters of what's usually done. Assessments would involve not just the productions themselves, but also reflective writing about the theory/practice dialectic, about producer choices, and about the incorporation of prior knowledge into the process.

Communication/media curricula are fragmented due to the field's placement within a multiplicity of academic divisions, including communication studies, journalism, English, speech communication, telecommunication, film studies, cultural studies, media arts, information science, and others. The study of communication is treated in various respects as part of the humanities, the social sciences, or as part of a professional school. We divide our students into tracks or sequences that tend to "silo" those students into discrete factions without a sense of the totality of a curriculum engaged with the vital whole of communication/media studies. This splintered condition, argue Sholle and Denski (1994), obstructs "possibilities for political and cultural debate ... and for students and faculty to work within a community that strives to see the educational situation as aimed at developing democratic citizenship skills" (p. 124). Through our modes of organizing learning in our courses, we can combat this fragmentation by reminding ourselves of the larger purpose of an education in communication/media. Our identities as instructors—and our core beliefs about teaching communication—are pivotal to the ability to design meaningful, significant learning experiences for our students.

References

Ambrose, S. A., Bridges, M. W., DiPietro, M., Lovett, M. C., & Norman, M. K. (2010). *How learning works: 7 research-based principles for smart teaching*. San Francisco, CA: Jossey-Bass.

Edwards, E. D. (2001). To be rather than to seem: Liberal education and personal growth through documentary production. *Journal of Film & Video, 53*(1), 9–19.

Fink, L. D. (2003). *Creating significant learning experiences: An integrated approach to designing college courses*. San Francisco, CA: Jossey-Bass.

Freire, P. (1970). *Pedagogy of the oppressed* (M. G. Ramos, Trans.). New York, NY: Seabury.

Jenkins, H., Purushotma, R., Weigel, M., Clinton, K., & Robison, A. J. (2009). *Confronting the challenges of participatory culture: Media education for the 21st century*. Cambridge, MA: MIT Press.

Nilson, L. B. (2007). *The graphic syllabus and the outcomes map: Communicating your course*. San Francisco, CA: Jossey-Bass.

Rhodes, L., & Roessner, A. (2009). Teaching magazine publishing through experiential learning. *Journalism & Mass Communication Educator, 63*(4), 304–316.

Sholle, D., & Denski, S. (1994). *Media education and the (re)production of culture*. Westport, CT: Bergin & Garvey.

Toohey, S. (1999). *Designing courses for higher education*. Buckingham, UK: Open University Press.

Wayne, M. (2001). Problems and possibilities in developing critical practice. *Journal of Media Practice, 2*(1), 30–36.

7
WAYS OF LEARNING IN COMMUNICATION/MEDIA

Most instructors have experienced teaching situations in which the audience seemed impenetrable. The instructor may leave wondering if she was able to communicate effectively with students. As communication/media faculty are acutely aware, we communicate *with* students, not *to* them. So, understanding how students learn best is vital to ensuring a learning environment that is responsive to them. Most people have a consistent way of responding to and using stimuli in the context of learning (Kolb, 1984). For philosopher John Dewey (1938), the way to absorb and process information is rooted in the individual's experience. For psychologist Kurt Lewin, a person must be active in learning by analyzing her/his own concrete experience (Kolb, 1984). For developmental psychologist Jean Piaget, intelligence is the result of the interaction between a person and the environment (Kolb, 1984). Taken together, the wisdom of these three theorists posits that learning involves knowledge and ideas, self reflection, and action in the world.

Creating a learning environment that is responsive to students requires an awareness that students process their learning in different ways. For example, some people learn best by reflecting deeply on concepts while others learn best by interacting with material in concrete ways. Faculty can incorporate an awareness of these differences into course design by developing teaching strategies that are derived not only from course goals and taxonomies of learning but also from a knowledge of *experiential learning*—that is, the collective ideas of Dewey, Lewin, and Piaget whereby meaning is derived from experience. How can we encourage students not only to master course content but to be able to use that content? How can we organize our teaching to accommodate differences in the ways students learn? Instructors tend to teach in ways that reflect their principal means of learning, so this chapter is devoted to creating an understanding of different patterns and traits of learning. This chapter will explore some practical strategies all instructors can use to reach the spectrum of learning modes but at the same time with the awareness that we cannot tailor learning to individual students. Rather, we can forge a student-centered, active learning classroom that is sensitive to the different types of learners within. If the instructor values experiential learning, it's useful to know what types of learners populate the classroom. Such an approach helps instructors reach everyone and fosters more effective, long-term learning for more students. What students learn is important, but understanding *how* they learn is equally essential. If we want our students to incorporate course material into their own experiences and their plans for acting within the world, we must engage students actively and with purpose. As noted elsewhere in this book, media are cultural artifacts, and active learning strategies compel students to extend beyond merely using culture in order to reflect upon it.

Media/communication instructors must make evident the connections between concepts we explore and activities we undertake in the classroom. For example, video production students may enter a course with a grasp of basic shooting and editing from having experimented with the manifold programs and apps available to them. But in class, they are exposed to theories of the aesthetics of photography and cinematography, and they may reflect upon their own experiences with video in accordance with these theoretical concepts. They may internalize these theories to influence their decision making in future projects. The process by which students undergo such a transformation will differ according to their dominant methods for learning new material and applying it in new contexts. Understanding how to reach our students as active learners means knowing how they approach learning, but it also means knowing what to do to facilitate learning in flexible ways. Gaining insight into the way we learn, and consequently, the way we teach, helps us to understand why some students seem frustrated or slow or uninterested while others are engaged and sharp.

What Are the Ways of Learning and Why Do They Matter?

Communication is a way of life as well as a target of study. As I have argued elsewhere in this book, media-inundated environments make the critical study of media a vital endeavor. Knowledge of communication nurtures the development of the whole person. If we accept Dewey's (1938) ideas about education as a means to promote positive cultural values, we must honor our students' individual communicative experiences as somehow interwoven into those cultural values. As we engage in conversations with our students about basic principles of communication, multiculturalism, discrimination, new technologies, industry changes, global information flows, communicative aesthetics, and other content areas, we recognize that our students have different experiences with communication. Those experiences inform student approaches to learning. For instance, a student who grew up in an environment where her only exposure to certain minority groups was mediated may approach learning about communication ethics and responsibility in a manner distinct from a student with a more cosmopolitan upbringing. Moreover, McLuhan's aphorism that "the medium is the message" demonstrates that the way in which information is communicated is as important as what is communicated. In recognizing the importance of form, Sprague (1993) cautions that we cannot develop or teach a universal communicative competency without a grasp of form as well as content in our pedagogies. Therefore, this chapter is not about strict adherence to a particular modality of learning but rather about knowing that visual, auditory, tactile, and kinesthetic learners exist. We must be conscious about being inclusive as we teach to these different perceptual proclivities.

The "ways of learning" are indicators of how students perceive, relate to, and respond to various learning environments and situations. Learners approach the learning enterprise through preferred means for processing, absorbing, and retaining information (Dunn & Dunn, 1999). Usually, we are unaware of our own preferences. Despite this lack of awareness, we are often able to identify basic modes of learning with which we feel resonance. For example, a student might comment that he needs to think concepts through before responding to questions in class or that she grasps material better with concrete examples of that material in use. Patterns of learning, whether innate or habituated, have been referred to as "learning styles" by many scholars (Dunn & Dunn, 1992; Kolb, 1984; Honey & Mumford, 1986; Grasha, 1996). Dunn and Dunn (1992) describe four categories of learning styles based on modality: visual, auditory, kinesthetic, tactile. Visual learners prefer to apprehend information through graphs, symbols, and reading. Auditory learners prefer lecture, discussion, and listening. Kinesthetic learners prefer to learn by doing through practices such as interviews and simulated life experiences. Tactile learners prefer to take notes or use their hands to interact with materials. For Grasha (1996), learning styles are founded less on sensory perceptions and more on student attitudes toward learning based on level of student responsibility, tendencies toward competition or collaboration with others, and dependence/independence when approaching learning. With a recognition of these different preferences and orientations as well as differences in structural, institutional, or environmental constraints, a larger pedagogical conversation has arisen (Coffield, Moseley, Hall, & Ecclestone, 2004) around the notion that there are learning preferences, that those preferences may be identifiable, and that instructors are responsible for attending to style in instructional delivery. Comprehending basic learning style preferences and incorporating them into teaching ultimately demonstrates an emphasis on inclusivity and a respect for students' individual differences and cultural experiences.

While students may have "dominant" learning modes, it is important to note that everyone learns through all sensory modalities. Because of life and educational experiences, some learning modes may become more prominent than others and are likely to be preferred. Lecturing may be denigrated for favoring students who have auditory styles and penalizing those who prefer other modalities; but a lecture can involve different sensory modalities as it embraces discussion and visuals. Students can *process* information using multiple modalities when it is delivered creatively and with a sensibility toward various representations. Instructors must provide cognitive access to material in multiple ways. For example, teaching web design by lecture alone makes little pedagogical sense, and an instructor would probably choose to lecture about design aesthetics, show examples of good design, and allow students to experiment with creating their own designs. Information in communication/media courses may be presented in different ways, and there may be optimum ways to present certain information effectively, but students will process information through their own preferred means. Concept mapping might be an expedient technique for understanding the logic of a particular aspect of copyright law, for instance, but lecturing works, too, as does group work that asks students to apply logic and reasoning to hypothetical legal cases. In communication/media courses that integrate theory and practice, the use of multiple learning modalities is clearly valuable. For true experiential learning along the lines of Dewey (1938), an instructor must appreciate that theory/practice integration and be able to construct flexible learning models. Students cannot learn experientially without action or without reflection. Dewey (1938) argued, "there is an intimate and necessary relation between the processes of actual experience and education" (p. 20). If we can provide rich learning environments using inclusive teaching strategies, students will have greater access to course material and a more comprehensive learning experience.

In addition to the sensory modes of learning, there are different conceptualizations of learning styles as means by which students attain and process information. Among some of the most well known are Honey and Mumford's (1986) model, the Dunn and Dunn (Dunn, Dunn, & Price, 1984) model, the Grasha-Reichmann Learning Style Scale (Grasha, 1996), and Kolb's (1984) experiential learning model, upon which some of the ideas in this chapter are based. These models acknowledge that cultural background and prior knowledge are important determinants of success in the classroom, but the concept of a "learning style" is based on the notion that students approach learning in myriad ways and that instructors desire to engage every student without alienating any. As instructors we have our own propensities and proclivities related to our preferred modes of teaching—some of us thrive on the lecture while others disdain it. Ultimately, we must try to transcend some of our own inclinations (and attendant biases) in order to reach the most students. A basic understanding of learning styles helps instructors to communicate with students that they can overcome habituated modes of learning and approach learning in new, sometimes uncomfortable ways.

Here, Bourdieu's (1990) concept of the *habitus* is useful in deconstructing habituated modes of learning so that we may become more reflective as both learners and instructors. Bourdieu's habitus is a type of world view that comprises more than just beliefs, but also an entire propensity for how a person thinks and behaves. The habitus prefigures personal behavioral choices, and thus action is a key component of the habitus. Deeply embedded into consciousness, the habitus is based on previous thoughts and experience. It is, using Bourdieu's words, "socially constituted nature" derived from social interaction. Thus, for the learner, the habitus encompasses identity, culture, perspective, lifestyle, gender, rituals, etc., that inform the practices surrounding learning attitudes and behaviors. The habitus dwells in the codes of conduct—implicitly understood—that are embodied in the learning environment. So students approach learning in ways that fulfill social expectations about the value of knowledge, relationships with educators, status within educational institutions, and patterns of behavior dictating the learning experience itself. An awareness of the habituated organization of practices—the ways we set goals, attack new information, process information into something useful, and map new information onto older experiences—can encourage the development of reflexivity about one's learning. There is flexibility within the habitus in that choices for action—although bounded in accordance with cultural, institutional, and experiential constraints—do exist. Because the concept of learning styles is tethered to action (for both the learner and the instructor), an understanding of them is particularly important for communication/media education since we create, respond to, consume, and exist within mediated environments. Moreover, Kolb (1984) argues, invoking Freire, that "the educational system is primarily an agency of social control, a control that is ultimately oppressive and conservative of the capitalist system of class discrimination." Changing that system means developing a critical awareness—"the active exploration of the personal, experiential meaning of abstract concepts through dialogue among equals" (p. 16). We want to cultivate enthusiastic students who are capable of resisting the lure to fall back on familiar patterns as they are made aware of alternative modes for learning.

The concept of learning styles is not without critique. Some scholars argue that no evidence exists showing that people truly have explicit propensities for different types of thinking and processing (Pashler, McDaniel, Rohrer, & Bjork, 2009; Coffield et al., 2004). Pashler et al. (2009) find that learning preferences do not automatically implicate particular instructional styles in reaching those learners. That is, they find no definitive correlation between expressed learning preferences and teaching styles directed toward those preferences. I do not claim that instructional strategies must be designed specifically to match each individual student's learning preferences (particularly since students may be unaware of their own preferences). Rather, I claim that the use of a variety of teaching styles will result in better learning outcomes for all students because, while we may have preferences for perceiving and processing information, we *all* learn in all the various ways enumerated in learning style theory. I argue that the use of multiple teaching techniques benefits all students because different techniques reinforce information in different ways. Thus, content may suddenly become clear to a student when it is presented through different modalities. Engaging with multiple means of apprehending information can encourage students to think in new ways, thereby working to fulfill learning goals that focus on creative thinking. Communication/media studies encompasses conceptual and practical learning and therefore must, by its very nature, welcome a variety of teaching modalities. As instructors, we want to present information in mutually reinforcing ways.

Coffield et al. (2004) claim that no consensus exists on particular pedagogical strategies derived from the learning styles research. Based on an examination of the theoretical suppositions and the instruments designed to assess learning styles of 13 different models, they conclude that little empirical evidence demonstrates the value of the concept of learning style models. They argue, "After more than 30 years of research, no consensus has been reached about the most effective instrument for measuring learning styles and no agreement about the most appropriate pedagogical interventions" (p. 137). They also critique the notion that learning styles are measurable, reliable, consistent, and stable. In a comment on Coffield's et al. (2004) critique of learning styles, Beetham (2007) remarks that

> it seems safe to state that learners have stable or slowly changing characteristics such as their identities, lifelong motivations and experiences of learning, physical and sensory access requirements, and related personal preferences, e.g., for particular kinds of information. But learners also have characteristics that develop in the process of learning, and that are dependent on the context in which they find themselves. Indeed, learning can involve fundamental changes in a person's outlook, values, social role, and identity. (p. 32)

Building on the concept of contextual learning, Beetham and Oliver (2010) claim that teaching practices and learning experiences have changed in digital media environments to account for new epistemologies. Because these new ways of knowing include critical techno-literacies, connectivism,[1] hypermedia literacies, and collaborative practices, they argue the concept of multimodal literacy—an integrated set of critical and social knowledge practices—has supplanted pedagogical discourse on learning styles. They argue that teaching strategies incorporating gaming and social media technologies, typical of multimodal literacy, epitomize "a critical engagement with ideas in different media … [now] understood as an essential skill for navigating the information age" (p. 159). This is a technologically deterministic argument, however, that fails to account for diversity of student experience and lodges the notion of various literacies within technological bounds only.

Also making a contextually based criticism of learning styles, Brockbank and McGill (2007) fault learning style inventories for inconsistency and for ignoring social and political aspects of learning, assuming that "learning takes place in a politically neutral context" (p. 44). This criticism is echoed by Smith (2010) about the Kolb experiential learning model, examined in greater depth in the next section. Smith questions the Kolb model's attention to the practice of *reflection*, a practice whereby self identity is formed through social interaction with others. He attributes a circularity to Kolb's model, saying that the learning styles map onto the dimensions of Kolb's experiential learning model in a convenient, if not particularly valid, manner. Like Brockbank and McGill (2007), Smith notes a lack of attention in Kolb's model to different cultural experiences and conditions. Lastly, Smith argues that the connection between learning process and knowledge is not well developed due to a lack of engagement with the nature of epistemology as contested and as socially situated. For Smith, a critical, culturally contextual aspect of learning is missing from Kolb's model. Smith does, however, concede the utility of Kolb's model for helping to design learning activities and engage learners. Coffield et al. (2004) similarly recognize that a grasp of learning styles can increase self-awareness among instructors and learners and an appreciation for the learning processes of others.

Kolb (1984) argued that learning experiences can be managed more easily if faculty share their theories of learning with students, attempt to identify and teach to the range of student learning styles, and reexamine their learning theories—in dialogue with the students. While it may not be practical or necessary to identify each student's learning style, I would argue that when individuals interrogate their own habitus of learning, they gain perspective on and control over their learning. I disagree with the overall character of much of the criticism of learning styles because it pinpoints the pedantic nature of learning style inventories while largely ignoring the usefulness of understanding learning preferences. I do not recommend that instructors assess student learning styles through inventories because I think it is superfluous. We all learn in multiple ways—we merely have some differences that become habituated. This means that learning styles are not consistent across learning conditions. People may use different learning styles for different kinds of tasks, materials, or learning situations. Thus, students may respond more strongly to a visual learning style for particular material and a kinesthetic style for another. Learning to take good photographs would be difficult without ever interacting with a camera. Preferences may not only change organically over time, but may be influenced by experience or by instruction itself. I advocate an approach of instructor awareness toward distinctive approaches to learning and distinctive ways of processing information. Instructors can therefore accommodate diverse types of learners in diverse learning environments with different learning experiences. Ultimately, a comprehension of learning styles can illuminate how process as well as content is important in teaching.

Beyond understanding how students access and process learning differently, instructors who want to encourage active learning environments must consider student motivations to learn, learning expectations, and prior disciplinary knowledge. The Kolb model is a useful starting point in media/communication education because it is based, in part, on Dewey's ideas about experiential learning as a valued aspect of communicative action. As students use cultural artifacts (in the form of mediated communication), create them, and deliberate about them, they are participating in the shared experience of public life. They are developing Dewey's (1927) sense of collective "common sense" around which we ascribe meaning to everyday life. Kolb's notion of experiential learning—the cycle of doing, reflecting, thinking, and acting—provides the context for enacting Dewey's ideas about action in a community and in a democracy.

The Kolb Experiential Learning Theory

If we accept that students enter our courses not as blank slates but as individuals actively seeking to learn, we are embracing experiential learning. Communication/media students have abundant opportunities to participate in an active, experiential curriculum as they write and research scholarly papers, critique mediated texts, perform in a variety of roles and contexts, and create their own media texts. Kolb and Kolb (2006) note that their conceptualization of experiential learning evolved from "the work of prominent 20th century scholars who gave experience a central role in their theories of human learning and development—notably John Dewey, Kurt Lewin, Jean Piaget, William James, Carl Jung, Paulo Freire, Carl Rogers and others—to develop a holistic model of the experiential learning process" (p. 47). These scholars—particularly Dewey, Lewin, Piaget, and Freire—emphasized progress "toward a life of purpose and self-direction as the organizing principle for education" (Kolb, 1984, p. 18). Contrasting experiential learning with behavioral models of learning that stress outcomes based on absolute elements of knowledge, Kolb (1984) argues, "ideas are not fixed and immutable elements of thought but are formed and re-formed through experience" (p. 26). Six propositions define experiential learning theory for Kolb and Kolb (2006), summarized here:

1. Learning is a process rather than an outcome. Feedback is important to the process, and education is a "continuing reconstruction of experience." (Dewey, 1897, p. 79, cited in Kolb & Kolb, 2006, p. 47)
2. "All learning is relearning" such that existing and new knowledge structures are integrated.
3. Conflict drives learning and so learning must be about resolving conflict. In the process of learning, we "move back and forth between opposing modes of reflection and action and feeling and thinking."
4. "Learning is a holistic process of adaptation to the world." It encompasses the whole person in terms of thinking, feeling, perceiving, and acting.
5. "Learning results from synergetic transactions between the person and the environment." Resulting from Piaget's theories, this principle involves the dialectic of integrating new experiences into existing thought structures and lodging those thought structures into new experiences.
6. "Learning is the process of creating knowledge." This is a constructivist model following Freire, Vygotsky, and others, as opposed to a transmission model (or "banking" model). Knowledge develops from the conversion of one's experience. (pp. 47–48)

According to these principles and to Kolb's (1984) original work on experiential learning, learning happens through a cycle whereby the learner grasps experience and then transforms it. First, the learner is involved in a specific experience. The learner reflects on the experience, and from the reflection, the learner makes judgments, creates constructs, and draws conclusions. Those judgments, constructs, and conclusions pilot the leaner toward behaviors that result in new experiences. Experience is *grasped* through one of two modes—concrete experience or abstract conceptualization (Kolb & Kolb, 2006). Experience is *transformed* through one of two modes—reflective observation or active experimentation (Kolb & Kolb, 2006). Thus, learners have preferences for dealing with information—either an abstract or concrete orientation toward dealing with tasks and either reflection or action for processing thoughts.

The grasping of experiential knowledge through "concrete experience" means knowing something by going through it. "Abstract conceptualization" means knowing something in a theoretical manner. The transforming of experience through "reflective observation" suggests creating meaning by thinking about knowledge and reflecting upon it. "Active experimentation" suggests creating meaning by putting knowledge into action (Kolb, 1984). Kolb and Kolb (2006) assert that experiential learning involves the cycle of "experiencing, reflecting, thinking and acting" (p. 48) in accordance with contextual demands but that preferences arise among individuals for particular learning modes. The diagram below depicts the experiential learning cycle based on Kolb's (1984, p. 42) design.

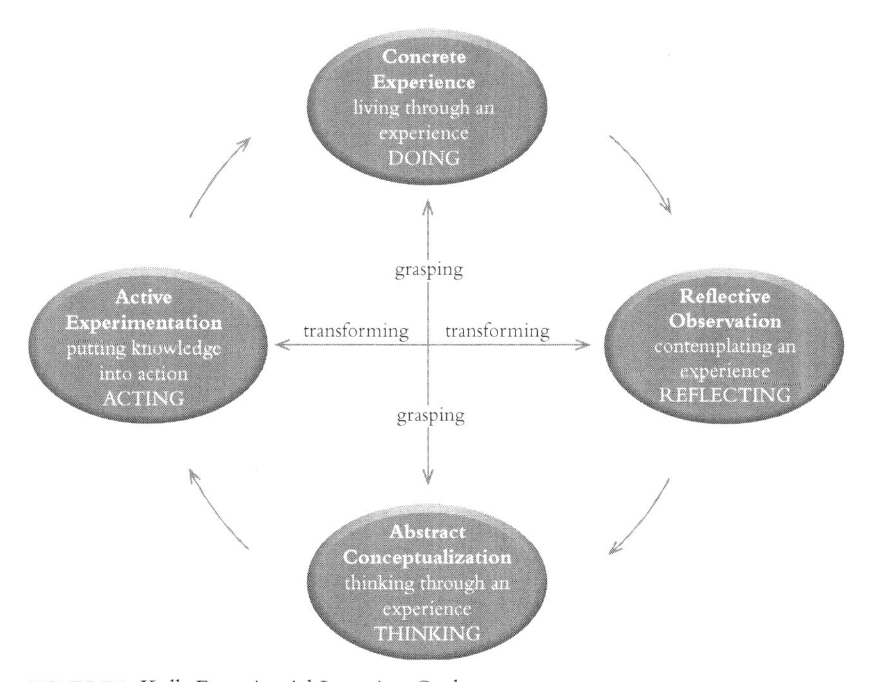

FIGURE 7.1 Kolb Experiential Learning Cycle.

Kolb asserted that learners' comfort levels in particular parts of the cycle constitute the preferences for certain learning modes. Understanding where an individual is comfortable on the scale of abstractness or concreteness (for grasping ideas) and on the scale of reflection or activity (for thought processing) indicates that person's learning style. Kolb formulated a "learning styles inventory" in which individuals may discover their preferred mode of learning, and he created a typology of the four different learning styles that constitute the cycle of experiential learning. He argues that preferred learning styles develop from "our hereditary equipment, our particular past life experience, and the demands of our present environment" (1984, p. 76). He defines the four styles, each of which represent a combination of two of the four learning modes.

> Through socialization experiences in family, school, and work, we come to resolve the conflicts between being active and reflective and between being immediate and analytical in characteristic ways, thus lending to reliance on one of the four basic forms of knowing: *divergence,* achieved by reliance on apprehension transformed by intention; *assimilation*, achieved by comprehension transformed by intention; *convergence,* achieved through extensive transformation of comprehension; and *accommodation*, achieved through extensive transformation of apprehension.
>
> (pp. 76–77, italics in original)

Kolb has since reformulated the language of the original styles to emphasize the dynamic nature of the learning cycle (Kolb & Kolb, 2006).[2]

Diverging Style—Concrete and Reflective

This learner sees concrete circumstances from multiple perspectives. This learner likes innovative and group activities, generating lots of ideas, being responsive to feelings, identifying problems, and being personally involved in the learning experience. This person tends to learn by listening, absorbing, and discussing. This instructor tends to motivate students to find their own incentives for learning.

Assimilating Style—Abstract and Reflective

This learner prefers abstract ideas and theories, creating conceptual models, designing experiments, systematic approaches to problem solving, considering alternative solutions, and structured activities. The learner prefers to think through ideas. As an instructor, this person tends to lecture.

Converging Style—Abstract and Active

This learner prefers decision making, discovering practical uses for ideas and theories, evaluating consequences, trial and error, and activities involving sequential steps. This learner prefers technical challenges rather than interpersonal situations.

This person may enjoy simulations, guest speakers, and "real world" applications and tends to learn by testing theories and questioning. This instructor teaches by facilitating and questioning.

Accommodating Style—Concrete and Active

This learner likes active learning, hands-on experience, risk taking, flexibility, sharing information with others, class discussion, debates, role playing, and group activities. The learner dislikes structure but works well with others. This individual learns by trial and error. As an instructor, this person teaches by staying in the background and encouraging students to do things.

Remembering that all individuals do learn in all of these ways, a basic understanding of these styles is useful in planning course activities that recognize tensions between opposing learning modes (acting and reflecting or concreteness and abstraction). Reaching students throughout the learning cycle is an ideal. Thus, the next section of this chapter examines practical approaches for addressing all types of learning styles. By providing a language for understanding the experiential learning process, the Kolb learning styles inventory can foster conversation among educators about constructing effective learning environments. Therefore, I view the Kolb learning styles inventory not as a "test" *per se*, but as an experience in comprehending different processes for learning. Scores on learning inventories are starting points for exploring how one learns best and how to address alternative learning preferences.

Techniques to Address All Learning Styles in the Communication Classroom

As you work to incorporate activities aimed at different learning preferences into your course, you will benefit from your previous efforts at prioritizing learning goals, coordinating assessments with those goals, and designing your course structure around the desired outcomes. Your teaching philosophy and experience as a student will also help guide the planning for accommodating different types of learners into your teaching repertoire. Brookfield (1995) calls this self-reflexive process the "autobiography of ourselves as teachers and learners":

> Analyzing our autobiographies as learners has important implications for how we teach. Our experiences as learners are felt at a visceral, emotional level that is much deeper than that of reason. The insights and meanings for teaching that we draw from these deep experiences are likely to have a profound and long-lasting influence. They certainly affect us more powerfully than methods or injunctions that we learn from textbooks or hear from superiors. We may think we're teaching according to a widely accepted curricular or pedagogic model, only to find, on reflection, that the foundations

> of our practice have been laid in our autobiographies as learners. In the face of crises or ambiguities, we fall back instinctively on memories from our times as learners to guide us in our responses.
>
> (p. 31)

Therefore, an instructor who may have been a reticent participant in class discussion as a student may recognize the tendency of such students toward reflective observation. So, using a learning inventory in concert with a reflexive stance about one's own teaching, an instructor can foster an awareness of his/her daily classroom operations. Because we are artifacts of our educational histories and experiences, we must consider several questions in seeking to create optimal learning experiences for all of our students.

- In what ways do media/communication students tend to learn best? Is this knowable?
- What strategies from my own learning preferences work well with my students?
- What approaches that are not part of my own educational history may be instructive for my students?
- What other experiences or influences might I draw upon to support learning in new ways?

These questions can help instructors be thoughtful about engaging all learners. We may even question the intersection of experiential learning theory with theories of communication. For example, Jarice Hanson (July, 2011), professor of communication at the University of Massachusetts Amherst, critiques the usefulness of educational theory but is reflexive about her own experiences teaching communication:

> I know a number of students from the School of Education (particularly grad students) are familiar with literature supporting different learning styles, but I don't seek this type of information out .... I draw much more from my experience with students, which I find makes me more adaptable to different situations in different contexts (big classes, little classes, activity-heavy classes, on-line classes). I don't disdain the educational/pedagogical literature—but I concern myself more with communication theory rather than educational theory.

Professor Hanson seeks out peer conversation about teaching by participating in small faculty discussion groups at the UMass Center for Teaching. Bonnie Brennan (July, 2011), Nieman Professor of Journalism at Marquette University, is similarly reflective about integrating communication theory into techniques for addressing diverse student constituencies:

> In my classes I help students to integrate theory with practice. In my qualitative methods classes, they use theory to help guide their research. In my

> ethics class, we analyze ethical dilemmas from a variety of philosophical perspectives. In my storytelling in public life course, students draw on a variety of conceptual tools to help them tell stories from different formats, perspectives and identities.

And Dustin Morrow (July, 2011), professor in the Department of Theater and Film at Portland State University, encourages students to be reflective about their own work as well as the work of others:

> Even in media production classes, I'm strongly in favor of writing exercises like creative journals and reasoned, analytical responses to texts and work. In the act of committing ideas to paper, even in something as short as an informal one-page essay, students are required to develop and organize their thoughts, which necessitates a significant level of wrestling with the material. But whether it is through writing or classroom discussion, students should always be responding to everything that is happening in a course—my comments, the comments and work of their classmates, the technologies, the written and audiovisual texts, and the processes of creating, presenting and discussing work. It is in this act of response that they become critical thinkers. As important as realizing an accomplished production is, the value of the producer is limited if he/she can't competently evaluate and discuss the work.

The recognition that a diversity of learning styles will accompany any group of students may be the best way to enact useful teaching practices. Putting together some instructional strategies specific to Kolb's learning styles, Sharp (2006) suggests that some strategies overlap styles, but for different reasons. For example, role playing appeals to different segments of learners—diverging students because they may experience concrete situations vicariously, thus gaining a new perspective; converging students because role playing allows the testing of actual concepts; and accommodating students who can focus on playing a part in a learner-created drama. Sharp's[3] (2006) strategies for Kolb's quadrants include:

Diverging style—concrete and reflective

- Brainstorming ideas
- Motivational stories
- Ask students what the material means
- In groups, have students define problems and imagine solutions
- Ask students to explain
- Class or group discussion
- Subjective exams
- Collegial learning environment
- Ask students "why?"
- Personal expression—how does the material relate to one's life
- Ask students to stop and reflect on material
- Role playing
- Field trips
- Peer reviews
- Listening and sharing
- Course-defined microblogging

Assimilating style—abstract and reflective	
• Demonstrations	• Ask students "what?"
• Gathering data and formulating theory	• Communicate your expertise to students
• Conduct independent research	• Critiquing material
• Problem solving by instructor	• Present material logically
• Provide time before asking questions	• Help students define problems
• Have students outline reading assignments	• Create models or maps of course material
• Thought provoking learning environment	• Asynchronous threaded discussion

Converging style—abstract and active	
• Devise practical applications for ideas	• Ask students "how?"
• Objective exams	• Ask for an oral summary of issues
• Examine or deconstruct objects or materials	• Field trips
• Problems worked on individually to develop procedures	• Laboratory or field simulations
• Active experiments or demonstrations to test concepts	• Worksheets
• Use augmented reality interfaces to test possibilities	• Coach students only after they've experimented on their own
	• Task-oriented learning environment
	• Demonstrate how material or concepts work in actuality

Accommodating style—concrete and active	
• Student-designed exams	• Ask students "what if?"
• Self-paced assignments	• Design problems to apply ideas to new situations
• Puzzles, apps, or games	• Group problem-solving
• Role playing	• Allow students to discover for themselves
• Have students draw or map concepts	• Encourage students to focus
• Provide materials for manipulation	• Class or group discussion
• Encourage risk-taking and creativity	• Student presentations
• Use social media for unstructured conversation	• Spontaneous learning environment

Based on these strategies for Kolb's categories, here is an example of a class on the First Amendment. For the diverging style, the instructor shows some racist or homophobic or misogynistic material online, asking the students to reflect on the nature of hate speech and why the First Amendment permits such forms of expression. For the assimilating style, the instructor lectures on case law involving hate speech, emphasizing the rationale (and its critiques) of the courts and of legal scholars in distinguishing between protected and unprotected speech. For the converging style, the instructor provides a set of facts that are organized into a hypothetical legal case involving the First Amendment and the limits of its protection with regard to hate speech. The students are split into groups and must work through the hypothetical to arrive at a decision, applying legal concepts to the case facts. For the accommodating style, the students work in groups or through social media to devise a legal regime under which hate speech is no longer protected by the First Amendment by attempting to define and regulate it. Such strategies are possible ways to engage all students in learning about the First Amendment.

A similar example follows for a class on successful introductions in argumentative writing. For the diverging style, students form groups to share and analyze their ideas about effective persuasive introductions, perhaps focusing on examples from their own experience. For the assimilating style, the instructor teaches the concept by explaining tactics for gaining attention in a credible manner. For the converging style, students can work together or alone to formulate some possible introductions for the same argument, explaining how each introduction works and why it might be effective. For the accommodating style, students can role play various introductions with one another, taking time to evaluate the possibilities of each approach. Or, students could create a game in which the objective centers on successful persuasion to move to the game's next level.

Several scholars have written about attention to different learning modes with specific suggestions for the media/communication curriculum. Willis-Rivera (2003) suggests techniques that engage kinesthetic, visual, and auditory learners in an intercultural communication course. Students can create a video documentary about a subject, using the kinesthetic mode in shooting the video, the auditory mode in editing the video, and the visual mode in writing a brief paper about the themes explored in the video. Another option would be for students to write a script about some intercultural communication issue and perform it. Kinesthetic learners are engaged in the performance of the script, auditory learners by the rehearsal of the performance, and visual learners by the writing of the script itself. Willis-Rivera's (2003) last option would be for students to attend a multicultural event and write a response paper to it. Visual learners are stimulated by writing the response paper, kinesthetic learners by presenting information from the event to the class, and auditory learners by attending the event itself. Class discussion or "debriefing" follows from each project that addresses course concepts, how the projects incorporated course concepts, and whether the projects helped the students learn the conceptual material better. According to Willis-Rivera (2003), students and instructors find this approach valuable:

> For the instructor, it can be especially gratifying and educational to see students take the knowledge from the course and apply it in a new and creative way. These options have also been well received by students. Many students

> appreciate the change from the traditional exam or project format; other students have found a new creative outlet through performance or video. Students who are not as proficient in taking objective examinations are excited to have other ways to demonstrate their learning that has occurred during the semester.
>
> (p. 4)

To build upon Willis-Rivera's techniques, an instructor can incorporate the use of QR codes (quick response matrix barcode) embedded in multiple locations as a storytelling device. Students generate QR codes and incorporate them into still images or text so that the user must interact with the text to allow the narrative to unfold. This method could be particularly useful in an intercultural communication course or a writing course where students develop story elements that may be used linearly or as modules. Another project that works across learning styles would involve the use of global positioning (GPS) for out-of-class activities. For example, a media history instructor could create a geocaching assignment in which students receive clues and references about various urban locations of historical significance. Students visit those locations in sequence as they decipher each clue or reference to the next location, with the help of smartphone locational technology. Students may work together to write the clues based on an instructor model. At the caching event's conclusion, students could write a paper or podcast explaining the significance of the endeavor. This activity involves logic and problem solving, concretizing abstract concepts or events, and application of specific skills and course materials into a larger context.

Matthew Lombard (June, 2014), a colleague at the School of Media and Communication at Temple University, reformulated his approach to teaching in multiple modes after consulting pedagogical literature on active learning. He describes his experiences with experiential learning:

> [The research] reaffirmed these ideas, and it's completely consistent with the scholarship in my area of psychological processing and telepresence—vivid and interactive experiences lead to simulated experiences that seem more real and are often more impactful. So I've tried in various ways to give students experiences that at least offer the chance to put ideas in practice even in small ways. My hope is that these experiences will help students understand key ideas in a more visceral and intuitive way, that the experiences will be enjoyable and interesting and so get them intrigued and motivated to learn more about the topic, and that these vivid experiences will be better remembered than a lecture or textbook.

Professor Lombard uses experiential learning most often in his course, Psychological Processing of Media, which often deals with the concept of telepresence, defined as "a sense of 'being there' in a virtual environment and more broadly defined as an illusion of nonmediation in which users of any technology overlook or misconstrue the technology's role in their experience" (http://ispr.info/). He uses a variety of techniques to appeal to multiple learning modes, including field trips, observational exercises, and class research projects. Here he describes a recent project:

> I show a lot of short videos to illustrate material and generate discussion; I put the links to them, as well as to news articles and scholarly readings, on the online syllabus, which I leave up after the course. Recently, I showed the students a PBS NewsHour story on EEG (Electroencephalography—recording the brain's electrical activity) measurement and applications (http://www.pbs.org/newshour/bb/science-jan-june12-neuroscience_01-02/). The report includes a discussion of the EEG and other bio sensor products of a company called NeuroSky (http://neurosky.com). I showed the students the web site, which highlights an interactive game made by Mattel called MindFlex Duel. The MindFlex web site (http://mindflexgames.com) promotes and describes the game this way:
>
> "Have you ever dreamed of moving an object with the power of your mind? Mindflex Duel™ makes that dream a reality! Utilizing advanced Mindflex Duel™ technology, the wireless headset reads your brainwave activity. Concentrate ... and the ball rises on a cushion of air! Relax ... and the ball descends. It's literally mind over matter! Mind vs. mind: Face off against another player ... Use the power of your thoughts to force the ball into your opponent's end zone to win!"
>
> Seeing that the students were intrigued, I purchased the game and brought it to the next class. I purposely didn't practice the game in advance or prepare a presentation about it because I wanted them to have the experience of exploring and learning about the technology and its applications themselves. Several students volunteered to play and it was pretty impressive (we all cheered) the first time one of them was able to raise the small ball using only her concentration. Eventually we had pairs of them competing to push the game's platform to their opponent's 'end zone.' I hope, and have some expectation, that everyone who was there will remember not just the experience but something about what EEG is and how it can be measured and used.

Professor Lombard's overall goal is to create vivid, poignant learning experiences in which students feel vested so that they internalize and reflect upon them after classroom instruction has ended.

FIGURE 7.2 An Immersive Experience: Sofia Lifts a Ball Using Her Concentration with the MindFlex Duel Game.

Dwyer (1998) assessed the value of learning styles in helping students who are apprehensive communicators. The study found that all students benefit from active learning strategies, suggesting that, echoing Kolb and others, a "cycle of instruction" should (1) connect new material to students' past experiences through discussion or interpersonal interaction, (2) provide opportunities for students to reflect and evaluate material through well-organized lecture and exposure to expert opinion, (3) allow students to test theories by applying concepts in class exercises, and (4) encourage creative involvement with course material through trial and error or occasions to teach other students. This cycle of instruction demonstrates the value of experiential learning in developing objectives based on student needs, encouraging student initiative, promoting openness among students about learning, and encouraging peer interaction to enhance student experiences.

Communication/media faculty have been at the forefront of using multiple modalities to connect with diverse student populations. Having a long history with the socioculturally embedded knowledge practices surrounding media, communication instructors understand how to teach students to encode and decode images, arguments, and ideas; to grasp theories of production, audience, and representation; to practice collaborative knowledge production; to regard communication technologies critically and ethically; and to reflect on one's own communicative practices. To develop in learners a sensibility toward critical reflexivity, authentic communicative practices, and evaluative skills, we must continue to address our students' disparate experiences and different learning preferences. Moreover, as Kolb (1984) claims, the tension students feel in the confrontation with multiple learning modes is what ultimately leads to transformation. Communication/media instructors may link the elements of the experiential learning cycle by questioning students about, for example, the connection between capitalistic imperatives of media institutions and the democratic process. In such questioning, the instructor invites the student to relate personal experience to theoretical knowledge and to make conclusions or judgments that can be transformative. Kolb (1984) sees this transformative possibility when students are provided an opportunity to

> stimulate growth in their ability to learn from a variety of learning perspectives. ... The aim is to make the student self-renewing and self-directed; to focus on integrative development where the person is highly developed in each of the four learning modes: active, reflective, abstract, and concrete. Here, the student is taught to experience the tension and conflict among these orientations, for it is from the resolution of these tensions that creativity springs.
>
> (p. 203)

The tension and conflict can challenge students to think in alternative ways or to think in ways with which they may be uncomfortable.

Active learning approaches make sense in a communication classroom where dialogic, communal models of teaching are becoming more familiar. In order to communicate effectively with our students, we must learn to do so in multifaceted ways. Without reflection about our own pedagogical practice, we succumb to teaching in habituated ways that seem most familiar or comfortable to us. Moreover, we may feel constricted by disciplinary convention regarding pedagogy. Kolb (1981) argues,

> [E]ducation in an academic field is a continuing process of selection and socialization to the pivotal norms of the field governing criteria for truth and how it is to be achieved, communicated, and used. ... Over time these selection and socialization pressures combine to produce an increasingly impermeable and homogeneous disciplinary culture and correspondingly specialized student orientations to learning.
>
> (pp. 233–234)

Kolb continues:

> [A] central function for the larger university organization is to provide the integrative structures and programs that counterbalance the tendencies toward specialization in student development and academic research. Continuous lifelong learning requires learning how to learn, and this involves appreciation of and competence in diverse approaches to creating, manipulating, and communicating knowledge.
>
> (p. 252)

Given the increasing diversity of the student population and the expectation to abandon or modify "stand and deliver" models of teaching, instructors may find reward in reviving teaching practices by bearing in mind learning styles. With the experiential learning models of Dewey, Lewin, and Piaget in consideration, faculty can motivate students to integrate course material into their own experiences and their plans for acting within the world.

Notes

1 Connectivism is a model of collaborative learning asserting that technology influences our thinking, that cognitive information processing is now supported by technology, and that knowing where to find information is paramount.
2 In addition, I prefer the language of styles rather than "types," which are reductive and oversimplified.
3 I have also added some of my own suggestions to Sharp's.

References

Beetham, H. (2007). An approach to learning activity design. In H. Beetham & R. Sharpe (Eds.), *Rethinking pedagogy for a digital age* (pp. 26–40). Abingdon, UK: Routledge.

Beetham, H., & Oliver, M. (2010). The changing practices of knowledge and learning. In R. Sharpe, H. Beetham, & S. DeFreitas (Eds.), *Rethinking learning for a digital age* (pp. 155–169). Abingdon, UK: Routledge.

Bourdieu, P. (1990). *In other words: Essays towards a reflexive sociology* (M. Adamson, Trans.). Cambridge, UK: Polity Press.

Brockbank, A., & McGill, I. (2007). *Facilitating reflective learning in higher education* (2nd ed.). Berkshire, UK: Open University Press.

Brookfield, S. D. (1995). *Becoming a critically reflective teacher*. San Francisco, CA: Jossey-Bass.

Coffield, F., Moseley, D., Hall, E., & Ecclestone, K. (2004). *Learning styles and pedagogy in post-16 learning: A systematic and critical review*. London, UK: Learning and Skills Research Centre. http://nwresearch.wikispaces.com/file/view/Coffield%20learning%20styles.pdf/246502619/Coffield%20learning%20styles.pdf

Dewey, J. (1897). My pedagogic creed. *The School Journal, LIV*(3), 77–80.

Dewey, J. (1927). *The public and its problems*. New York: Henry Holt.

Dewey, J. (1938). *Experience and education*. New York, NY: Macmillan.

Dunn, R., & Dunn, K. (1992). *Teaching secondary students through their individual learning styles*. Needham Heights, MA: Allyn and Bacon.

Dunn, R., & Dunn, K. (1999). *The complete guide to the learning styles inservice system*. Boston, MA: Allyn and Bacon.
Dunn, R., Dunn, K., & Price, G. E. (1984). *Learning style inventory*. Lawrence, KS: Price Systems.
Dwyer, K. K. (1998). Communication apprehension and learning style preference: Correlations and implications for teaching. *Communication Education*, *47*, 137–150.
Honey, P., & Mumford, A. (1986). *Manual of learning styles*. Maidenhead, UK: Peter Honey Publications.
Grasha, A. (1996). *Teaching with style*. Pittsburgh, PA: Alliance Publishers.
Kolb, A. Y., & Kolb, D. A. (2006). Learning styles and learning spaces: A review of the multidisciplinary application of experiential learning theory in higher education. In R. R. Sims & S. J. Sims (Eds.), *Learning styles and learning* (pp. 45–91). New York, NY: Nova Science Publishers.
Kolb, D. A. (1981). Learning styles and disciplinary differences. In A. W. Chickering and Associates (Ed.), *The modern American college* (pp. 232–255). San Francisco, CA: Jossey-Bass.
Kolb, D. A. (1984). *Experiential learning: Experience as the source of learning and development*. Englewood Cliffs, NJ: Prentice-Hall.
Pashler, H., McDaniel, M., Rohrer, D., & Bjork, R. (2009). Learning styles: Concepts and evidence. *Psychological Science in the Public Interest*, *9*(3), 105–119.
Sharp, J. E. (2006). Rationale and strategies for using Kolb learning style theory in the classroom. In R. R. Sims & S. J. Sims (Eds.), *Learning styles and learning* (pp. 93–113). New York: Nova Science Publishers.
Smith, M. K. (2010). David A. Kolb on experiential learning. *The encyclopedia of informal education*. http://infed.org/mobi/david-a-kolb-on-experiential-learning/
Sprague, J. (1993). Retrieving the research agenda for communication education: Asking the pedagogical questions that are "embarrassments to theory." *Communication Education*, *42*(2), 106–122.
Willis-Rivera, J. (2003). Production, performance, and portfolios: A final project for diverse learning styles. *Communication Teacher*, *17*(3), 1–2, 4.

8

ETHICS AND CITIZENSHIP IN TEACHING COMMUNICATION

With Brian McFadden[1]

Media technologies help people to connect with each other and participate in communal relationships. Technological advances influence how we communicate with each other by eliminating the once-restrictive barriers limiting community participation. Although these advances allow for increased community involvement, the seeds of communal activity do not always blossom into civic participation and vigor for the democratic process. Accordingly, it is important that we, as communication faculty, contemplate the ways we can help to combat such a reality. Looking beyond terminal course goals and toward enduring lessons may have a lasting positive effect on our students' futures. For this reason, media and communication educators should consider how the communication field might empower our students as future citizens of a democracy.

In this book, I have examined pedagogy and practice, from establishing philosophies of teaching to designing courses with goals that align with those philosophies to understanding communication/media students as learners. I assert, along with former ICA president Larry Gross (2012), the pivotal nature of the study of communication and its connection to citizenship:

> If the goal of the liberal arts is the acquisition of basic intellectual skills, combined with knowledge of the historical roots and cross-cultural variations in human behavior and institutions, then communication is necessarily at the center of such an education. ... Communication studies can rightfully claim a central role not only in the basic general education of an informed citizenry, but also in understanding and clarifying many of the central challenges of our rapidly changing world.
>
> (p. 924)

This means that we study the ways in which the world constitutes itself. And, we can point to recent examples of communication technologies as a vehicle for civic empowerment in the form of the Arab Spring protests. Driving these campaigns were clearly defined protest goals in the form of the desire for new governmental leadership. In the United States, the Occupy Wall Street protests attempted to follow a similar blueprint. However, without leadership or clearly defined goals, the movement fizzled. Today, community participation involving communication technology tends to revolve around deciding the winners of competitive reality television programs rather than taking meaningful civic action. As educators, we should encourage our students to participate in actively engaging *real* issues.

Communication/media education can play a central role in involving students in issues of equality, justice, and public importance to combat a consumerist ethos of personalized lifestyle markers as indicators of community participation. Citizenship is marked by the social contract between people and the collective society; as Dewey (1916) argued a century ago, education is part of the social contract that builds the wisdom and knowledge necessary for civic engagement. Citizenship is about human agency, social capital, and acting within the world. Citizenship is not about spectatorship or noncommittal online clicking. Education's role in promoting citizenship is about confronting civic ills such as corruption, racism, discrimination, and injustice; it helps us to recognize that human equality is a public good. As Griebling and Shaw (2011) note, "if [educators] do not nurture a passion for knowledge ... they will fail to produce thinkers with the intellectual expansiveness necessary to deal with the moral and practical complexities of contemporary life" (p. 15). With the more recent emphasis on active learning, I argue that the prevailing assumption in academia is that of a more collaborative learning environment. Students' acknowledgment of an inherent responsibility for their own education has lasting repercussions that transcend their time in the classroom. Our personal education can and should occur every day.

As media/communication educators, we have an ethical responsibility to encourage civic participation among our students. In the introduction to this book, I invoke John Dewey to illustrate the long-lasting cultural effects classroom instruction can have on students—that educators not only communicate cultural values to perpetuate them but also, perhaps more importantly, to reflect upon them. Sprague (1990) insists that "our collective survival demands that the best ideas of the past be kept alive, not in a few museums or libraries, but in the consciousness of a large segment of society" (p. 20). Similarly, Reich (2008) asserts that those ideas passed along typically hold some degree of communal value (p. 61). And Campbell (2008), reasserting Dewey's notion that community and education work together to reinvigorate democracy, adds:

> It is necessary for our educational institutions to both introduce the young into the shared values of their society and to give them some distance from their common life. In a democracy, education must prepare the young for

> their lives as future citizens. It must be moral, not just intellectual; emphasize judgment, rather than just skills of calculating; aim at wisdom, rather than just knowledge; and foster cooperation rather than "getting ahead."
>
> (p. 24)

When we consider these points together, it becomes clear that we, as educators, play a vital role in informing the cultural values of the future. According to Sholle and Denski (1994), teaching media studies forces us to contemplate our location within a democracy. As we consider and reconsider our own place in the world,

> our lives have become increasingly compartmentalized. As the personal, the professional and the political are shunted into separate spheres, one of the more pressing tasks we face involves the subsequent reintegration of our lives as teachers with our lives as citizens. In that we can never purge the personal, ethical and political from the discourse of curriculum, we must seek strategies which offer us reflexive moments within which we might examine our own subject positions as educators.
>
> (p. 7)

They claim that cultural politics is an important part of thinking critically about media education for an egalitarian society. Communication/media educators have recognized the struggle within the academy for legitimacy based on the field's interdisciplinary roots, its theoretical and methodological diversity, and its identity as a practical subject affiliated with industry in contrast to its identity as a scholarly avenue of inquiry. So communication/media studies is a field well positioned to host a critical conversation about citizenship, ethical action, and education for democracy. This chapter's goal is to consider how instructor identity, teaching philosophy, and the classroom environment work together to inspire communication/media students to take responsibility for their own education. This chapter will conclude by considering the positive effects such education can have on democracy, egalitarianism, and active citizenship. Ultimately, as educators, we have a public responsibility to inspire and nurture a thirst for learning and participation within our students.

Teaching Philosophies and Ethical Frameworks

As noted in the chapter on teaching philosophies, communication faculty seeking to develop compelling pedagogical philosophies must grant a role to communicative practices in articulating our approach to education. We understand that students need to reflect on the repercussions of creating and consuming media. We understand that media construct and reconstruct culture. And we understand that our teaching philosophies must recognize the faculty's position in the professional growth of students as well as the meaningful examination of communication in culture so as to contribute to a democratic, civically valuable education.

Communication/media faculty are key in assisting students to develop as citizens and to grasp distinctions between ethical, authentic communication and manipulative demagoguery. A teaching philosophy reconciling the societal push toward developing students professionally with an emphasis on meaningful exploration of communication in culture will help galvanize Dewey's vision of democracy.

Ethical teaching in communication/media invokes what Nussbaum (2002) argues is an education for citizenship in a globally connected world. She advocates a humanity-centric, empathetic, and reflective approach to education that, at its core, is ethical and sensitive to human diversity. These characteristics mark much of the effort of communication/media educators, who grasp that communication is culture and that media permeate our lives. In Nussbaum's (2002) call for higher education to foster democratic citizenship, she observes that global communication directs our attention toward issues of cultural diversity and human connection. This worldwide conversation brought about by globalized media systems has, however, tended to be characterized by the norms of market exchange rather than an ethos of human fellowship. She suggests three core ethical values for higher education: critical self-examination in the vein of Socrates, in which we question our own beliefs and habits; the notion of the world citizen in which we are bound, locally and globally, to others "by ties of recognition and concern" (p. 295); and the cultivation of "the narrative imagination" (p. 299) in which we empathize with others' positions, stories, and feelings. Nussbaum's ideals for higher education are often explored in communication/media curricula through courses in media production, analysis, rhetoric, multiculturalism, policy, and ethics.

Similarly, Nixon (2011) exhibits a general philosophy that advocates the notion of higher education as a public good for a civil society. For Nixon, the purpose of higher education is to contribute to the public good in the face of encroaching privatization and commodification evident within contemporary university environments. Echoing Dewey, he claims that education must go beyond "transmitting the collective resources of human capability, human reason and human purposefulness" (p. 117). It must be a force for social transformation. Nixon provides us with foundational ideas that can help us craft teaching philosophies that elicit the potential for positive social change within our students.

During my first semester of doctoral studies, my cohort and I were required to take a class about teaching in higher education. The instructor[2] designed the course in such a way that it challenged us to consider all the work that goes into designing, developing, and teaching a course. Some assignments, like creating a syllabus or fair grading rubric, exposed us to the clerical components of the profession. Other assignments challenged us to reflect on and contemplate our academic identities. One example of this assignment variety was our final examination: Write your personal teaching philosophy.

The assignment challenged students to contemplate their identity as an academic—a difficult task for a first year doctoral student who, at that point of his or her academic life, likely denotes academic identity as his or her research interests. Upon completing this assignment, I was keenly aware that there was more to my academic identity than the research I conduct or papers I write. Instead, an educator's academic identity is symbiotic to the extent that one's teaching self and research self go hand in hand. I would argue that we should take time to reflect on our academic identity's ethical implications. I encourage instructors to think about how academic identity meshes with desired classroom outcomes and, more importantly, whether those outcomes are sensitive to our ethical obligation as educators toward nurturing our students' passion for egalitarianism and civic participation.—Brian McFadden

Faculty Identity within an Ethical Context

Anthony Giddens (1991) offers the idea of a *reflexive* identity that is enacted through the individual's personally constructed narrative. It is the story of the self and is integrated with everyday experiences. It is made and remade. Giddens says,

> The "identity" of the self ... presumes reflexive awareness. It is what the individual is conscious "of" in the term "self-consciousness." Self-identity, in other words, is not something that is just given, as a result of the continuities of the individual's action-system, but something that has to be routinely created and sustained in the reflexive activities of the individual. (p. 52)

Therefore, an academic identity does not exist within a bubble. Academic identity—or any identity—acts, reacts, and interacts with neighboring identities in a given setting. The university, campus, and classroom are all settings in which we perform our academic identities. In these places, we negotiate our identities with the people we encounter, like our students, colleagues, or administrators. For this reason, it is an uninformed assumption to think that educators possess one fixed academic identity. Instructors draw upon disciplinary inspiration and personal credo to form understandings of teaching and learning. By being reflexive about her or his experiences as a scholar, teacher, and individual, a faculty member engages with an authentic, critical academic position that students can access. But, as noted in the introduction to this book, our identities as educators and as scholars are inseparable. As instructors develop their academic identities through professional norms, institutional cultures, and everyday experiences, the opportunity to be ethical presents itself. To communicate the substance of researching and evaluating the role of media and communication in contemporary life is part of an ethical, lifelong, and democratic educational mission.

Carr (2011) argues that problems arise when educators ask students merely to reproduce orthodoxy or to trust only their own experiences without reflection. Moreover, extrinsic pressures make demands on academics to regulate their identities. Institutional and community values dictate how instructors function as do our own commitments to particular epistemologies or knowledge frameworks. Recently, the goals, values, and practices of higher education have been challenged by constituencies questioning the worth of a university education, the motives of those in academia, and legitimacy of educational ideals such as individual and cultural growth.[3] As other societal sectors and internal structures exert more control over faculty identity, instructors may find themselves succumbing to demands for instrumentalist educational goals rather than more ideal aims. For communication and media instructors, this has meant a stronger emphasis on skill development at the possible expense of less tangible goals such as reflection and critical analysis. Nevertheless, to be conscious of Giddens' notion of reflexive identity requires that faculty be able to adapt to the changing nature of the academy while upholding their principles of educational philosophy. Demonstrating this flexibility, Luthra (2007) asserts that navigating through course content can be a "[collective] process of exploration … with no predetermined end points" (p. 204). She acknowledges the challenge of holding "freewheeling discussion" (p. 211) amid the contradictory impulses to protect free expression and to recognize that the classroom sphere is influenced by external social forces. This reminds us that there is no one right way to realize one's desired course goals and that an awareness of such external factors helps students grasp the nature of civically minded education. Maintaining a flexible academic identity, then, may help students to invest more into a course since they have a stake in the its direction. Luthra (2007) says that this teaching philosophy sets her communication classes "on a quest for solutions" (p. 204) rather than a replication of her own critiques or analyses. In this instance, flexibility and fluidity invite student contribution to the course learning goals in an effort to inspire students to take responsibility for their education.

To be clear, this is not a call for a complete overhaul of how we think about our teaching philosophies. Consideration of our ethical position within our teaching philosophy may nurture student attitudes toward education. Blumberg (2009) argues that when a teaching philosophy features a learner-centered focus (or the idea that instructors should "overcome the tendency to do things for the students" (p. 131)), it increases the opportunity for students to invest in their own learning. Therefore, if we focus our efforts on how to best inspire student action, we come closer to aligning our teaching philosophy with our ethical obligation to our students and to the public. Shifting to a learner-centered teaching philosophy should be easy for communication instructors because, as Ramsey (1993) explains, we "accept and teach the role of the 'active audience' in almost all … courses" (p. 75).

Regardless, Ramsey (1993) asserts that communication educators often have difficulty according such a status to their own students (p. 75). Perhaps the best course of action for escaping this paradoxical abyss is for communication faculty to view the classroom as a staging area for future members of the public. In this way, our students experience what it means to be a part of and work within a community of their peers. If we tie this idea of the classroom as staging area into our academic identity, our educational philosophy has the potential to fulfill our ethical responsibility to prepare students to be an active and beneficial part of the public. Thus, communication/media faculty are positioned to tackle vital questions like "how does knowledge about communication relate to social agency?" and "how does an understanding of media make us better citizens?" and "how can knowledge about communication expose and abrogate gaps between society's advantaged and disadvantaged peoples?"

Aligning Faculty Identity with Ethical Aspirations

To endorse democratic values within our courses and curricula, ethical action based on a consideration of the welfare of others is a necessity. Ethical action is bound to the values of social justice and equality through faculty whose academic identities involve citizenship. Kogan (2000) points out that academic identities are multifaceted but that they ultimately contain a communal aspect. Individual faculty have their unique histories and moral frameworks that inform their professional identities. Moreover, individual faculty possess identities within their various communities and institutions whose values, practices, and mythos define and shape these identities. As noted above, external communities and internal bureaucracies shape academic identity, but Kogan (2000) claims that those externalities may strengthen internal academic communities as well as challenge them. Faculty, regardless of disciplinary identity, are a community loosely bound together by expertise, standards, and a commitment to students. I argue that part of the communal identity of faculty is also informed by civic connections that are negotiated through multiple functions. Communication and media departments, for example, routinely forge partnerships with local media outlets for internships, community events, or scholarships. Our academic identities are both formed by and enacted within a holistic conceptualization of knowledge production as teaching, research, and citizenship. These ideas are inspired by Dewey's works on democracy and education: he connects pedagogy to personal philosophy by advocating the formation of a governing principle that underlies one's educational techniques and practices.

Also, Dewey's (1916, 1927) views on public citizenship stem from his assumptions that participation is essential to democracy, that public communication fuels participation, and that both communication and democracy are tied to education. These views are linked to an ethical sensibility wherein the university could promote community action by contributing academic expertise to debates about matters of public importance (Dewey, 1927). Applying Dewey's conceptualization of a democratic public to how we approach classroom instruction, it seems that educators should privilege class interaction as a means toward inspiring students to feel a sense of duty for civic action. A civically minded teaching philosophy, according to Barkley (2009), should consider promoting a sense of community among students such that they feel safe to test and share beliefs and opinions. Amankwah (2008) speaks to the importance of seeking "ethical dialogue" in class because it will undoubtedly house a variety of opinions (p. 45). Asking whether ethical dialogue is truly an obtainable outcome in the communication classroom, Amankwah nevertheless claims that to reach an ethical dialogue, the students and instructor must not privilege any opinion or person; all opinions and people should be equally valuable in the classroom community. In attempting to reach this ideal, the students comprising this community will feel freer to participate through sharing and understanding the opinions and views of their peers.

Other scholars have considered alternate ways of promoting participation as a means of having their students learn how to interact publicly and productively. Rheingold (2008) claims that for communication students, this means learning about the difference between private and public voice. According to this logic, students can find their own identities and style of individual expression by "consciously engaging with an active public" (p. 25). In the communication classroom, educators have the platform to enact a public sphere of sorts to help students discover their public voices. It is through these public voices that students can become engaged citizens—first in the classroom and eventually in our democracy. Rheingold (2010) advocates a critical perspective for the public voice by noting that democratic participation (via social media in particular) permits a student to become "an active citizen rather than simply a passive consumer of what is sold to you, what is taught to you, and what your government wants you to believe" (p. 18). Although Amankwah and Rheingold approach building a classroom community differently, it is clear that their teaching philosophies are both geared toward the same end: to prepare students to apply their education toward becoming informed citizens.

In the media and communication curriculum, there are numerous opportunities to practice the tenets of public citizenship. "Democracy is constructed in and through the everyday narratives of living and learning" (Nixon, 2011, p. 121), and those narratives are often communicated through a culture of media. Various prognosticators have cited the digital revolution as a means toward enhanced democracy and equality. However, communication educators realize that other communication revolutions (telegraph, radio, television) have prompted similar promises toward equality and human emancipation. The promises heaped upon communication technologies to usher in a renewed society are similarly heaped upon communication/media education to elevate civil society. But those everyday narratives of living and learning that constitute democracy are *found within* the communicative sphere and are *of* the communicative sphere. In the chapter on categorizing thinking, we see that Bloom's taxonomy offers a way to incorporate Dewey's (1916) ideas about reflective thinking[4] into the curriculum. For example, instructors teaching argumentation or media production will move beyond basic understanding to reveal the relationship that evaluating and creating have to fundamental communicative practices and concepts. So students need to learn the conventions of narrative construction and be able to decipher contextual meaning so as to make value judgments about media and to make new media. As noted in the chapter on categorizing thinking, when students grasp the basics, they comprehend how and why those basics endure throughout the study of communication. And when they make links between those basics and their relevance in complex communicative processes, students can then use "higher order" skills to create new media forms with sophistication. In this process, faculty provoke students to think reflectively about course content from their individual viewpoints and experiences. This is an opportunity for students not only to grow but also to situate themselves within the larger arena of civil society.

Exercise to Structure Reflective Thinking

This is an in-class exercise I use in my PhD seminar, *Teaching Communication.* The exercise is based on this citation: King, P. M. (2000). Learning to make reflective judgments. In M. B. B. Magolda (Ed.), *Teaching to promote intellectual and personal maturity: Incorporating students' worldviews and identities into the learning process* (pp. 15–26). *New Directions for Teaching and Learning.* San Francisco, CA: Jossey-Bass. The goal of the exercise is to provide instructors with a typology of reflective thinking activities based on communication/media course topics.

King argues that complex reasoning among students develops over time. Because faculty want to encourage reflective thinking, three factors should be considered in helping students to learn to make interpretive arguments:

1. understanding the knowing process in complex and encompassing ways
2. accepting uncertainty without being immobilized by it
3. learning to use evidence to reason toward conclusions and make "best judgments" (p. 24)

To accomplish the goal of helping students become effective at constructing, reflectively, their knowledge claims about the world, King identifies suggestions for instructors:

1. show respect for students' assumptions
2. discuss controversial, ill-structured issues with students throughout their educational activities

3. create opportunities for students to analyze others' points of view for evidentiary adequacy and to develop and defend their own points of view
4. teach students strategies for systematically gathering data, assessing the relevance of the data, evaluating data sources, and making interpretive judgments based on the data
5. give students frequent feedback
6. help students address issues of uncertainty in judgment making and examine their assumptions about knowledge and how it is gained
7. encourage students to practice their reasoning skills in many settings (p. 24)

Our task: in pairs, construct an example of how you might approach these seven suggestions using a topic related to communication. You may choose your own topic, or choose from these topics below.

- The importance of the First Amendment to the U.S. Constitution in democratic society
- The impact of assumptions about [sexuality, race, gender, religion, age] in mainstream media
- Can ICTs (Information & Communication Technologies) transform economically disenfranchised communities?
- Is digital art "real" art?
- What are the social consequences of the "bottom-line" economic mentality governing mainstream media?
- What are the benefits or detriments of media globalization for audiences and cultures?

Ethics and the Media/Communication Classroom

The communication classroom is an environment capable of fostering feelings of both community and marginalization. As we address questions and confront difficult issues about our shared cultural ecosystem (the media), we invariably cope with our own cultural identities, positions, and power. The room's physical assemblage (including online "rooms") contributes to such feelings to the extent that a space can promote or limit student participation. For example, a lecture hall with fixed seats facing the front of the classroom is inherently less participatory than a seminar room where students can see their peers or instructor on an equal level. However, the extent to which a classroom promotes or limits participation spans beyond its architecture. An instructor's pedagogical approach can override the benefits or detriments of the classroom space. Since we, as educators, ultimately hope to empower our students, we have an ethical responsibility to create a classroom environment conducive to this end. The classroom itself is a socially constructed space wherein power and identity are negotiated by all participants. In this way, an inclusive and ethical pedagogy recognizes the possibilities for public expression, social advocacy, and democratic engagement. Students tend to cognitively separate academic and social spaces, and they may be uneasy communicating a personal perspective relating to knowledge production when asked to adhere to formal guidelines of evidentiary support. They must manage their identities across spaces but feel comfortable advocating their positions within the classroom. If we believe, with Mahoney (2008), that instructors have an obligation to "fulfill the highest expectations of our students and their parents, [their] colleagues, and our public" (p. 157), we acknowledge our ethical responsibilities. Mahoney's quote points to the big picture: our students become the future voices informing public opinion. Hence, the classroom serves as a training ground for our students' future democratic participation. For this reason, educators should consider the following elements of the communication classroom: the diverse nature of the participants in the classroom space, the existence of embedded power systems, and how to best align our pedagogical philosophies to these sensibilities.

The Nature of the Diverse Communication Classroom

The interdisciplinary nature of communication/media studies guarantees an academically diverse classroom. This intersection of academic disciplines presents both a benefit and a challenge to the communication classroom. Some of the most fruitful learning experiences occur in a classroom containing a variety of academic identities. Academic orientation, of course, is only one way to account for the communication classroom's diverse composition. Race, gender, sexuality, age, economic status, and many other identity markers also contribute to class heterogeneity. These multiple and varied identities carry with them diverse beliefs that inform thoughts and opinions during class discussions. An ethical sensibility toward diverse perspectives can encourage transformative educational experiences.

According to Mortenson (2007), a transformative education in communication and media is one that encourages students to examine their own assumptions by contemplating various perspectives as a measure toward reflective action. Like the active learning model, transformative education yields broadened thinking and sensitivity toward diverse viewpoints. Brockbank and McGill (2007) see transformative learning as a social process since all meaning is created in concert with others:

> The ability to become a reflective learner, to be able to shift across paradigms of knowledge and self as well as perceive and act in ways that may transcend understandings in the past requires the capacity to be able to reflect on what is known, felt, and acted upon. Being able to undertake reflection alone is necessary but not sufficient. The tendency to self-deceive, collude and be unaware is ever present. (p. 4)

For Mortenson (2007), "transformative education teaches students how to use their logic and intuition to interrogate the habitual ways that they perceive and respond to their world and to develop frames of sense-making and action that consciously reflect personal values and greater awareness" (p. 402). Writing about interpersonal communication education, Mortenson's comments can be extended to all media/communication education since both have transformative educational potential. Courses in communication engage with issues of lived experience, self-perceptions, meaning, and action. When students are able to formulate their own questions about meaning and ideas in addition to reframing their habituated interpretations and behaviors, they undergo transformative, democratic learning.

One way for educators to establish a transformative learning environment that takes advantage of its diversity is to promote inclusion via class participation. Jenkins, Purushotma, Weigel, Clinton, and Robinson (2009) suggest a classroom with "low barriers" for student expression, "strong support for creating and sharing," and "members who believe their contributions matter" all help to foster class participation (p. 6). Increasing constructive class participation requires a concomitant increase in student sensitivity toward the classroom community. This recommendation is a surface-level means toward the egalitarian classroom, and so the following examples are included to address the complex practicalities of promoting an inclusive class experience.

Luthra (2007), a critical pedagogue, describes her way of embracing inclusivity while defending against alienation, coercion, or marginalization. In her communication courses, Luthra attempts to bolster students' power by "allowing them to explore the issues on their own, to work with their own rubrics, insights, and vocabulary to understand current problems and create alternative visions" (p. 204). In this example, the educator sets the inclusive tone for the class by selecting media texts for analysis that have potential to change the way students think about mainstream culture and popular opinion.

This model, from Arlene Dallalfar (2011), illustrates how the instructor's political perspectives and choices inform her desire to transform conceptual learning into action:

> [A]n important site for enhancing cross-cultural and multi-cultural understanding in this era of rapid globalization is the arena of media (both informational and entertainment) in communicating and framing international affairs. As an ethnographic filmmaker, I am interested in exploring how global mass media impacts cultural identity, and how visual literacy combined with cultural analysis can be used as a pedagogical tool in teaching. Students are asked to bring two distinct images of the "other" to class. As a group, we discuss the images, what is being framed, and what is being illustrated, that is, context and misrepresentation in the media, films, and TV at that particular historical conjecture. Exploring ways to understand

> the persistent and powerful negative images and notions of different groups and cultures within our society and worldwide is an important component of the interdisciplinary pedagogical approach used in my teaching and scholarship.
>
> (p. 122)

Dallalfar's exercise is a useful means of examining mediated representations in ways that respect students' lived experiences and critical reflections. However, the study of media and communication encompasses more than content representations. Instructors must consider how all facets of the study of communication—its practices, its institutions, its audiences—are sites of inquiry for diverse student populations. Moreover, as both cultural and institutional dictates require us to engage with social media technologies, we must problematize their ubiquity so that students can think about them in ways that encourage respect for alternative perspectives and identities.

In this example from Adrienne Shaw (June, 2014), faculty in the School of Media and Communication at Temple University, the classroom culture of her *Mobile Media* course is shaped by the use of an "inclusivity policy" to negotiate a responsible and safe environment for discussion.[5] The policy states:

> Sometimes during the semester we will discuss ideas that might produce strong emotional responses. This may include addressing issues or ideas that some students might find offensive. Although we will not avoid such discussions, it is important that everyone in the room is sensitive to how they communicate ideas. In particular, everyone in the class is expected to avoid language that is pejorative or perpetuates stereotypes about gender, age, race, religious affiliation, class, sexuality, national origin, dialect or disability (this is not an exhaustive list, please let me know if more should be added).
>
> Differing opinions and perspectives are crucial to effective discussion, however I insist that everyone in this class remain mindful of, and take responsibility for, their speech and behavior. This course is committed to creating and maintaining an inclusive and safe space for all students, guests, and instructors. This means every step will be taken to ensure no one is mistreated or disadvantaged because of ability, socioeconomic status, race, sexuality, age, gender, nationality, religion, or any other factor.
>
> I recognize that many people are coming to this class with different understandings of privilege and social oppression, and mistakes may happen. Because of this, it is paramount that you tell me when you can about something that has bothered you (including anything I say), and for those who misstep to be open to correcting their behavior. This is going to, hopefully, be a lively and friendly classroom where everyone treats each other with respect.

Here are some guidelines to follow:

- Always wait for a speaker to finish speaking before you reply.
- Be sure to actively listen to others and not dominate discussion.
- Avoid making assumptions about other people's identity including but not limited to, race, sex, gender, and sexuality. Let others disclose the information they choose to, and if you absolutely must know something (like preferred gender pronouns), don't single a person out for their information, offer yours first, and if you're in a group of people, pose your question to the entire group.
- Do not use any slurs. This includes terms and language that are racist, sexist, homophobic, heterosexist, classist ("white trash"), transphobic/cissexist ("tranny" and "she-male") and ableist ("crazy," "lame" and "retarded").[6]
- Ask respectful questions if you do not understand or are unfamiliar with a term someone is using to describe their experience. Better yet, there are many online resources you can make use of to learn the answers to your questions. Do not make any individual responsible for educating you about people "like them." Educate yourself, google your questions or terms you don't know, and remember that being inclusive is not a passive activity.
- The terms we use to describe our experience are always changing. I ask that you respect everyone's right to define and communicate their identity in whatever way they see fit.
- Be aware of your own privileged position(s), and learn to be comfortable having people politely tell you if you are unintentionally acting insensitive to others. (try taking the Social Privilege test).[7]

If you see people behaving inappropriately I ask that you refrain from any kind of public shaming and allow us to respond to the situation as a community. This class actively opposes all forms of harassment and hate speech. If you experience any marginalizing or silencing behavior, please come to me and we will discuss how best to approach the situation. In most cases I will respond to all issues by addressing the class as a whole so we can learn together.

This statement shows how the classroom culture can be modeled in ways that encourage ethical action, reflexivity, and egalitarianism. Students are presented the opportunity to discuss social identities and positions in terms of potential social advantages, power asymmetries, unequal representations, and disproportionate access to social resources. These quotes from Professor Shaw's *Mobile Media* student evaluations demonstrate the effectiveness of the inclusivity statement for learning:

Professor Shaw always made sure that everyone was included in the discussions we had. If someone made a problematic or misinformed statement about race/ethnicity/gender/etc., she was quick to correct the student and inform them why their discourse was offensive or incorrect. She also makes

> her students sign an inclusivity policy at the start of the course in which we promise to not use derogatory/offensive language towards others who are different from us, and if there is something we are unfamiliar with about another gender/culture/sexuality, we make an effort to educate ourselves.
>
> When touchy subjects were discussed she approached them in a great way and made sure the class didn't become a political argument, it was all educational.
>
> She made sure everyone was comfortable in the class. In the beginning we even had to sign a form to agree to be fair and understand the diversity in the class when speaking.
>
> She had us sign in the beginning of class to be mindful of all genders, races and cultures. So, it's fair to say she respects everyone and hopes to keep a respectable classroom.
>
> So great! Loved the agreement we signed at the beginning, I actually told friends and family about how cool it was.
>
> Very respective (sic) of peoples differences. Actually gave a disclaimer about hate speech in class, how it was not going to be tolerated. Great job.

As Freire or Giroux would remind us, an awareness of and respect for multiple viewpoints is a first step toward correcting power imbalances within both the educational and wider cultural environments. Within the communication/media classroom, human agency is often a topic of inquiry; courses in theory, policy and law, rhetoric, media production, institutions and economics, globalization, and audiences each consider, in some form, the ability of people to communicate on equal terrain. When instructors create classroom cultures that enable student potential for empathy, participatory culture, justice, and an ethic of humility, students recognize their own voice and their own communicative power. They become connected to the larger civic community.

Connecting Pedagogical Philosophy with Issues of Diversity and Ethics

In the introduction to this book, I highlighted an argument by Sprague (1993) for a context-specific pedagogy for communication. Part of her argument connects communication with cultural identity through culture-specific codes of communicative competence. She claims that personal identity is shaped through the extent to which these competencies are mastered or rejected. The creation of identity is, according to Sprague, a potent communicative act that we often recognize in our pedagogies. Beetham and Oliver (2010) examine how competencies with digital literacies impact student identity:

> One important strength of "traditional" academic teaching in disciplines is that it recognizes learning not as the collection of competences but as the emergence of an identity. Particularly in higher education, learning

> involves taking up a personal stance in relation to subject knowledge and expertise. In a digital age, learners need to practice and experiment with different ways of enacting their identities, and adopt subject positions through different social technologies and media. These opportunities can only be supported by academic staff who are themselves engaged in digital practices and questioning their own relationships with knowledge.
>
> (p. 166)

For Beetham and Oliver, the academic identities of both students and instructors are more fully developed when both groups position themselves within the contemporary communication/media studies curriculum. To the extent that a teaching philosophy is a type of professional judgment that accrues over time, it is forged from our individual academic identities and the goals we set for student learning. In order to address contemporary realities within communication and media, faculty must recognize their own subject positions within the curriculum and the larger culture of diverse perspectives.

By articulating a teaching philosophy infused with an ethical responsibility and that is sensitive to diversity within the classroom and the culture, we expose our students to a microcosm of those things they will encounter outside of higher education. This philosophy is evident in Dustin Morrow's (July, 2011) strategies for teaching his production courses at Portland State University:

> And students must learn that media production involves a great deal of interpersonal interaction, not only with their own production teams, but with members of the public whose knowledge of the production processes will be limited. An awareness of the responsibilities and sensitivities required of a good media producer is always foregrounded in my courses. Recently, I had a group of students shooting documentary footage in a large working children's hospital, talking to patients and doctors under incredible stress; I've had students shooting in some of Philadelphia's most run-down communities, in formerly drug-infested neighborhoods of Dublin, in politically unstable parts of Africa; and students that I taught in a Northern Irish documentary course conducted interviews with former political prisoners and convicted terrorists. All these experiences provided the students with a crash course in how to operate with grace and discretion in politically and emotionally fragile environments as responsible media professionals.

Professor Morrow is encouraging ethical behavior among his future professional students while preparing them for participation in a diverse public sphere. His philosophy is one in which students learn skills in communication along with an ethical critique of the practices of media. Writing about the confluence between universities and the media in performing the functions of a public sphere, Slavko

Splichal (2011) emphasizes the importance of an ethical education in attaining Dewey's notion of a public community linked with democracy and communication. Splichal emphasizes the importance of both the university and the media as sites for public deliberation and argues that both institutions, confounded by market constraints, are obstructing the democratic process. However, he sees a role for the university in the pursuit of a participatory democratic sphere that is not corrupted by the principles of markets. This ethical stance must be emphasized in the communication classroom—students studying communication need to understand the vital role media industries and social media play in the functioning of a democracy as envisioned by Dewey. Too often, communication faculty forget, in light of the daily concerns of teaching, that all democracies conceptualize an exalted and essential role for the media.

To clarify our own goals as faculty of communication and media studies, to locate ourselves within disciplinary culture, and to make decisions about our teaching practices, we turn to our educational philosophies about communication education. Our philosophies demonstrate our commitment to principles of democratic responsibility. According to Giroux (2011), educators have an obligation to inspire students to participate in the public sphere through sound moral judgment and socially responsible action. For Giroux and other critical pedagogues, this means providing "students with the skills, knowledge, and authority they need to inquire and act upon what it means to live in a substantive democracy, to recognize anti-democratic forms of power, and to fight deeply rooted injustices in a society and world founded on systemic economic, racial, and gender inequalities" (p. 72). Although idealistic about these potential returns, Giroux does well to paint a portrait of what an ethically inspired pedagogy may instigate within our students. Recognizing that democratic participation is sometimes limited by restrictive power systems, such as lack of access, communication educators are well positioned, by effort of understanding communication as a social process, to clarify these issues for students. Splichal (2011) contends that educators can lead by example through participation in societal "debates beyond their own 'ivory towers'" (p. 57). This advice, parting shot included, serves as an important reminder that, as educators, we should not forget that some of the lasting impressions we leave with our students are those in which we lead by example. Our education as teachers continues *with* that of our students. The ideal result is one where instructor and student participate together within a learning community where they become aware of issues affecting them individually and those overlooked issues affecting other members of the learning community. A large part of community awareness means an appreciation for group diversity. As such, it would best serve us to account for these issues of diversity in our teaching philosophies. Communication is a complex process, and we must inculcate in our students a deep understanding of communicative patterns and how they operate in a democratic culture.

Dewey (1963) understood the important linkage between communication, education, and democracy by advocating the idea that all people have rights to participate in the public sphere, to speak for themselves, and to be respected for their opinions. Simultaneously, Dewey believed learners should be granted the same opportunities to participate actively and reflectively in the construction of their own learning as individuals with varied backgrounds, experiences, and interests. Striving for a sensitivity to diversity within one's teaching philosophy not only means striving to help students develop their own sensitivities toward differences within their learning community, but also demonstrating an interdependence within the classroom that makes the learning community more successful when it considers the opinions and experiences of its members. A teaching approach that favors this ideal benefits students of communication who can learn to be responsible communicators as well as responsible critics of the communicative process. Equipping our students with the ability to look past popular trends by lending a sensitive ear to marginalized voices benefits both the individual and the greater community. Reich (2008) says that students cognizant of these issues are the future citizens that make democracy achievable:

> To make democracy possible, learning must never be confined to but one view of one interpretive community. It must always involve different variations, extensions, and reconstructions of knowledge or imagination within a community of learning, and it must give learners a chance to explore diverse lines and perspectives of observing and acting. Learners must have the possibility to come to know other communities outside of the norms and values they are used to. This possibility must include ways of cross-border communication, understanding, and participation. Such leaning will succeed most readily if a democratic community of practice exists and indeed allows for practical partaking of all learners in choosing and constructing contents, relations, and methods of learning.
>
> (p. 79)

Reich's observation encapsulates why connecting our teaching philosophies to issues of ethics and diversity is so important. As educators, we should motivate our students to exercise their civic responsibility to participate in a democracy. Educators have a secondary function to enrich democracy by promoting a sense of community, respect, and social justice in our classrooms. In this way, we can inspire students to exercise their duty to civic participation and communicate the importance of egalitarianism within a democracy.

While Dewey's ideal democracy presumes the appreciation of differences as a requisite condition of democratic communication, he was not unaware of the relationship among varied social interests in terms of power imbalances in the development of democratic communication. Thus, we must recognize connections between communication and power within our pedagogies. Communicative behaviors assist or oppose existing power arrangements, and our students must explore these practices both analytically and ethically.

The Construction of Power Systems

Power is inherent in systems. To some extent, systems of higher education are subject to a market rationality that is supplanting the ethos of education as a public good. Market imperatives affect all aspects of the educational mission—from institutional funding to student support to faculty hiring to the use of technology—and have resulted in the expansion of a consumerist attitude reminiscent of service industries such as banking. Traditionally, a university education permitted students to reflect on ideas and events in an environment independent of market rationality. But the systemic power that increasingly characterizes all of the higher educational experience in the United States is felt in communication in two notable ways. First, because of its interdisciplinary status, the study of communication is informed by multiple theoretical traditions and is thus varied in its epistemologies. Faculty have a responsibility to be mindful of the interdisciplinary tradition and what it means in terms of power structures. Because disciplines are bound by epistemological assumptions, interdisciplinarity may challenge these assumptions in ways that may influence social power. For example, we assume that media are worthy objects of study in part because of their ubiquity. This is a system of knowledge—a claim to truth—used as a form of power. Traditional disciplines contain their power, in part, within monopolies of knowledge or at least claims to particular intellectual turf. To some, communication as an interdisciplinary field is unfocused because it is theoretically and methodologically diverse and includes professional as well as scholarly dimensions. The second way that systemic market power is evident in communication and media studies is within the curriculum. Communication is based on a curriculum in which students learn to create and manage media while simultaneously learning to critique the industry and its products. This means that industry power systems sometimes influence the curriculum, and students are likely to feel a dichotomy between professionalism and intellectualism. Students may learn how profit motives dictate the quality of mediated messages or how the delivery of media is determined by technology policy strictures while they are, at the same time, doing internships at major media outlets. Students may learn about media industry competition, hierarchies, and dubious practices from communication programs that have been credentialed by professional industry organizations and populated by faculty whose expertise is sanctioned by them. Overall, then, communication faculty must respond to power structures in ethical ways that allow students to contest such structures outside the classroom.

One way to address ethical perspectives on power in our teaching is by being transparent about the ways in which power asymmetries are evident in everyday forms of communication. Maria Simone (June, 2014), Associate Professor at Rowan University, articulates how she weaves power concerns into her courses:

> I like to think of my courses—especially my *Political Communication* course—as a "citizen's survival guide." I think it's important for students to understand how power circulates by and through communication, and how the ways in which we socially construct meaning have very material consequences for power, citizenship, and interaction.
>
> But even beyond the specifically political context, I think it's important for students to understand their subjectivity in relationship to others—and that's the civic perspective. We are interconnected, and the activities of even just one person can have repercussions for many, often unknown others. So, I think it's important for students to understand how the choices we make are 1) constrained and enabled by the power relations with others, and 2) effect the choices that others recognize as part of the realm of the possible.

Professor Simone displays a Freirian sensibility toward empowering students to not only understand and question power arrangements, but also to grasp the power dynamics embedded within the processes and forms of communication. Such a lesson is vital for future communication professionals to absorb.

I noted in the introduction to this book that, because communication is an element of the system of cultural routines that constitute society, faculty and students have a duty to challenge the practices and messages of media. How we as educators respond to power structures of all types is important for communicating to our students an agenda of civic responsibility. An interrogation of power in the communication/media studies classroom can reveal the ideological realities of the media industries as the prevailing agents of cultural production and reproduction. But it can also reveal an understanding that resistance to ingrained forms of power is a type of power in itself. According to Giroux (1988), this understanding is part of the method of democratic learning that includes:

> The basic skills students will need to work and live in the wider society, but also knowledge about the social forms through which human beings live, become conscious, and sustain themselves, particularly with respect to the social and political demands of democratic citizenship This relates to knowledge about power and how it works, as well as to analyses of those practices such as racism, sexism, and class exploitation that structure and mediate the encounters of everyday life. . . . The point here is not merely to denounce such stereotypes but rather to expose and deconstruct the processes through which these dominant ideological representations are produced, legitimated, and circulated in society. (p. 103)

An example of a class exercise that confronts dominant aesthetic practices within major media could involve the creation of mobile phone videos (see Keegan & Bell, 2011).

Students can use mobile devices in original ways or in previously inaccessible spaces in order to create narratives that are outside the norms of video-making conventions and aesthetics. The videos can be shared on social media platforms as part of participatory culture. When students are able to surmount barriers to ingenuity and creativity, they not only contest traditional modes of production but also learn to resist them in empowering ways. This is a form of experiential learning that has transformative qualities (per Mortenson, 2007).

Such an exercise can also be used to think about product as well as process, i.e., students may be challenged to problematize mainstream culture and their assumptions about segments of ignored or overlooked voices. Students may be learning about new media practices and texts, but the deeper lesson is acknowledging the existence and contestation of power systems. In this way, instructors can move away from traditional education as a vehicle for, as Freire (1970) notes, the mere preservation of preexisting power structures and the preparation of students to enact preexisting modes of oppression. The communication classroom can be a site of confrontation between competing discourses of power such that students can participate in a model public sphere.

Media texts themselves are helpful to instructors looking to articulate the existence of power systems beyond the classroom. Allowing students to relate to mediated texts using their own terms is an act of combating an already existing power system and has implications beyond a lesson about a given media text. Thus, educating students to critique media texts (and even processes) in terms provided by the instructor (and other experts) *as well as* students' own vernacular lays bare the linguistic power structures that characterize the ways we think about and talk about communication. Making students feel welcome to use their own relational frames or terms also helps to create "an open atmosphere for robust discussion," according to Luthra (2007), who points to such a classroom environment as "a must for critical media education" (p. 210). Communication faculty can help students understand ways to challenge extant power structures and increase their own agency by examining avenues toward social justice. The exercise in the box below can help instructors to theorize ways to contest systems of power and, ultimately, to formulate course goals and practical strategies around those theories.

Exercise on Empowerment

This is an in-class exercise I use in my PhD seminar, *Teaching Communication*. The exercise is based on this citation: Triece, M. E., Hill, P. S., Clark, K. D., Lin, L., & Spiker, J. A. (2002). Pedagogies of empowerment. In J. S. Trent (Ed.), *Included in communication: Learning climates that cultivate racial and ethnic diversity* (pp. 57–75). *American Association for Higher Education*. Washington, DC: Stylus. The goal of the exercise is to help instructors strategize means of student empowerment in communication courses.

According to the Triece et al. article, pedagogies of empowerment involve the use of theoretical perspectives on empowerment to point out the concrete, lived experience of oppressed people in an attempt to secure social justice both inside and outside the classroom.

The article uses two overarching critical perspectives: (1) materialist critical perspective; (2) standpoint theory.

Materialist critical perspective explores pedagogical practices that maintain or legitimate the status quo, thereby continuing the cycle of oppression of disenfranchised people.

Standpoint theory is a framework for analysis of daily, quotidian life experiences as a means for understanding social power—marginalized groups can inform class content to be more representative of diverse perspectives.

Our task: to devise some teaching strategies that incorporate these two perspectives into a classroom experience. Form groups of three. Discuss the procedures below in your groups, taking approximately 15 minutes.

Procedure:

1. Choose a course topic as the basis for the experimental strategy.
2. Devise an exercise for both perspectives to use in the classroom. The goal is to develop theoretically informed class discussion/exercises to sensitize students toward social justice/diversity issues.
3. A materialist critical exercise should challenge mainstream values, assumptions, beliefs about racial/sexual/religious/gender practices.
4. A standpoint theory exercise should "emphasize experiential learning strategies which link theory more meaningfully to direct experience and practice and empower students of color to think and speak critically" (pp. 61–63 of Triece et al., 2002. Sterling, VA.).
5. Report on your exercises to the class, specifically describing the goals and desired outcomes of the exercises.

Teaching Communication, Democracy, Egalitarianism, and Citizenship

Translating lessons from classroom to public is not an easy task for our students. This chapter has explored the influence our teaching identity and instructional practices can have on our students. It addresses how these lessons transfer from the communication/media studies classroom to the larger community through two pools of related scholarship: First, John Dewey reminds us that, through education and communication, our students will come to learn that democracy is an interactive way of life—not a political system. Second, critical pedagogy reminds us that educators can work to provide agency for students within society's many incarnations of power. The ideal result for these critical scholars is a society rich in the principles of democracy and egalitarianism. This chapter concludes by linking these model ends to communication to the extent that communication is vital to civic participation, egalitarianism, and an ethical idea of what democracy should be.

John Dewey (1927) believed that citizens in the 1920s had a false sense that democracy was failing amid the technocratic impulses of fascism. Dewey combated this assertion by shifting the focus from what democracy lacks to a larger discussion about working together, through communicative action, to make democracy broad and robust. The challenge facing this shift is that, for the most part, the popular—and narrow—interpretation of democracy is that it functions as a political system. For Dewey (1927), citizens have a responsibility instead to think of democracy as *a way of life*. Dewey (1963) advocated that, as with many societal issues, change starts in the classroom:

> [T]he greatest of all pedagogical fallacies is the notion that a person learns only [what he or she] is studying at the time. Collateral learning in the way of formation of enduring attitudes ... is much more important than the spelling lesson or lesson in geography or history. ... For these attitudes are fundamentally what count in the future.
>
> (p. 48)

In other words, when we accept the responsibility that comes with being an educator, we accept the responsibility to shape those enduring attitudes our students take into the future. These sentiments point to the purpose of this chapter: To remember that instructors have an ethical responsibility to value democratic and egalitarian principles—the "collateral" lessons that persist. When we construct a teaching identity and a classroom assemblage, we do so with sensitivity toward inspiring community participation and appreciating diversity of opinion. A sensitivity to these issues also helps fulfill the promise of a public sphere by producing learned citizens capable of "communicat[ing] their opinions in concert with other citizens in a productive manner" (Rheingold, 2010, p. 20). By doing this, our students have the potential to participate in Dewey's concept of a "lived democracy" rather than a "representative [one]" (Reich, 2008, p. 68). To this end, Reich (2008) claims citizens can come to realize the significance and benefit of socially consequential decision making. Bromley (2011) calls this a process of cultivating "thick citizenship" or the idea that "continual civic participation" is a necessary ingredient in democracy's dynamic and complicated mixture (p. 107). These ideas about civic participation in a democracy illustrate how vital communication is for the potential of democracy.

Toward this end, Jarice Hanson (July, 2011), Professor of Communication at the University of Massachusetts at Amherst, discusses how she contextualizes her teaching in terms of democracy and citizenship:

> I teach so many courses that involve media and technology as filters and prisms for democracy and citizenship, and we often talk about key themes;

> what is democracy? How does it function or not function? Why should we be concerned about it? Do we expect technology or media to solve the hard problems? Virtually every course I teach examines contemporary democracy (and historical roots and situations) from some angle, and every time, I stress that we as citizens have responsibilities to think and act according to our beliefs—but that our beliefs all come from somewhere.

Professor Hanson works to promote the idea of authenticity in civic deliberation. She instills the notion of citizenship into her students but does so by accentuating the skills of deliberation in a technologically complex culture. She demonstrates the central role for communication and media studies in educating students for contemporary citizenship.

Based on Dewey's concepts, I argue that education in media and communication is essential for a revitalized democracy and for a democratization of social institutions. Citizens must understand the media—including social media—in order to exert their own power, to make determinative decisions, to act toward ethical change, and to insert themselves into the mediated environment. An education in media and communication inspires students to question the structure and functioning of not just media institutions but all social institutions and arrangements. What is the nature of contemporary democracy? What public responsibilities do citizens carry? In what ways are professional communicators accountable to the public? In what ways do financial and legal arrangements of media institutions influence the democratic process? Media and communication students must understand that the context of democratic politics is not defined by consumer choice but by citizens themselves, independent of market forces.

This chapter has presented arguments from various scholars about the purposes of general education and of communication/media education in the preparation of students for lives of social responsibility, citizenship, and creativity. Part of the logic of an education in communication and media is that learners need to understand how to "read" the world around them. Our instruction helps students to develop the habits of mind and vocabulary of expression to read their worlds and to communicate those readings to other public constituencies. Rheingold (2010) calls this a "literacy of participation" (p. 20). Moreover, communication educators must encourage students to critique these habits of mind, ways of knowing, and ways of acting in the world. So students are exposed, through cognitive and affective and psychomotor ways of learning, to a range of understandings about communication, about other disciplines, and about how their own life experiences influence their academic learning. This type of learning involves students in contemporary democracy. It means that learning for citizenship entails, with Dewey, not just knowledge and ideas but also self-reflection and action in the world. For Nixon (2011),

> Democracy is constructed in and through the everyday narratives of living and learning together. Experiencing democratic processes and practices is

> then critical in building collective responsibility and ensuring individual and social development. Education conceived as a transformative process helps create the democratic conditions necessary for its own sustainability. (p. 121)

This transformative process signifies a return to the public, according to Nixon.

Bromley's (2011) conceptualization of thick citizenship in a lived democracy embodies the connections between democracy, citizenship, community, and transformation that characterize media studies and communication education. A critical pedagogy derived from Dewey's notions of democratic community seeks a disruption of anti-egalitarianism toward a transformative agenda of social justice, equality, and human emancipation. Because the study of media and communication—in ways inspired by Dewey—privileges student creativity and action, students are ideally empowered to forge a democratic consciousness that they carry throughout other pedagogical spaces.

Drawing together ideas about reflexivity, transformative learning, and action in a democracy, critical pedagogy helps clarify the role of educators in moving future citizens toward a more egalitarian democracy. Critical pedagogy's claim is that classrooms are staging areas for democracy's future civic participants and that educators have a public responsibility to engage significant issues. Ideally, citizens recognize systems of social power and understand the attendant social inequalities. As a result, citizens are poised to enact a progressive democracy. Giroux (2011) explains that "[higher education] is also one of the few spheres in which students are provided with the tools not only for citizen participation in public life, but also for exercising forms of critical leadership" (p. 121). In this sense, critical leadership does not necessitate individual leadership. Rather, a community of individuals is needed to position democracy on a course toward a more just future. Therefore, critical pedagogy's design focuses on informing cultural beliefs and practices. For Giroux (2011), among other critical pedagogues, the ideal outcome is an education that "enable[s] individuals to … nurture a democratic society that takes equality, justice, shared values, and freedom seriously" (p. 4). However, as Carr (2011) argues, seeking a more democratic society through a critical education necessitates "the belief that people can, ultimately, function together without self-destruction" (p. 203) and that students must "reflect on the meaning of democracy, and to accept, with humility, that there is not simply one way to conceive of the human condition" (p. 189). Communication and media studies play a role in this effort, in part, by teaching students to critique the "marketplace of ideas," to create messages ethically, and to participate actively in the public sphere of diverse opinions.

We want our students to be educated in ways that help them to be thoughtful citizens, to act ethically in the world, to be conscientious communicators, and to embrace their own power in defense of social justice. Dewey (1916) argued that "not only is social life identical with communication, but all communication (and hence all genuine social life) is educative" (p. 5). He understood that community building, through education and communication, is the path to an open democracy. It is essential to recognize that our teaching is fundamental to our work in the academy and to the wider world.

Overall, this book has sought to engage educators, practically and philosophically, to examine the how and why of teaching media studies and communication. If we understand communication/media education to be a type of social good, contributing to a democratic public sphere, that assumption will affect our pedagogical practices, knowledge, and learning goals. This book entreats educators to take notice of the construction and realization of educational goals through the context of communication/media pedagogy. Understanding our academic identities helps us to do the work of teaching communication and media studies. Developing our positions on technology given the cultural and institutional imperatives to incorporate it into our pedagogies helps us to do the work. Understanding taxonomies of knowledge to help form goals, and knowing how students learn helps us to do the work. Doing the work of communication/media education is about the connections we make in an interdisciplinary field for our students. It is about understanding how our academic practices connect to larger political, economic, and cultural concerns. These mandates all coalesce within an ethical, democratic, reflexive educational mission.

Notes

1 Brian McFadden is a PhD student in Media and Communication at Temple University.
2 The course, taught by Jan Fernback, is Teaching Communication in Higher Education.
3 See, for example, David Horowitz's *Reforming Our Universities: The Campaign for an Academic Bill of Rights*, published by Regnery Publishing in 2010.
4 Reflective thinking is careful consideration of a subject in order to understand the meaning of the subject and to internalize the values accompanying such an understanding.
5 Professor Shaw based her inclusivity policy, in part, on statements from the Queerness and Games Conference (http://www.qgcon.com/) and the Different Games Conference (www.differentgames.org).
6 Links to these terms are: http://en.wikipedia.org/wiki/List_of_ethnic_slurs; https://www2.stetson.edu/secure/history/hy10302/nongenderlang.html; http://en.wikipedia.org/wiki/List_of_LGBT_slang_terms; http://en.wikipedia.org/wiki/Heterosexism; http://ws405.blogspot.com/2011/01/class-and-classism.html; http://thoughtcatalog.com/samantha-allen/2013/07/7-ways-to-be-a-trans-ally/; http://www.autistichoya.com/p/ableist-words-and-terms-to-avoid.html
7 http://www.helloquizzy.com/tests/the-social-privilege-test

References

Amankwah, J. (2008). Ethical dialogue in the classroom. In M. A. Cook and A. M. Holba (Eds.), *Philosophies of communication: Implications for everyday experience* (pp. 41–56). New York, NY: Peter Lang.

Barkley, E. F. (2009). *Student engagement techniques: A handbook for college faculty*. San Francisco, CA: Jossey-Bass.

Beetham, H., & Oliver, M. (2010). The changing practices of knowledge and learning. In R. Sharpe, H. Beetham, & S. DeFreitas (Eds.), *Rethinking learning for a digital age* (pp. 155–169). New York, NY: Routledge.

Blumberg, P. (2009). *Developing learner-centered teaching: A practical guide for faculty*. San Francisco, CA: Jossey-Bass.

Brockbank, A., & McGill, I. (2007). *Facilitating reflective learning in higher education*. (2nd ed.). Berkshire, UK: Open University Press.

Bromley, M. (2011). iPhones and eyeshades: Journalism and the university's role in promoting a dynamic public sphere. In B. Zelizer (Ed.), *Making the university matter* (pp. 104–112). New York, NY: Routledge.

Campbell, J. (2008). The political philosophy of pragmatism. In J. Garrison (Ed.) *Reconstructing democracy, recontextualizing Dewey* (pp. 19–30). Albany, NY: State University of New York Press.

Carr, P. R. (2011). The quest for a critical pedagogy of democracy. In C. S. Malott & B. Porfilio (Eds.), *Critical pedagogy in the twenty-first century: A new generation of scholars* (pp. 187–210). Charlotte, NC: Information Age Publishing, Inc.

Dallalfar, A. (2011). Teaching women's lives: Feminist pedagogy and the sociological imagination. In A. Dallalfar, E. Kingston-Mann, & T. Sieber (Eds.), *Transforming classroom culture: Inclusive pedagogical practices* (pp. 111–126). New York, NY: Palgrave Macmillan.

Dewey, J. (1916). *Democracy and education: An introduction to the philosophy of education*. New York, NY: Macmillan.

Dewey, J. (1927). *The public and its problems*. New York, NY: Henry Holt.

Dewey, J. (1963). *Experience and education*. London, UK: Collier Books.

Freire, P. (1970). *Pedagogy of the oppressed* (M. G. Ramos, Trans.). New York, NY: Seabury.

Giddens, A. (1991). *Modernity and self-identity: Self and society in the late modern age*. Stanford, CA: Stanford University Press.

Giroux, H. (1988). *Schooling and the struggle for public life: Critical pedagogy in the modern age*. Minneapolis, MN: University of Minnesota Press.

Giroux, H. (2011). *On critical pedagogy*. New York, NY: Continuum International.

Griebling, B., & Shaw, A. (2011). Introduction: Models of teaching and learning. In B. Zelizer (Ed.), *Making the university matter* (pp. 15–16). New York, NY: Routledge.

Gross, L. (2012). Fastening our seatbelts: Turning crisis into opportunity. *Journal of Communication 62* (2012), 919–931. doi:10.1111/j.1460-2466.2012.01679.x

Jenkins, H., Purushotma, R., Weigel, M., Clinton, K., & Robinson, A. J. (2009). *Confronting the challenges of participatory culture: Media education for the 21st century*. Cambridge, MA: MIT Press.

Keegan, H., & Bell, F. (2011). YouTube as repository: The creative practice of students as producers of open educational resources. *European Journal of Open, Distance and E-Learning (EURODL), 10*. http://www.eurodl.org/?p=special&sp=articles&article=456

Kogan, M. (2000). Higher education communities and academic identity. In I. McNay (Ed.), *Higher education and its communities* (pp. 29–37). Buckingham, UK: Open University Press.

Luthra, R. (2007). Media education toward a more equitable world. In A. Nowak, S. Abel, & K. Ross (Eds.), *Rethinking media education: Critical pedagogy and identity politics* (pp. 203–215). Cresskill, NJ: Hampton Press.

Mahoney, D. (2008). *Ethics in the classroom: Bridging the gap between theory and practice*. New York, NY: Rowman & Littlefield.

Mortenson, S. T. (2007). Raising the question #7: Should we teach personal transformation as a part of interpersonal communication? If so, how is it done? *Communication Education, 56*(3), 401–408.

Nixon, J. (2011). *Higher education and the public good: Imagining the university*. London, UK: Continuum.

Nussbaum, M. (2002). Education for citizenship in an era of global connection. *Studies in Philosophy and Education, 21*(4–5), 289–303.

Ramsey, S. (1993). The active learner and a cycle of involvement. *Journalism Educator, 48*(2), 74–80.

Reich, K. (2008). Democracy and education after Dewey—Pragmatist implications for constructivist pedagogy. In J. Garrison (Ed.), *Reconstructing democracy, recontextualizing Dewey: Pragmatism and interactive construction in the twenty-first century* (pp. 55–88). Albany, NY: State University of New York Press.

Rheingold, H. (2008). Using social media to teach social media. *The New England Journal of Higher Education, 23*(1), 25–26.

Rheingold, H. (2010). Attention, and other 21st-century social media literacies. *Educause Review, 45*(5), 14–24.

Sholle, D. & Denski, S. (1994). *Media education and the (re)production of culture*. Westport, CT: Bergin & Garvey.

Splichal, S. (2011). University in the age of a transnational public sphere. In B. Zelizer (Ed.), *Making the university matter* (pp. 55–63). New York, NY: Routledge.

Sprague, J. (1990). The goals of communication education. In J. A. Daly, G. W. Friedrich, & A. L. Vangelisti (Eds.), *Teaching communication: Theory, research, and methods*. Hillsdale, NJ: Lawrence Erlbaum Associates.

Sprague, J. (1993). Retrieving the research agenda for communication education: Asking the pedagogical questions that are "embarrassments to theory." *Communication Education, 42*(2), 106–122.

LIST OF INTERVIEWEES

Chapter 2
John Campbell (July, 2011)
Dustin Morrow (July, 2011)
Andrew Mendelson (August, 2011)
William Walter (June, 2011)

Chapter 3
Dustin Morrow (July, 2011)
Terry Harpold (June, 2011 and May, 2014)
William Walter (June, 2011)
Tom Johnson (June, 2012)
Jack Klotz (June, 2012)

Chapter 5
Kim Bissell (August, 2011)
Maria Simone (August, 2012)
William Walter (June, 2011)
Dustin Morrow (July, 2011)
Jarice Hanson (July, 2011)
Nancy Morris (August, 2013)
Terry Harpold (June, 2011 and May, 2014)
Kristine Weatherston (August, 2013)

Chapter 6
Dustin Morrow (July, 2011)

Chapter 7
Jarice Hanson (July, 2011)
Bonnie Brennan (July, 2011)
Dustin Morrow (July, 2011)
Matthew Lombard (June, 2014)

Chapter 8
Adrienne Shaw (June, 2014)
Dustin Morrow (July, 2011)
Maria Simone (June, 2014)
Jarice Hanson (July, 2011)

INDEX

Printed by PGSTL